MACHINE TRANSLATION

LINGVISTICÆ INVESTIGATIONES: SUPPLEMENTA

Studies in French & General Linguistics /
Etudes en Linguistique Française et Générale

This series has been established as a companion series to the periodical "LINGVISTICÆ INVESTIGATIONES", which started publication in 1977. It is published jointly by the Linguistic Department of the University of Paris-VIII and the Laboratoire d'Automatique Documentaire et Linguistique du C.N.R.S. (Paris 7).

* * * * *

Volume 15

John Lehrberger and Laurent Bourbeau

Machine Translation

MACHINE TRANSLATION

Linguistic characteristics of MT systems and general methodology of evaluation

by

John Lehrberger
Laurent Bourbeau

JOHN BENJAMINS PUBLISHING COMPANY
Amsterdam/Philadelphia

1988

Library of Congress Cataloging in Publication Data

Lehrberger, John.
Machine translation.

(Lingvisticæ investigationes. Supplementa, ISSN 0165-7569; v. 15)
Bibliography: p.
1. Machine translating. I. Bourbeau, laurent. II. Title. III. Series.
P308.L44 1988 418'.02 87-17441
ISBN 90 272 3124 9 (alk. paper)

TABLE OF CONTENTS

ACKNOWLEDGEMENTS

The content of this book on machine translation owes much to the experience acquired by the authors as members of the group for research in automatic translation at the University of Montreal (TAUM). We would therefore like to express our gratitude to the Department of the Secretary of State of Canada, which financed R & D at TAUM from 1973 to 1981, and to all our colleagues who took part in that research during those years.

The first sketch of the present volume began in December 1981 and the final corrections were finished in December 1986. Most of the work was financed by the Translation Bureau of the Secretary of State. Our thanks go to Alain Landry, Assistant Under Secretary of State, for his support during this long period, and to Gregory Gauld and Fernand Gobeil in the Planning, Management and Technology Branch for putting the project into operation and making the necessary financial resources available.

We are grateful to Françoise Dompierre and Lise Girard for their help in mobilizing human and technical resources involved in word processing for the numerous versions of our text, and to Lucie Legault, Louise Shpak, Monique Grenier, Francine Joanisse, Joanne Derouin and Diane David-Bergeron for their valuable assistance.

Finally, we wish to thank Pierre Isabelle, Marcel Paré and Gilles Stewart for their critical comments on our manuscript.

The opinions expressed and the scientific positions taken in this book are those of the authors; in particular, the authors do not speak in the name of the Canadian Government.

John Lehrberger
Laurent Bourbeau

PREFACE

Mechanical translation is perhaps the first attempt to apply computors to the simulation of a (nonnumerical) human activity. The amount of interest and support for this idea, which was developed in the 1950s has varied according to times and countries, but it has always been closely tied to political interests. The Cold War was the motivation for Russian to English translation in the early sixties; Canada had linguistic problems in the seventies; the Japanese language is a linguistic barrier to communication with America; and the European Economic Community has placed its different languages on the same footing for the communication of reports.

All these national or international patterns have caused a surge in the amounts of translation felt to be necessary by governments. In each cited case, mechanical translation has been seen as providing a solution, regardless of the state of advancement of the various scientific and technological domains involved.

Early research on machine translation suffered from a structural ambiguity. On the one hand, there were many basic problems that should have been studied:

- the construction of electronic dictionaries,
- the construction of electronic grammars.

It was then assumed, in many research centers, that the nonformalized dictionaries (monolingual and bilingual) and grammars available in bookstores and libraries were sufficient for computer applications, provided that they were transferred to some magnetic support in the proper format. A lot of superficial studies were then produced, mainly on the morphology of words. No serious effort was then brought to bear on the deeper linguistic aspects of the problems, and this aroused criticism from the community of theoreticians (e.g. Y. Bar-Hillel 1960: The Present Status of Automatic Translation of Languages, in F.L. Alt ed.: *Advances in Computers*, Vol. 1, New York: Academic Press, pp. 1-163).

From the viewpoint of computer technology, many fundamental problems were approached:
- construction of large memories (G. King's photoscopic disk), access to large data bases by hash-code like techniques (T. Ziehe at the Rand Corporation),
- a variety of models of natural language flourished, and parsing algorithms were developed for them.

On the other hand, the amount of support given to these research projects was motivated by the production of a final program which was to be evaluated on some economical basis. In 1966, the Peirce report (John R. Peirce ed. *Language and Machines*, Washington D.C.: National Academy of Sciences, National Research Council, publication 1416, 124p.) provided this evaluation of the field, which resulted in the ending of massive financial support in the United States, and in some other countries.

In the past five years, mechanical translation has once more raised the interest of potential users, mainly in Europe and Japan. As already mentioned, the wave of the 1960s covered a variety of research topics which were aimed at high-quality translation. As such, they involved many fundamental aspects of linguistics and computer science. Today, these questions are no longer seen as prerequisites, and on the contrary, the present movement is concerned with building cost effective systems that make no claim about quality, but that stress the increase of productivity (1) that organizations or individuals willing to use them would benefit from.

Whereas aspects of early experiments and of their failures seem to be remembered, the Canadian experiment is only rarely referred to. The Canadian Government supported the TAUM project at the University of Montreal consistently for about 8 years. A large amount of work on English and on French has been accomplished, both fundamental and practical, aimed at the translation of texts of a particular technical domain. When in

(1) Productivity appears to be due more to the improvement of text processing systems, including desk top printing, than to the linguistic tools.

1981 the project came to an end, the results obtained went through a remarkable process of evaluation, both from the Government and from private interests.

I think that there is a lot to learn from this experience for both ongoing and future projects, and I am particularly happy to preface this book by John Lehrberger and Laurent Bourbeau which goes systematically into the theoretical steps and the economics of the main approaches to machine translation.

Few specialists are in the position of having made substantial contributions to a project and of being able to follow it up to the end, through an assessment of its merits and deficiencies. Thus, the two authors present us with the first handbook of the field. They describe all the basic components of MT systems, and they review the main approaches from a user's point of view, not from the naive buyer's point of view who would only be interested in the return provided by his investment. They do this from the view point of specialists who will have to improve a system by extending both its vocabulary and grammar, and by customizing and maintaining them. Above all, the authors never forget the finality of MT systems: their ergonomy. This book should be read carefully.

Maurice Gross

1. INTRODUCTION

The use of the computer in translating natural languages ranges from that of a translator's aid for word processing and dictionary lookup to that of a full-fledged translator on its own. Translators are generally somewhat skeptical about the possibility of computers turning out high quality translations, without human intervention, in the foreseeable future. Linguists disagree about the best role to assign to the computer in automating the translation process. Meanwhile the layman receives contradictory reports: automatic translation is impractical ("just look at the ridiculous translation..."); computer translation is so fast it will undoubtedly replace the human translator in the not too distant future; the computer will never replace the human translator; etc. Adding to the confusion, the interested spectator has to cope with a number of terms that are not always clearly defined: machine translation, computer-aided (or -assisted) translation, computerized translation, automatic translation, fully automatic translation, interactive translation systems, and so on. We have tried in this book to sort out the different approaches to the use of computers in translation and to explain the different types of systems that result. In order to understand the limitations of various types of systems it is necessary to examine some of the linguistic phenomena that make the computer's task non-trivial.

The obstacles to translating by means of the computer are primarily linguistic. To overcome them it is necessary to resolve the ambiguities that pervade a natural language when words and sentences are viewed in isolation. Texts are normally not ambiguous to their readers; the challenge for researchers is to develop computer programs with something like the ability of the ordinary human reader to extract the intended meaning from the string of words that forms a text. To put the matter another way, the computer must be taught to **understand** the text - a problem in artificial intelligence.

Apparent ambiguity on the word level fades as we take into account the implicit relations between the linguistic elements in a text, the tacit assumptions due to knowledge shared by the text writer and readers, and the restrictions imposed by the text domain, i.e. the subject matter itself. The problem then is to formalize, in the computer, these aspects of natural language understanding.

Machine translation (MT) has been around for several decades and in spite of having been declared impractical, impossible and even dead, it shows no signs of disappearing from the scene. On the contrary, a number of commercial companies are now providing this service in the business world, while various long range projects are in the works (e.g., the European Economic Community's EUROTRA and fifth generation projects in Japan). Why, then, is there such diversity of opinion about the feasibility of MT? One reason is that MT means different things to different people (see **CHAPTER 2**, Section 1); another is that the criteria for what constitutes acceptable output from an MT system depend on the type of text and the needs of the user of that output. In order to get a clear picture of what MT is and what might be expected of it we shall examine the characteristics of different types of systems, the linguistic concepts underlying these systems, the linguistic obstacles that still plague machine translation, and the factors that enter into linguistic evaluation of MT systems.

The evaluation of an MT system can quickly turn into a complex operation when the system is examined from all angles. MT is a multidisciplinary application bringing together computer science, linguistics, translation and terminology. This application is now part of a new discipline known as computational linguistics. Computational linguistics is a term applied to any type of computer-assisted treatment of natural languages. Machine translation also involves another discipline known as artificial intelligence (AI). Computational linguistics and artificial intelligence have given rise to specific techniques and theories. In addition, these new disciplines often employ a hybrid terminology, as when a special term is borrowed from or refers to a specific linguistic theory, computer technique or a recognized translation practice. In this book we try to use a non-specialized terminology as much as possible; an extensive bibliography is provided for the reader who feels in need of further clarification.

The evaluation methodology described here recognizes three distinct types of system evaluation: evaluation by the system's designer, on the one hand, and cost/benefit evaluation and linguistic evaluation by the user, on the other. The main emphasis in this presentation is on the linguistic aspects of the task. It is not a recipe for system evaluation, but an overview of the subject backed up by a discussion of the principal linguistic concepts related to the evaluation of MT systems.

The authors try to show how, from a linguistic point of view, one may form some idea of what goes on inside a system's black box, given only the input (original text) and the raw output (translated text before post-editing). Many examples of English/French translation are used to illustrate the principles involved.

Any evaluation of an MT system is made up directly or indirectly of three parts: an evaluation of the quality of the translation produced by the system, an evaluation of the underlying linguistic model for the actual descriptions that constitute the system's dictionaries and grammars, and an evaluation of the computational model used to implement these grammars and dictionaries. For each of these three aspects the evaluation should determine not only the actual performance of the system with particular texts as input, but its **potential** as well. Of course, if we are aware of the potential of a system we are also in a position to understand its limitations.

This study provides a certain amount of technical information which serves to complement a strict cost/benefit evaluation: identification of the main characteristics of a system, classification on the basis of degree of automation, description of the various linguistic components, determination of the potential and limitations of a system, and insight into a too-often neglected area - the requirements and constraints of translation itself as well as the working environment of the translator.

In **CHAPTER 2** systems are classified along a number of dimensions: the degree of automation inherent in the system, the depth of linguistic analysis of the source language, the type of information transfer between source and target languages, the organization of processing phases in the translation chain, and the lexical and syntactic dependence of the system on the domain of application. This classification forms the basis for a multi-dimensional comparison between a system being considered for acquisition and others that are available. It also furnishes information basic to understanding the potential and limitations of a system.

CHAPTER 3 looks more closely at the characteristics of a system by giving an idea of its internal organization in terms of the major linguistic components: lexical (dictionary or dictionaries), morphological, syntactic and semantic. In order to understand the function and scope of these components, relevant linguistic phenomena are defined for each and illustrated with examples. Of course, the components are not isolated and independent of one another, but are interrelated. We must therefore take these relations into account as we examine each component to determine what it does, how it does it, and the nature and structure of its specific linguistic information.

CHAPTER 4 discusses two diametrically opposed approaches to designing a system: the corpus-based approach and the standard grammar approach. The advantages and disadvantages of each are explained. These two approaches have a direct effect on determining the content of the linguistic information present in the dictionaries and grammars of a system. Knowing which approach the system designer has chosen also gives us some idea of the extendability of the system to different domains.

CHAPTER 5 deals with the methodology for linguistic evaluation: identifying the needs and constraints of translation, evaluating the performance of the linguistic components of the system and evaluating the potential of a system. In addition, because of the importance of taking into account the man/machine relation in computerized translation, i.e. the effect on the human translators and revisers who must use the machine, the evaluation of the user environment is also discussed. The authors suggest steps to be followed in deciding on the acceptability of a system and then summarize the fundamental aspects and limitations of the proposed methodology for evaluating translation systems. They conclude with a discussion of the viability of MT, its future prospects and the impact of evaluation methodology on those prospects.

A preliminary study of evaluation methodology is contained in **Appendix A** (written in 1981) and a detailed flowchart of a typical second generation MT system in **Appendix B**.

2. IDENTIFICATION OF SYSTEM CHARACTERISTICS

The following classification of system characteristics is intended to provide a framework for discussing the features of particular systems and their capabilities. The parameters involved in this classification are: (1) the degree of automation of the translation process, (2) the depth of analysis of the sentences processed, (3) the type of transfer from source to target language, (4) the relation between phases in the translation process, and (5) the extent to which the system is limited to translation of texts from particular domains. The nature of the individual linguistic components of a system (lexical, morphological, syntactic and semantic) will be discussed in Chapter 3, and the relation between the approach used in building a system (corpus-based VS standard grammar) and its domain of application will be examined in Chapter 4.

2.1 DEGREE OF AUTOMATION

The degree of automation expresses the relative contribution of the machine and the human translator to the translation process. If a system is not fully automatic, there is some intervention by the human translator before obtaining the "raw output" (unrevised translation). In such an interactive system there are various ways in which the interaction can take place, resulting in different degrees of automation for the system as a whole. A rough idea of the degree of automation can be obtained by measuring the time spent by the human translator interacting with the machine to produce the raw output; this measurement forms part of a cost-effectiveness study.

But here we shall examine interactivity from the point of view of linguistic evaluation: which aspects of linguistic analysis are performed by the machine alone, and which require human intervention. This will help provide information needed to determine the limitations and improvability of the system.

2.1.1 MACHINE-AIDED HUMAN TRANSLATION (MAHT)

MAHT is basically human translation with only limited assistance from the machine. At the lower end of the scale of what might be called "computerized translation" the machine may consist simply of a word processor with provision for looking up translation equivalents of source language words. This may be faster than writing out the translation by hand (or typing it with an ordinary typewriter) and thumbing through a dictionary for unfamiliar terms, but it does not remove from the translator the burden of actually performing the translation. Following are some features that may be included in an MAHT system.

(i) Word processor with provision for dictionary lookup (translation equivalents).

(ii) KWIC facility. The KWIC (Key Word In Context) can be used to show the contexts in which a word occurs in the texts under translation or in texts from the same domain. This helps the translator to understand how a word is used in that domain and may therefore help in the resolution of homographs.

(iii) Grammatical information. In addition to providing translation equivalents, the machine might also supply, for each word in its dictionary, grammatical categories (i.e., parts of speech), subcategories, and various syntactic and semantic properties of the word. The structure of the dictionary (or dictionaries) will be discussed in section 3.1; for the moment we simply note that in an MAHT system the availability of such information to the translator-operator does not imply that the machine itself uses the information to produce a translation of the text.

(iv) Morphological analysis.

(v) Corpus of translated texts. The translator can be provided with easy access to previously translated texts for reference in the current task.

(vi) Spelling and grammar correction.

We might think of MAHT as a system in which the human translator has control; the machine is simply a tool to be used at the discretion of the translator. On the other hand, computers can be made to seem quite human by sufficiently sophisticated programming. Thus we can have a man-machine system in which the computer has control while the human translator is used to supply information at the discretion of the machine. This is, in fact, the situation described in the next section (Human-Aided Machine Translation).

2.1.2 HUMAN-AIDED MACHINE TRANSLATION (HAMT)

In the case of HAMT the human translator supplies limited information to "fill out" the machine translation. After being supplied with the necessary data by the translator, the machine completes the translation, producing a raw output suitable for human revision. This can be accomplished in several ways. The required human assistance may take place before machine processing begins, during the translation process, or afterward. The machine may pause in mid-sentence to query the operator and then resume its processing of the remainder of the sentence, or it may make more than one pass through the whole sentence, with the operator inserting the appropriate information between passes.

The need for some human assistance arises primarily from the fact that certain linguistic structures have proven extremely difficult to parse automatically and words with multiple meanings add to the difficulty. Thus the machine may call on the translator:

- to decide on the scope of a conjunction (i.e., "what groups of words are connected by 'and', 'or', 'but'?");

- to bracket or translate a string of nouns in a sentence;

- to decide whether an occurrence of a preposition is part of a verb-particle combination, or whether it introduces a prepositional phrase modifying some noun in the sentence, or whether it introduces a prepositional phrase that functions as a sentence adverbial;

- to resolve homography problems;
  etc.

The boundary between HAMT and MAHT is difficult to draw. The designers of an interactive system may refer to it as "machine translation", but if the machine requires too much assistance, the translator may be effectively providing the translation. In that case, regardless of any claims made by the system's designers, it may be classed as MAHT rather than HAMT. Furthermore, phenomena such as those mentioned in the preceding paragraph are so prevalent that having the translator supply just that information may slow down the process to the point where the number of words per hour in the output is not significantly greater than that of the translator working without the help of automatic analysis (e.g., using the machine only for dictionary lookup and KWIC display, but not for analysis). And, given the present state of the art, raw output from the machine is likely to place greater demands on the reviser than would the output from the human translator.

Finally, it must not be assumed that if the machine asks for certain information and this is, in fact, supplied by the translator-operator, then the machine will be able to use the information; it is much easier to program the questions than to write programs that furnish correct analyses of the source text.

2.1.3 FULLY AUTOMATIC MACHINE TRANSLATION (FAMT)

In FAMT there is no human intervention between the input of the original text and the final raw machine output of the translated text. Of course, revision of the raw output may be required, just as it is for the output of a human translator; "fully automatic" does not imply that human post-revision is eliminated. However, there is at least one FAMT system (METEO) in which the machine itself decides which of the sentences submitted to it are to be revised, all others being translated and considered suitable as finished text ready for use.

2.2 DEPTH OF ANALYSIS

The ability of a machine to translate texts depends on its ability to analyze them syntactically and semantically. Without analysis there can only be word for word substitution, which is of little value. On the other hand, high quality fully automatic translation requires full analysis of the source text. The machine's capacity to produce, on its own, translations comparable to those of human translators is limited by the depth of the analysis it can perform. Depth of analysis, like depth of understanding, is a matter of continuous gradation; however, for the purpose of making a broad classification of computerized translation systems we will, for the moment, distinguish between systems in which the machine analyzes the whole sentence and those in which it performs only a local analysis.

2.2.1 LOCAL ANALYSIS

A local analysis is restricted to certain contexts within the sentence. Limited context may be helpful in translating certain words. For example, in translating from English to French, 'the' becomes 'les' before plural nouns, and either 'le' or 'la' before singular nouns. Choice of 'le' or 'la' depends on the gender of the noun in French, and further adjustments such as elision depend on the immediate context in French (e.g.,the tree ——► le arbre ——► l'arbre). This seems rather straightforward and easy to program until we encounter sentences such as (a) and (b):

(a) **The passenger flight arrival time changes every summer.**
(a') **L'heure d'arrivée des vols/voyageurs change tous les étés.**

(b) **The passenger flight arrival time changes will be posted.**
(b') **Les changements d'heure d'arrivée des vols/voyageurs seront affichés.**

Before translating 'the' in these sentences the computer must find the **head** of the noun phrase in each case, for the head noun will be placed immediately after the definite article and will determine whether 'le', 'la', or 'les' replaces 'the' in the French equivalents (a'), (b'). Of course, the computer could be programmed to look for the last noun when there is more than one, since that is the head noun in English. But with this last-noun-in-a-sequence strategy the computer will have difficulty locating the head noun in (a): it must consider the possibility that 'changes' is a plural noun, although 'changes' is, in fact, a verb in (a) and 'time' is the head noun. Furthermore, in both (a) and (b) the computer must eliminate the possible interpretation of 'time' as a verb. Only by examining the entire sentence can we (or the computer) be sure that the head of a noun phrase has been correctly identified. Examples like (a) and (b) are not rare, and the syntax of the noun phrase is further complicated by the fact that a noun phrase may contain **embedded** sentences in various forms.

Local analysis may work in very simple cases, but few texts are very simple. And the claim that analysis can be localized to a particular constituent type (noun phrase, verb phrase, prepositional phrase, etc.) is misleading, for only an analysis of the whole sentence reveals what its constituents are.

2.2.2 FULL SENTENCE ANALYSIS

Experience with machine translation has shown that few local problems can be solved without knowledge of the overall sentence structure. If such information is obtained by the computer, this amounts to full sentence analysis; if it is supplied by a human translator interacting with the computer, the benefit gained from local analysis by the computer must be weighed against the demands placed on the translator. The discussion of full analysis here applies to the computer's contribution, not to the translator's (presumably, a human translator routinely performs a full analysis when translating a sentence).

The expression **full sentence analysis** needs some explanation. If it is taken to mean that **every aspect of sentence structure** is accounted for, no automatic analysis is likely to fall in that category. However, certain global aspects, at least, should be accounted for, such as those involved in

(a) the identification of major sentence types (declarative, imperative, interrogative),

(b) the identification of major sentence parts (main verb, subject and objects, if any, and sentence adverbials),

(c) the identification of embedded clauses and their major parts.

Other phenomena such as grammatical agreement, modifier-head relations, pronominal reference and scope of conjunction cannot be dealt with in isolation from these global considerations. For example, it makes no sense to try to establish subject-verb agreement without knowing which noun phrase is the subject of a given verb in a sentence.

Assuming that a computer is programmed for full sentence analysis, the **depth** of that analysis may vary considerably: there may be semantic as well as syntactic analysis, there may be a treatment of inflectional morphology only or both inflectional and derivational morphology, there may or may not be a strategy for determining the internal structure of noun strings, etc. These matters will be discussed further in **Chapter 3**. From a linguistic point of view, the intractable problems still remaining in automatic translation require a very deep analysis for their solution. And there are some problems that cannot be dealt with by analyzing sentences in isolation. An ambiguity in one sentence may be resolvable only in the light of information from preceding sentences. Unfortunately, text grammars are still in a primitive stage of development compared with sentence grammars.

2.3 TYPE OF TRANSFER

A system may be characterized as either a direct transfer or pivot language type, depending on whether or not it makes use of an intermediate representation ("pivot" language) between the source text and its translation in the target language. The terms **direct transfer** and **pivot language** are suggestive, but they stand in need of further explanation.

Regardless of which type of system is used, as a sentence is processed it goes through various intermediate stages before it finally emerges as an equivalent sentence in the target language. This being the case, what kind of an intermediate stage constitutes a pivot language representation? And what is the significance of a pivot language? How does it facilitate transfer? From the user's point of view, what are the advantages and disadvantages of the two types of systems?

To answer these questions we will begin by examining the direct transfer type of computerized translation system and finding the reasons for introducing a pivot language. We will also distinguish different kinds of pivot languages and discuss the merits of each.

2.3.1 DIRECT TRANSFER

A direct transfer system attempts to take the shortest, or most direct, route from a sentence in the source language to its equivalent in the target language. That route is determined essentially by two processes: **replacement** and **adjustment**. Such a system might consist of

(i) a bilingual dictionary that provides potential replacements (target language equivalents) for each word in the source language,

(ii) rules for choosing the correct replacements, and

(iii) rules of adjustment for putting words in the right order in the target language, adding or deleting words where necessary, etc.

These would seem to be the minimum requirements for a machine capable of producing reasonable translations on its own: (ii) is necessary since a word in one language usually has more than one equivalent (or translation) in another language; (iii) is necessary since word order may differ from language to language, some languages require articles or prepositions where others do not, and so on.

Suppose we submit the sentence 'Fresh water enters the small reservoir' to a hypothetical system of this type and try to imagine what would take place in translating the sentence into French. We needn't concern ourselves with the details of how the software performs each task or the exact order in which they are performed: those details may vary considerably in actual systems. In (i) the English words are given, along with the part of speech to which each belongs, and the potential French equivalents that could be listed in a bilingual dictionary just on the basis of the form of the English word.

(i)	fresh	water	enters
	ADJ	NOUN	VERB [transitive]
	frais [m,sg,pl]	eau [f,sg]	entre [3,sg,pres]
	fraîche [f,sg]		pénètre [3,sg,pres]
	fraîches [f,pl]	VERB [transitive]	monte [3,sg,pres]
		arroser [infinitive]	
		arrose [1,3,sg,pres]	
		arroses [2,sg,pres]	
		arrosons [1,pl.pres]	
		arrosez [2,pl,pres]	
		arrosent [3,pl,pres]	

the	small	reservoir
DEF ARTICLE	ADJ [prenominal]	NOUN
le [m,sg]	petit [m,sg]	réservoir [m,sg]
la [f,sg]	petite [f,sg]	
les [m,f,pl]	petits [m,pl]	
	petites [f,pl]	

The word «water» is listed as both a noun and a verb. A human translator would immediately take it to be a noun in this sentence but the machine would try both interpretations. To make the correct choice the machine needs to know that the interpretation ADJ + VERB + VERB + DEF ART + ADJ + NOUN does not yield a coherent sentence. Thus even in a direct transfer system the program for choosing the correct dictionary entry for a word in a sentence must incorporate or have access to rules of grammar. Direct transfer without some form of grammatical analysis of the sentence would result in a huge amount of garbage in the output.

Assuming, for the moment, that «water» has been identified as a singular noun in the given sentence, the French translation is then uniquely determined: eau [feminine,singular]. Similarly there is just one possibility for the noun «reservoir»: **réservoir** [masculine,singular].

Only one morphological form is given for each French verb corresponding to 'enters' since the English form can only be third person singular present tense; if the form had been 'enter' there would have been six potential forms for each French verb (e.g., entrer, entre, entres, entrons, entrez, entrent).

(ii)	**fraîche**	(agrees in number and gender with 'eau')
	petit	(agrees in number and gender with 'réservoir')
	le	(agrees in number and gender with 'réservoir')
	entre, pénètre, monte	(agree in number and gender with 'eau')

At this point we note that on the basis of the information available from (i) 'entre', 'pénètre', 'monte' and any other verb that is a translation equivalent of the transitive verb 'enter' in some context must also be considered compatible with the rest of the sentence. Without further information of some sort there will be multiple replacements for 'enter' and multiple translations of the original sentence. We will have more to say about this problem of choosing correct replacements after examining the rules of adjustment required for completing the translation into French.

(iii)	**fraîche eau** →	**eau fraîche**	(Change of word order for ADJ + NOUN if ADJ is not marked [prenominal])
	→	**la eau fraîche**	(Addition of definite article before nouns not otherwise marked, e.g. [proper], or pre-modified by certain determiners, etc.)
	→	**l'eau fraîche**	(Elision of final vowel of article before words beginning with a vowel or mute h)

The translation is still not complete since the preposition 'dans' must be inserted after the verb before obtaining (1b).

(1) (a) Fresh water enters the small reservoir.
(b) L'eau fraîche (entre dans, pénètre dans, ...) le petit réservoir.

But the addition of the correct preposition following a verb (when one is required), as well as the correct choice of verb in French, depends on the context of the verb in a rather complex way. This becomes evident when we consider the following related sentences.

(2) (a) The student enters the classroom.
(a') L'étudiant entre dans la salle de cours.

(b) The robber enters the house.
(b') Le voleur s'introduit dans la maison.

(c) The man enters a horse in a race.
(c') L'homme engage un cheval dans une course.

(d) The thought never entered my head.
(d') Cette pensée ne m'est jamais venue à l'esprit.

(e) The young man enters the service.
(e') Le jeune homme s'enrôle dans les forces armées.

(f) The bookkeeper enters an item in the ledger.
(f') Le teneur de livres inscrit un article au grand livre.

(g) The lawyer enters an action against the accused.
(g') L'avocat intente un procès contre l'accusé.

(h) The defendant enters a plea of not guilty.
(h') Le défendeur plaide non-coupable.

If the computer is provided with a sufficiently sophisticated program for analyzing the contexts in which different French equivalents of 'enter' can occur and deciding which prepositions (if any) are appropriate, then it may succeed in turning out the desired translations. But it is evident that in a direct transfer system the mapping from source sentences to target language equivalents may be very complex; direct does not mean simple substitution! Even in the case of short sentences that present no difficulty for the human translator the direct transfer path may be strewn with obstacles for the machine.

The above example illustrates an important fact: the correct translation of a verb, in general, requires information about the nature of admissible subjects and objects (arguments) of the verb, i.e. selectional restrictions. It is highly desirable to have this information available in a form that makes it readily accessible to transfer rules. We will examine several lines of evidence that point to the need for building up a structure where a variety of information about the sentence being processed is presented in a form convenient for the application of transfer rules.

HOMOGRAPHY

Transfer rules become much more complicated in a direct transfer system when words are encountered that belong to more than one part of speech. The existence of these homographs complicates the choice of replacements by forcing the rules to take into account more of the syntactic environment of the replaced word. This was the case with 'water' in (1a); likewise, if the word 'empty' had occurred in (1a) rather than 'small' then the machine would have had to decide whether 'empty' was an adjective or a verb in that context. The latter possibility could have been eliminated by programming the rejection of 'empty' as a verb in the syntactic environment ARTICLE _____ NOUN. Now adjective/verb homographs are fairly common and we do not want to repeat such a rule for every dictionary entry where it might apply. Rather we would prefer to obtain the same result by means of a general constraint on structures that are built up during the translation process. There are various ways to accomplish this, but for the moment we merely note that a general constraint on intermediate structures is considerably better than hundreds of similar constraints sprinkled around among the algorithms for choosing target language replacements for individual words.

The frequency of occurrence of homographs is very high in most texts and the environmental constraints, syntactic or otherwise, that can be used to resolve homographs are numerous indeed. The readers of these texts are seldom bothered by homography, and probably benefit from the economy it brings to natural language; but it is the bane of researchers in MT since the computer, which never tires of going down the garden path, diligently pursues every possibility that is open to it. It would be extremely cumbersome and repetitious if, for each homograph, all the constraints relevant to the transfer of the homograph into the target language had to be packed into the transfer rule for that particular item. A more practical approach is to bring together in one place any general constraints that would appear in many rules. Unfortunately, such a gathering place is not part of the scheme in a direct transfer system.

VERB + PARTICLE

There are many verb + particle combinations in English where French equivalents cannot be obtained by translating the verb and the particle separately.

(3)	**pick up**	**ramasser, relever**
	shake up	**secouer, agiter**
	fill in	**combler, remplir, remblayer**
	tune in	**régler, se mettre à l'écoute**
	check out	**retirer, vérifier**
	turn off	**fermer, couper, éteindre**
	jack up	**soulever, hausser**

This problem cannot be solved merely by entering the verb + particle in the dictionary as a single lexical item, since the particle may be separated from the verb by another word or phrase:

(4) (a) **John picked up the coin.**
(a') **Jean ramassa la pièce.**

(b) **John picked the coin up.**
(b') **Jean ramassa la pièce.**

(c) **John picked it up.**
(c') **Jean la rammassa.**

If 'pick up' were listed as a unit, then it would not be detected in (4b) and (4c). On the other hand, we might try writing a more complicated transfer rule for the verb 'pick' which would include look-ahead instructions that trigger a search for 'up' in the rest of the sentence, uniting it with 'pick' if found. The trouble with this solution is that even if 'up' is found somewhere in the sentence following the verb 'pick' there is no guarantee that the two words form a verb + particle combination; for example,

(5) (a) She picked the mushrooms that came up after the rain.
(a') Elle cueillit les champignons que la pluie avait fait pousser.

(b) He picked a fight with the guy up the street.
(b') Il en vint aux coups avec le gars de l'autre bout de la rue.

As a further illustration of the complex environmental factors that influence the interpretation of potential particles, consider the following occurrences of 'fill ... in'.

(6) (a) He filled it in.
(a') Il l'a rempli.

(b) He filled it in haste.
(b') Il l'a rempli à la hâte.

(c) He filled it in yesterday.
(c') Il l'a rempli hier.

(d) He filled it in the morning.
(d') Il l'a rempli durant l'avant-midi.

In (6a) and (6c) 'in' belongs with the verb 'fill', but in (6b) and (6d) 'in' plays the usual role of a preposition introducing a prepositional phrase. Reference to context is required not only to decide whether the preposition belongs with the verb, but also to decide on the interpretation (hence the target language equivalent) of the verb + particle combination. Both of these factors are illustrated by the occurrences of 'turn ... on' in (7).

(7) (a) She turned on the light.
(a') Elle a allumé la lumière.

(b) She turned on the gas.
(b') Elle a ouvert le gaz.

(c) She turned on the radio.
(c') Elle a ouvert la radio.

(d) She turned on the slippery road.
(d') Elle fit demi-tour sur la route glissante.

(e) She turned on her attacker.
(e') Elle se retourna contre son agresseur.
(e'') Elle surexcitait son agresseur.

When the verb occurs in a complex sentence (Section 3.3.2) with complex constituents (Section 3.3.3), identification of the relevant context can be an extremely complicated process. To account for relevant contexts in the transfer rule of each verb that has an associated particle (or particles) would be a formidable task. A more practical alternative would be to include a stage, prior to the application of transfer rules, where the context is analyzed and the results presented in a normalized form that can be easily "interrogated" by transfer rules for individual verbs to obtain the necessary contextual information.

ACTIVE/PASSIVE

There are thousands of transitive verbs in English that can occur in either the active or passive form. Because of the difference in position of the arguments of a verb in active and passive sentences, any constraints on the translation of a verb that refer to its arguments must be stated differently for the active and passive forms - if the statement is made in terms of the actual positions of these elements in the sentence. Two examinations of context are therefore required for dealing with passives: one to determine whether the verb is, in fact, being used in the passive[1], and another to identify the arguments of the verb (which may be complex noun phrases whose boundaries are not obvious (see section 3.3.3)). These intricate searches should not be part of the transfer algorithm for each verb; rather the system should include a general facility for identifying passives and checking the constraints on the arguments of the verb. This information, once obtained, can be given a standard representation at some intermediate stage so the transfer rules can refer to that representation in a simple uniform manner without repeating constraints on subjects and objects for active and passive forms[2]. But there is no such intermediate stage in a direct transfer system.

TRANSITIVE/INTRANSITIVE

Many transitive verbs in English can be used intransitively simply by deleting the object of the verb in a transitive sentence and keeping the same subject:

(8) (a) John reads books.
(a') Jean lit des livres.

(b) John reads.
(b') Jean lit.

There is an important subclass of transitive verbs in English whose intransitive use can be obtained from the transitive use by deleting the object and replacing the subject with the deleted object:

(9) (a) John opens the door.
(a') Jean ouvre la porte.

(b) The door opens.
(b') La porte s'ouvre.

(10) (a) John moves the stone.
(a') Jean bouge la pierre.

(b) The stone moves.
(b') La pierre bouge.

(11) (a) The sun melts the ice.
(a') Le soleil fond la glace.

(b) The ice melts.
(b') La glace fond.

(12) (a) Too much force will bend the metal.
(a') Trop de force fera plier le métal.

(b) The metal will bend.
(b') Le métal pliera.

(13) (a) The change of polarity discharges the condenser.
(a') Le changement de polarité décharge le condensateur.

(b) The condenser discharges.
(b') Le condensateur se décharge.

(14) (a) The friction that develops during re-entry into the earth's atmosphere heats up the surface of the vehicle very rapidly in spite of the heat shield.
(a') La friction qui se produit pendant la rentrée dans l'atmosphère

terrestre réchauffe très rapidement la surface du véhicule malgré son écran protecteur.

(b) The surface of the vehicle heats up very rapidly in spite of the heat shield.
(b') La surface du véhicule se réchauffe très rapidement malgré son écran protecteur.

This phenomenon presents a problem similar to the one discussed in the case of the active-passive relation: just as we wished to avoid duplicating the statement of argument restrictions for the passive form of the verb, in the present case we would like to avoid duplicating the statement of restrictions for the intransitive use of the verb. Since the same restrictions that hold between the verb and its direct object in the transitive occurrence also hold between the verb and its subject in the intransitive occurrence, it would be preferable to state this restriction just once (say as a restriction on the second argument of the verb) and note that the second argument is direct object when the verb is used transitively and subject when it is used intransitively. To program the necessary analysis of context and the relation between transitive direct object and intransitive subject, and include such programming in the transfer rule for each such verb, would be impractical at best.

The problems discussed so far do not necessarily occur in isolation from one another; several may crop up in the same sentence. The ubiquity of homographs is well known, the passivization of verb + particle combinations and verbs of the type illustrated in (9)-(14) is common, and this latter subclass of verbs also includes some verb + particle combinations (as illustrated by 'heat up' in (14) and by examples (15)-(20) below).

(15) (a) The driver slows the car down.
(a') Le conducteur ralentit la voiture.

(b) The car slows down.
(b') La voiture ralentit.

(16) (a) The runner speeds up the pace.
(a') Le coureur accélère l'allure.

(b) The pace speeds up.
(b') L'allure s'accélère.

(17) (a) Heat peels the paint off.
(a') La chaleur fait s'écailler la peinture.

(b) The paint peels off.
(b') La peinture s'écaille.

(18) (a) The attendant is filling up the tank.
(a') Le préposé remplit le réservoir.

(b) The tank is filling up.
(b') Le réservoir se remplit.

(19) (a) We checked the audio circuit out.[3]
(a') Nous avons entièrement vérifié le circuit audio.

(b) The audio circuit checked out.
(b') La vérification du circuit audio a été complétée.

(20) (a) The return line drains off the lighter liquid.
(a') Le conduit de retour vidange le liquide le moins dense.

(b) The lighter liquid drains off.
(b') Le liquide le moins dense se vidange.

IDIOMS

The dictionary in a practical machine translation system usually contains many idiomatic expressions (see section 3.1.4). If a string of words is entered in the dictionary as a single lexical item, the string as a whole is translated rather than the individual words that make it up (if it is translated both ways, a lot of garbage will result). But a string which is an idiom in one context may not be so in certain other contexts[4]:

(21) (a) Position AC hydraulic pump on **shock mount**.
(a') Positionner la pompe hydraulique CA sur le support d'amortisseur.

(b) To prevent **shock mount** equipment as described in 1B.
(b') Pour éviter un **choc poser** l'équipement comme il est indiqué au paragraphe 1B.

(22) (a) On finding the error he **hit the ceiling**.
(a') Lorsqu'il trouva l'erreur, il sortit de ses gonds.

(b) The ball bounced up and **hit the ceiling**.
(b') En rebondissant, la balle a frappé le plafond.

(23) (a) It has happened time and again.
(a') Cela s'est produit maintes et maintes fois.

(b) It happened at that time and again the next day.
(b') Cela est arrivé à ce moment-là et encore le jour suivant.

(24) (a) He is not all there.
(a') Il n'a pas tous ses esprits.

(b) The money is not all there.
(b') Tout l'argent n'est pas là.

(c) Is that all there is?
(c') Est-ce que c'est tout.

If the computer is to decide whether or not a potential idiom really is an idiom in a given sentence, it must first examine the context. As the above examples show, such an examination may amount to a full parsing of the sentence — which is not a task for individual idiom transfer rules. Thus we see that for idioms as well as for other lexical items transfer rules require an analysis of the sentence and a normalized representation of the sentence from which the relevant contextual information can be readily obtained.

* * * * * * * * * *

The sentences encountered in practice are seldom simple (see section 3.3 for a detailed discussion of simple vs complex sentences). We have seen ample evidence that lexical transfer requires the extraction of a great deal of contextual information from the sentence. The presence of complex constituents (see section 3.3.3) makes the identification of relevant context enormously complicated.

There are two methods for dealing with this problem:

(i) abandon direct transfer and include in the system a parser which analyses the sentence, labels the constituents and builds up a simplified but highly informative representation of the sentence (a normalized structure);

(ii) leave the choice of target language equivalents for lexical items to a human translator and let the computer do the rest.

The second method (ii) seems fairly straightforward, although the consequences of its adoption may not be so obvious. It results in an interactive system (see **section 2.1.1** and **section 2.1.2**) whose degree of automation depends on a variety of factors in addition to the manner of choosing target language equivalents for lexical items in the source text. The question of interactivity will be examined further in **Chapter 5** when we look at projected levels of automation, constraints on the quality of translation, and evaluation of a system's potential. For the moment, however, let us examine the consequences of adopting (i) as a solution to the problems facing direct transfer systems.

2.3.2 PIVOT LANGUAGE

We have seen that lexical transfer requires considerable contextual analysis. The context ranges over the entire sentence, as in the case of checking for the arguments corresponding to a given predicate. Nor is the relevant context necessarily contiguous with the word whose translation is in question (a predicate may, for example, be separated from one of its arguments by an adverbial or a non-restrictive relative clause). And the context is not likely to be stated in terms of particular words, but in terms of relational concepts such as subject, direct object, indirect object, modifier, head, agent, instrument, etc. And to make matters worse, these elements are themselves often quite complex. The only sure way of obtaining all the information necessary for lexical transfer is to analyze the entire sentence.

Any attempt to avoid complete sentence analysis by restricting the analysis of context to just those cases where the translation of a word requires it will result in many **overlapping analyses**. This follows from the fact that several words in the same sentence may require information from the same constituent for their translation. For example, in each of the following sentences it is necessary to locate and analyze the subject of 'seemed' in order to obtain the appropriate French equivalent of that verb; it is also necessary to locate and analyze the element that is modified by the adjective 'hard' in order to choose its French equivalent. But the subject of 'seemed' and the element modified by 'hard' happen to be the same.

(25) (a) The pie crusts she made yesterday seemed to be very **hard**.
(a') Les croûtes de tarte qu'elle a faites hier **semblaient** être très **dures**.

(26) (a) The problem she solved yesterday **seemed** to be very **hard** for her.
(a') Le problème qu'elle a résolu hier **semblait** être très **difficile** pour elle.

(27) (a) Making good pie crusts yesterday **seemed** to be very **hard** for her.
(a') Ça **semblait** très **difficile** pour elle hier de faire de bonnes croûtes de tarte.

Note also that because of the position of the adjective 'hard' in these sentences, its translation requires an analysis of the whole sentence to locate the element that it modifies.

An obvious way to avoid these problems is to analyze the whole sentence once at the outset and make the results available to transfer rules in a normalized form. Transfer rules can then simply mention the kind of information needed (subject, object, modifier, head noun, etc.) without having to analyze the original sentence (possibly several times) to find it.

In light of the above discussion let us suppose there is a single parse of the whole sentence. There are many ways that this parsing can be done: top down, left to right, bottom up, parallel, single pass, multiple pass, etc. To say that a sentence should be analyzed just once does not imply single pass parsing anymore than it implies top down or bottom up. It is the analysis as a whole that should be done only once, whatever method is used. We are not concerned here with the details of the parsing device, but with the representation of the sentence that is built up (we will refer to that representation as the "normalized structure" of the sentence) and the role it plays in machine translation.

It will be instructive to review the purpose of **normalized structure** from the point of view of the preceding discussion before looking at the broader implications for machine translation.

PURPOSE OF NORMALIZED STRUCTURE:

(A) To provide information relevant to the transfer of individual lexical items.

(B) To avoid multiple analyses of the same material to obtain this information.
(C) To provide for ease of access to this information.
(D) To provide an unambiguous representation of the sentence.
(E) To provide for the expression of general constraints on syntactic structures.

(A) and (B) have been covered in some detail in this and the preceding section. Further comments are needed concerning (C), (D) and (E).

(C) Normalized structure often takes the form of labeled trees. Algorithms for operating on tree structures are well known in computer science and in linguistics. Many linguists feel that trees are the most natural form for the information structure of sentences. But whatever form is used, a basic requirement is that it be as simple and clear as possible in order to facilitate the writing of transfer rules. This is very important since those rules tend to be rather complicated and it should be possible for linguists or terminologists to write them, as well as computer scientists. Writing transfer algorithms requires considerable knowledge of linguistic structure and special terminology, and it is very time-consuming. As a system is used new words are constantly being entered in the transfer dictionary. A well-designed normalized structure will make it easier to expand the domain of texts that can be handled by the system (assuming that the parser is capable of analyzing the input) by simplifying the writing of transfer rules. This enhances the versatility of the system.

To illustrate the kind of representation we have been discussing, consider the normalized structure used in the TAUM-AVIATION machine translation system. Every sentence, regardless of its complexity, is taken to consist of a predicate (verb or adjective), its arguments (one for intransitive verbs, two or three for transitive verbs), and possibly some circumstantial elements (sentence adverbials). The basic structure, which is a tree, has the general form[5] shown in (28):

(28)

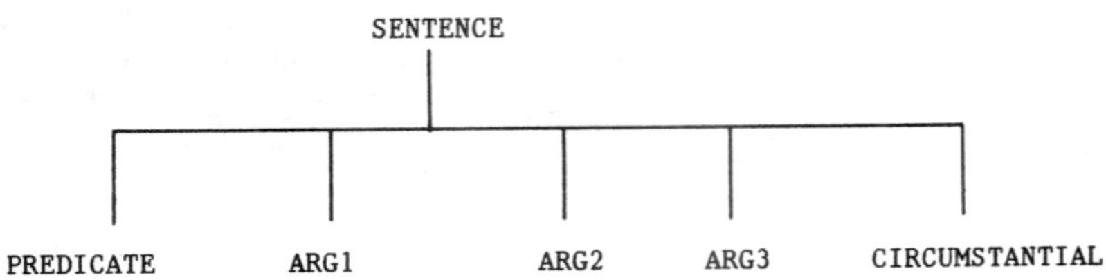

where the order of these elements is always the same regardless of the order in which they occur in the source sentence or in its target language equivalent. Although the number of arguments is limited, there may be any number of circumstantials or none at all.

Following are a few examples of this basic structure, omitting some of the details. The sentences are: (29) It snowed. (30) Yesterday it snowed according to a report which was issued by Environment Canada. (31) John loves Mary. (32) Mary is loved by John. (33) John gave Mary a ring. (or: John gave a ring to Mary.)

(29)

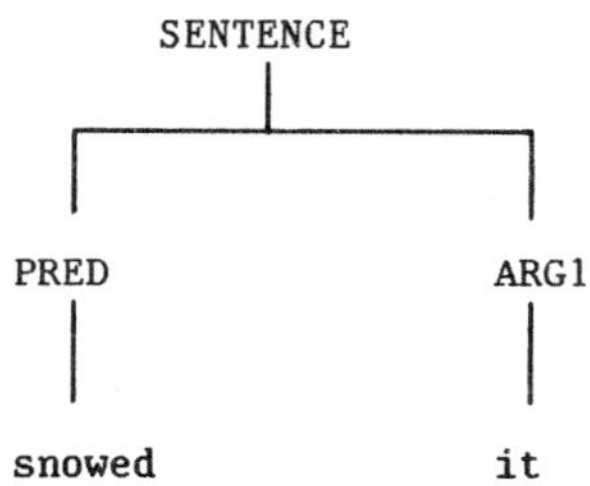

(30)

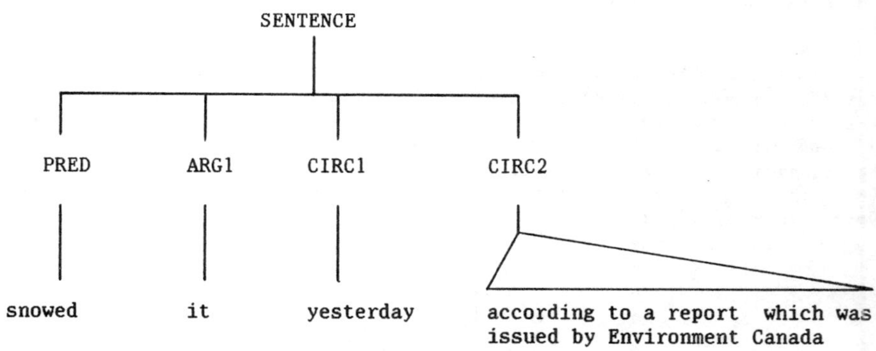

(31)

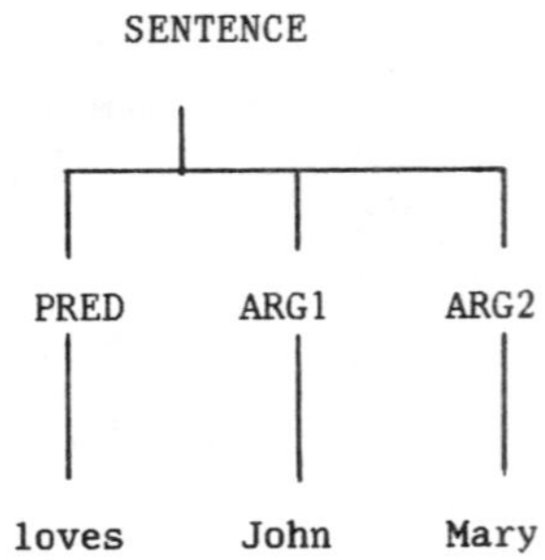

(32)

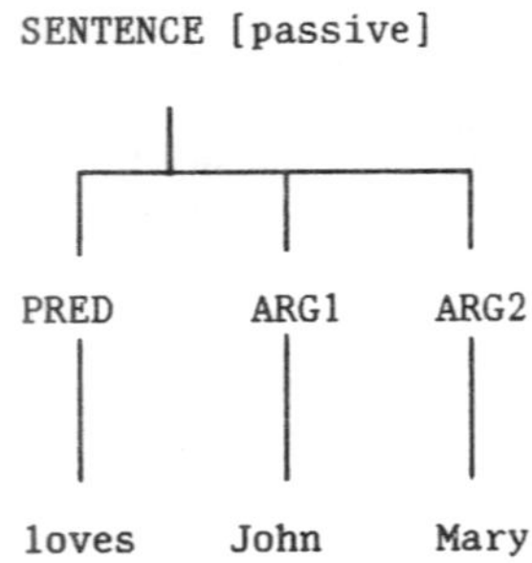

(33)

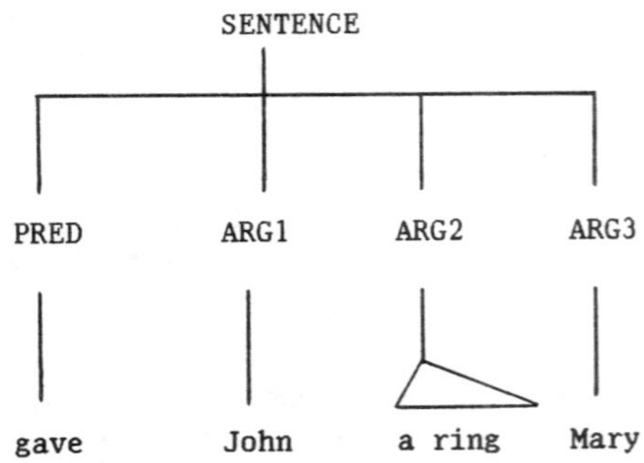

(29) illustrates the basic structure of a sentence whose main verb is intransitive and in (30) two circumstantials have been added. (31) and (32) show that the representation of a passive sentence differs from its active counterpart only by the presence of the feature [passive] attached to the SENTENCE node. (33) illustrates a sentence with both a direct and an indirect object; ARG2 is the direct object and ARG3 the indirect object, regardless of the order of these elements in the sentence.

The second CIRC in (30) and ARG2 in (33) represent phrases rather than single lexical items, hence there will be subtrees branching out from those nodes. Since the CIRC2 in (30) contains a relative clause and relative clauses are considered as embedded sentences, the subtree under CIRC2 will include a node labeled SENTENCE which will be the top node of another tree conforming to (28); in this case the features [passive, relative] will be attached to the SENTENCE node. Thus a tree may contain a subtree, which may contain another subtree, and so ad infinitum - depending on the depth of embedding in the sentence. The important fact is that every subtree branching from a node X must conform to the normalized structure specified for X (where X may be SENTENCE, NOUN PHRASE, PREPOSITIONAL PHRASE, DETERMINER, etc.).

This normalized structure also leaves a place for deleted elements, as illustrated in (34) for the agentless passive 'The fort was captured':

(34)

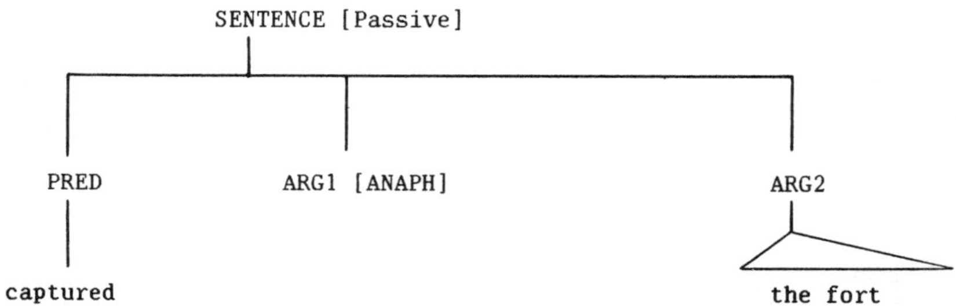

The feature [ANAPH] indicates that ARG1 is to be considered as referring to an unknown element somewhere in the discourse (i.e., a kind of anaphora). There are many different types of deletion in English and it occurs frequently in normal usage. By creating nodes in normalized structure for elements that do not occur in the original sentence, but which can be inferred, a more uniform representation of sentence structure results and the check for contextual information by transfer rules is greatly simplified.

(D) Normalized structure is an **unambiguous** representation of the sentence. If analysis reveals more than one possible interpretation, then each one is assigned its own normalized structure. Transfer rules are applied to each representation separately and separate sentences are generated in the target language. In such cases a reviser can decide which output is appropriate and reject the others. In practice, total disambiguation of a sentence is not always attainable. It sometimes happens that for a particular language pair an ambiguity in the source language carries over into the same ambiguity in the target language. In this case, a single normalized structure may be used to represent more than one reading of a sentence. Given the present state of the art, human translators are still much better at resolving ambiguities than the machine is - and they are likely to remain so for some time. The translator is able to keep track of the discourse preceding the sentence in question and extract the information needed to resolve the ambiguity, but automatic text analysis beyond the sentence boundary is still at a very primitive stage of development. In addition, a good translator has a large store of knowledge of the world which he can bring to bear on the problem of ambiguity. (One of the major questions in computerized translation is whether to go all out for a fully automatic system with only post editing by human translators, or to permit human intervention during the translation process. We will return to this question later.)

The important point about normalized structure being an unambiguous representation is that it simplifies the statement of transfer rules.

(E) It is not the function of normalized structure to represent all the grammatical details of the sentence that has been analyzed. Many of the details that have to be taken into account during analysis may not have to be given explicit representation for the purpose of transfer and generation. Thus normalized structure does not specify word order in either the source or target language; the analysis grammar and the generation grammar take care of that aspect of syntactic structure. We have also seen that bits and pieces of the original sentence may be omitted in normalized structure, their contribution being signalled by a feature on the SENTENCE node. For example, in (32) the word 'is' disappears from the predicate and 'John' loses the agentive marker 'by'. The transfer rules can obtain the information furnished by these words simply by checking for the feature [passive] on the SENTENCE node, which eliminates a good deal of searching through the tree. This is all part of the process of forming the simplest possible structure for transfer rules to operate on - without loss of critical information.

Certain general syntactic constraints are expressed through normalized structure. For example, (35) and (36) are legitimate, but (37), (38) and (39) are not.

(35)

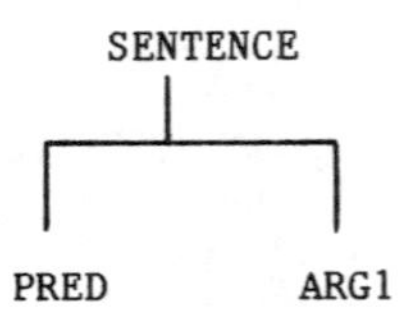

(36)

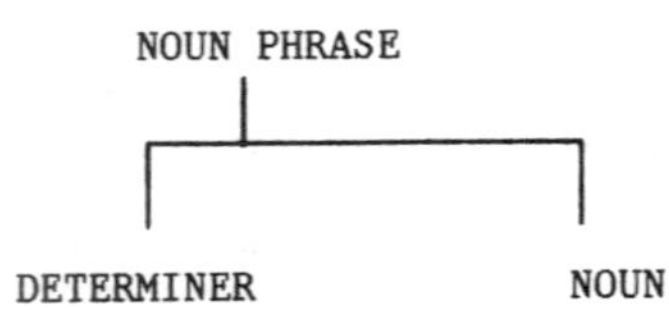

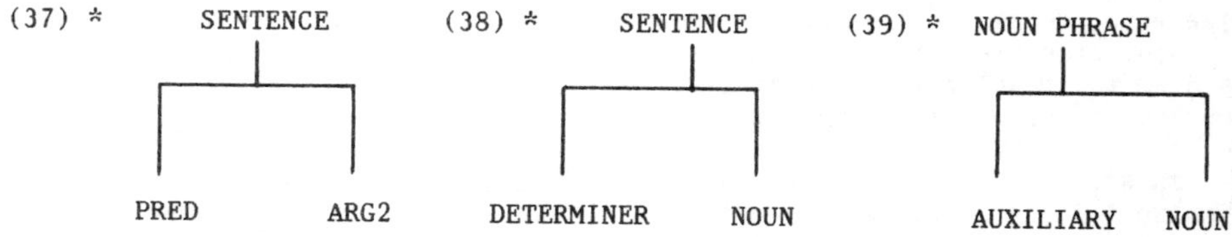

The constraints on normalized structure can be codified in the form of an official syntax; in other words, the set of sentence representations that we have called normalized structure conforms to definite rules. These rules, in fact, constitute a context free generative grammar in the TAUM system. Like any other generative grammar, this one generates a set of strings over a given vocabulary and assigns a structure to each string it generates. The resulting set of structured strings is therefore a language which stands between the source and target languages. It is pivotal in the translation system: instead of source sentences being converted directly into their target language equivalents, they are first expressed in this pivot language and then mapped into the target language.

THE ROLE OF PIVOT LANGUAGES

The attempt to overcome the limitations of direct transfer led to the concept of a pivot language. We have looked briefly at one pivot language, but there are other versions in operation and on the drawing board. Researchers in machine translation have various ideas about just what a pivot language should consist of and what role it should play in the development of new systems.

If a system is designed for a specific pair of natural languages and a particular kind of text, a pivot language may be tailored to fit that situation. A good example of this is METEO, which was designed only for the translation of weather forecasts from English to French. The pivot language in METEO reflects the limitations inherent in this situation.

Of course, the vocabulary in the sublanguage of weather bulletins is rather small - on the order of 1,300 words, including morphological variants (there is no morphological analysis of words in METEO, because of the very limited use of inflectional endings in the English sentences). But it is not just the small vocabulary that affects the pivot language; after all, it is possible to construct sentences of arbitrary syntactic complexity using a much smaller vocabulary (linguists have been doing precisely that for many years). Let us see what other factors are present.

The examination of many weather bulletins in English led researchers at the University of Montreal to identify five different sentence types; consequently there are five classes of tree structures in METEO representing those sentence types. Two of them are trivial: one consists of place names that are given before the forecast (a single name is treated as a sentence in that position) and another consists of a stereotyped heading in which only the names, dates and times of day vary. The other three classes of tree structures are illustrated by (40), (41) and (42)[6]. The basis for this classification is semantic and there are only a few different message types involved.

(40)

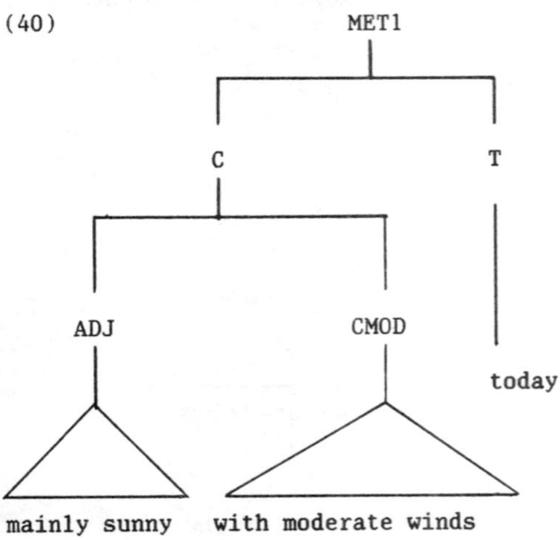

MET1 expresses the meteorological condition for the day.

C = condition (meteorological)
CMOD = complement (modifier)
T = time
NP = noun phrase

(41)

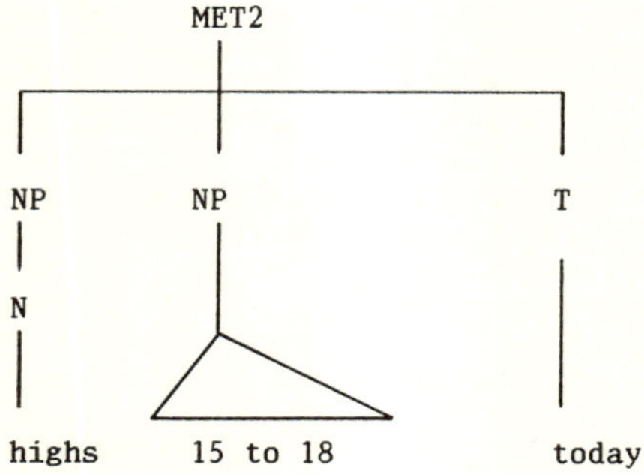

MET2 expresses maxima and minima.

(42)

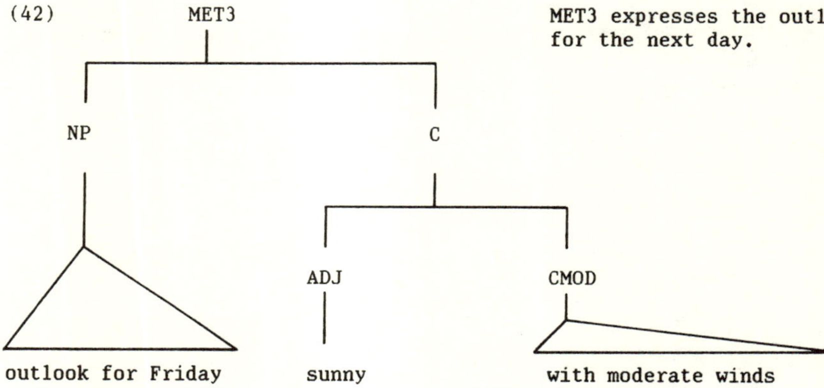

MET3 expresses the outlook for the next day.

The relative simplicity of this set of structures is also a result of the telegraphic style of weather forecasts. Most grammatical words are omitted, there are no relative clauses, subordinate clauses or passives, and the sentences are short. The syntax of these short telegraphic sentences is much the same in English and French. Needless to say, this happy circumstance does not prevail in most situations where machine translation is contemplated.

Even in the restricted domain of maintenance manuals for aircraft hydraulic systems - a domain that was studied intensively by researchers on Project TAUM from 1976 to 1980 - no such simple classification of sentence structures suffices. The semantic range is far more extensive than that of weather bulletins. There is some use of telegraphic style in sections of the manuals consisting of instructions for carrying out maintenance procedures (mostly imperative sentences with much deletion of definite articles), but the descriptive sections are more like standard English. Throughout all sections there are extremely complex nominal compounds that still defy automatic analysis. And problems involving the scope of conjunction and attachment of prepositions abound.

At the opposite end of the spectrum from METEO are systems designed to translate a wide variety of texts between many different languages. One such multilingual system, now in the planning/development stage, is EUROTRA, which is a cooperative effort among the European Communities[7]. Analysis of texts will be based on dependency grammar which produces representations in the form of dependency tree structures. The characteristic of these structures is that in each constituent there is a "governor" (the head, or main part) and the other parts are related to (or modify) this head. The dependency trees form the basis for an interface structure which adds the following types of information to the dependency relations:

(i) surface syntactic function (subject, object, etc.)
(ii) semantic relations (manner, source, etc.)
(iii) valency boundedness (closeness of the connection between the predicate and other constituents)
(iv) morphological, morpho-syntactic and syntagmatic information.

EUROTRA is a modular system with independent modules for analysis, transfer and generation (see section 2.4 for a detailed discussion of modularization). The interface structure provides linkage between these modules. The overall program is very ambitious, although the planners recognize certain limitations due to linguistic problems whose solutions are not within sight.

A UNIVERSAL PIVOT LANGUAGE?

In a multilingual environment where the design of a transfer system can not, in general, take advantage of similarities between source and target languages, the question of the possibility of a universal pivot language naturally arises. Is it feasible to design a pivot language that is completely independent of any particular natural language, even to the extent of replacing lexical items with semantic primitives?

Researchers in the field of artificial intelligence have made various proposals for semantic languages and universal representations. Their main concern has been with **natural language understanding** and with the use of inferencing, but these concerns have become increasingly important in machine translation too as traditional methods of sentence analysis, largely syntactic, have been pushed to the limit.

During the 1970's Roger Schank, of Yale University, developed the theory of **conceptual dependency.** Schank (1975, 1977) believed that the ease with which people could translate from one language to another indicated an interlingual representation of meaning, "language free", that was available to the mind. He was interested in machine translation and hoped that a psychologically correct meaning representation would be useful there. In his theory a predetermined set of possible relations (conceptual rules) are used to predict conceptual items implicit in the sentences of a natural language.

Yorick Wilks developed a machine translation system in which **templates** are the fundamental units of meaning representation - i.e. basic messages of the form agent-action-object. In Wilks' theory of meaning representation (Wilks 1973, 1975a, 1975b), templates are constructed from formulas which represent the **senses** of individual words; underlying these formulas are the **semantic primitives** (cause, have, use, want, do, etc.), less than a hundred in all. Everything is ultimately constructed out of these primitive elements by functions and predicates ranging over them.

The search for a truly universal interlingua to serve as the pivotal element in a multilingual machine translation system continues, but there is still much skepticism about the use of such an interlingua in a large scale practical application. If, on the other hand, we look at the syntactic aspect of pivot languages apart from the semantic representation, it can be seen that considerable universality has already been achieved in the former. Transfer systems such as that of TAUM-AVIATION make use of pivot languages whose syntax is relatively independent of any particular natural language. But semantic analysis and the representation of meaning are not nearly as well developed, and the conversion of lexical items of the source language into semantic primitives is hardly considered for practical applications.

Researchers generally agree that a deeper semantic analysis of the source texts is essential to further progress in machine translation; there is somewhat less agreement about what form semantic representation should take. Transfer systems already make use of representations that are quite abstract and this trend will probably continue. However, in the immediate future, truly universal interlinguas are not likely to replace separate transfer modules for individual language pairs in multilingual systems.

2.3.3 SUMMARY: ADVANTAGES AND DISADVANTAGES

The strategies underlying direct and pivot language transfer systems are indicated by (43) and (44) respectively.

(43)

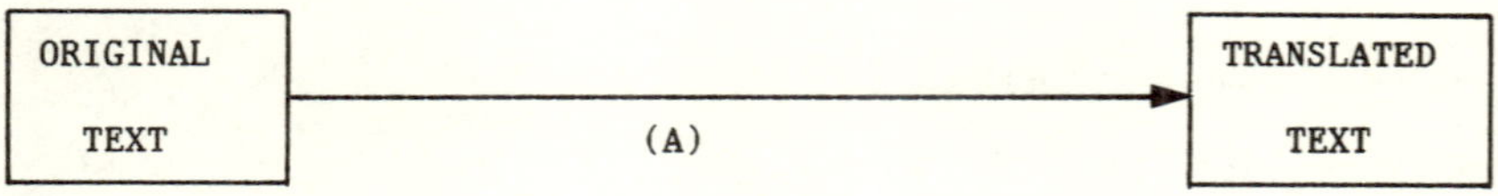

(A) Substitution of target language equivalents for lexical items.

(44)

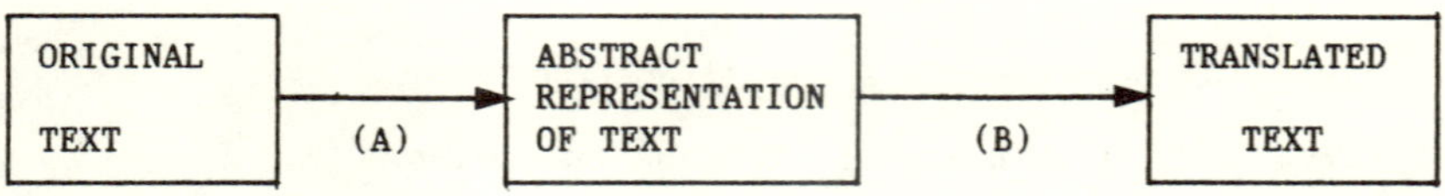

(A) Analysis of text and construction of abstract representation of text.

(B) Lexical substitution, restructuration, and generation of sentences in the target language.

At first glance, (43) appears much simpler than (44); if this simple strategy could be implemented, it would, presumably, cost less. But, as we saw in sections 2.3.1 and 2.3.2, such a strategy encounters many problems:

- Proper choice of lexical equivalents for words in the original text cannot be made without knowledge of their context.

- Relevant context for lexical substitution ranges over the entire sentence.
- Individual rules for lexical substitution would have to incorporate an analysis of the whole sentence in many cases.
- Since the grammatical structures of source and target language sentences differ, restructuration of sentences must take place as well as lexical substitution.

The last point is illustrated by the following examples in which structural changes accompany the transfer from English to French.

```
(45) (a)    Check the wooden box.
                      ADJ  N
     (a')   Vérifier la boîte en bois.
                         N   P   N

     (b)    Check filters for contamination.
                         P       N
     (b')   Vérifier si les filtres sont sales.
                     C                   VP

     (c)    Be sure doors are free of obstructions.
            V  ADJ
     (c')   S'assurer que rien n'obstrue les portes.
              V

     (d)    There are no leaks in the system.

     (d')   Il n'y a aucune fuite dans le circuit.

     (e)    The extension is pointed in the same direction as the wrench.
                          BE  Ved
     (e')   La rallonge se dirige dans le même sens que la clé.
                         V [reflex]

     (f)    While he plays the guitar, they will sing.
                         V [pres.]
```

(f') Pendant qu'il jouera de la guitare, ils chanteront.
V [fut.]

(Note that in (f) the information needed to determine the change in tense of the verb in the first clause comes only at the end of the second clause, and the verb phrases are not contiguous.)

(g) She must be sick.
MODAL V [inf.]

(g') Elle sera malade.
V [fut.]

It is obvious that the apparent simplicity of the strategy in (43) is misleading. Direct substitution would, at best, yield a sequence of sets of target language equivalents for the sequence of words in the original sentence. In this strategy the choice of the correct equivalent from each set would have to be made by a human translator to obtain any degree of accuracy. Furthermore, restructuring the sentence and ensuring grammatical agreement between various sentence elements would also require analysis extending over the whole sentence; if the machine does not perform the required analysis, it cannot handle those operations automatically.

In short, strict adherence to a direct transfer strategy results in a system that depends heavily on human intervention in the translation process. If a high degree of automation is desired, then a strategy more like that of (44) is called for.

Full sentence analysis and construction of an abstract representation of each sentence prior to transfer offers several advantages:

- Lexical transfer rules can be stated more easily on a uniform, simplified, perspicuous and unambiguous representation of the sentence (normalized structure) than on the original sentence where grammatical structure is only implicit;

- The structural transformations involved in restructuring a sentence to correspond to the grammar of the target language can be stated more simply on the domain of normalized structure;

- The use of a single structure to represent related sentence forms such as active/passive permits greater economy in the statement of selectional restrictions between predicates and their arguments;

- Dependence on human assistance can be minimized; i.e., a higher degree of automation can be attained.

As for the use of a universal pivot language, this would result in practical advantages for multilingual translation systems. In translating from any one of n different languages to any of the remaining (n-1) languages, n(n-1) different transfer modules would ordinarily be required. For example, five languages would require 5 x 4 = 20 transfer modules and ten languages would require 10 x 9 = 90 transfer modules. But consider the economy obtained if a universal pivot language could be implemented: transfer into each of the n target languages would use only the universal pivot language as input; hence only n encoders from the source languages into the universal meaning representation and n decoders from the universal meaning representation into the target languages would be required. For example, five languages would require five encoders and five decoders instead of twenty transfer modules. For the present, unfortunately, a truly universal interlingua does not appear to be feasible for large scale practical applications.

Finally, apart from the question of universality, the pivot language concept is an important element in the modularization of the translation process. The advantages of modular systems will be discussed in the next section.

2.4 TRANSLATION MODULARIZATION

In order to solve the problems inherent in direct transfer systems (without resorting to human intervention in the translation process) the minimum requirement seems to be full sentence analysis. It was shown in section 2.3 that local analysis does not suffice; the relevant context for determining the choice of a lexical equivalent is not confined to the immediate environment of the item to be replaced. The requirement that the whole sentence be analyzed leads naturally to the separation of the operations of analysis and transfer, i.e., to the creation of independent modules within the translation system. It has also been suggested that transfer operations be separated from those involved in generating the target language sentences with proper syntax, morphological forms, grammatical agreement, etc. The resulting system then contains three modules, referred to simply as analysis, transfer and generation (or synthesis).

The separation of transfer and generation has been the subject of some debate. It may be argued that generation of the target language begins with the substitution of lexical equivalents in the normalized structure that constitutes the output of analysis. In that case, there is only analysis of the source language and generation of the target language, with normalized structure serving as the interface between analysis and generation. The two points of view are illustrated in (46) and (47); cross-hatched areas indicate communication between modules.

(46)

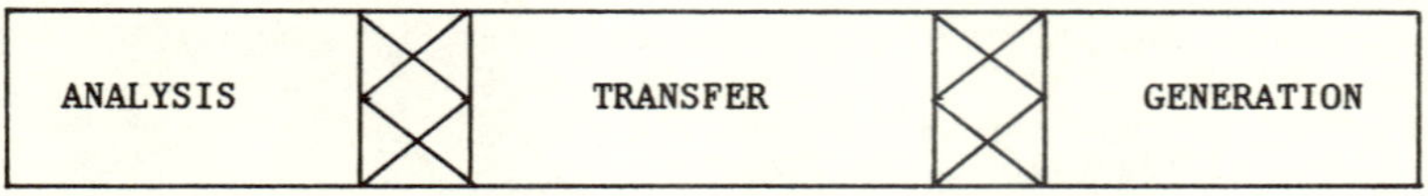

(47)

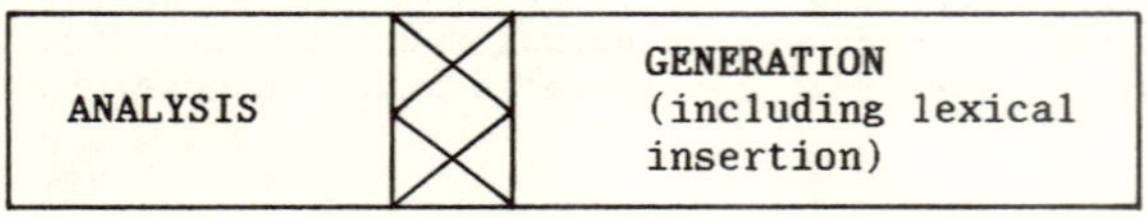

At first glance, the difference between (46) and (47) might appear to be merely terminological, with the transfer and generation modules in (47) being referred to jointly as GENERATION. However, there are some substantive issues involved and we shall return to this question later.

2.4.1 SEQUENTIAL PHASES

Each of the three modules in (46) has a specific task to perform - one that is well defined in the translation process. Of course, there must also be some form of communication between modules so the results obtained at one stage are available for use at another stage. The link is provided by an interface structure that we have referred to as normalized structure. This is shown more clearly in (48).

(48)

(A) Original text.

(B) Normalized structure with lexical items of the source language included.

(C) Normalized structure with lexical items of the target language included.

(D) Translated text.

As mentioned before, some restructuration may take place at transfer in addition to substitution of lexical equivalents, but the resulting structure must conform to the general constraints on normalized structure (i.e., the syntax of the pivot language) so that it can serve as input to generation.

The arrows in (48) indicate that communication between modules in this case is unidirectional: all the operations of analysis are completed before sending the results to transfer and all the operations of transfer are completed before sending the results to generation. There is no jumping back and forth between phases, so to speak. We will say that a modular system of this type has **sequential phases**. Note that (46), unlike (48), is non-committal about that aspect of processing; the interpretation of (46) in terms of **non-sequential phases** will be examined in section **2.4.2.**

SUBMODULES

The tasks that are performed by analysis, transfer and generation can be broken down into certain well-defined subtasks corresponding to subdivisions of grammar such as morphology and syntax. Some grammarians refer to these subdivisions as **linguistic levels**, emphasizing the "layered" aspect of language structure. The notion of independent levels has important consequences for the processing of texts in a computerized translation system. For example, an analysis module may itself contain independent submodules for morphological and syntactic analysis. Within these submodules, particular problems of morphology or syntax may be isolated and dealt with in a simpler manner than would otherwise be possible.

The general plan of a modular system with sequential phases, and submodules corresponding to various linguistic levels, has been carried out in the TAUM-AVIATION system. In (49) we have summarized each module of this translation chain to give an example of a modular system with sequential phases. A detailed flow chart of this second generation MT system is contained in Appendix B.

(49) **ANALYSIS**

INPUT = ENGLISH TEXT.

I. **Preliminary Processing**

Word and sentence boundaries of the English text have been identified. Periods used in abbreviations (rather than end of sentence), punctuation marks, numerals and other types of symbols have been identified.

II. **Morphological Analysis**

Words of the text have now been put into their base form (e.g. 'books' is transformed into 'book' [+ PLURAL], 'ran' into 'run' [+ PAST], etc.)

III. **English Dictionary Look-up**

Words have been assigned grammatical categories (NOUN, VERB, ADJECTIVE, etc.), semantic and syntactic features (ABSTRACT, HUMAN, DATIVE, DEMONSTRATIVE, etc.), and the number and types of possible arguments for predicate words have been indicated.

IV. **Syntactic - Semantic Analysis**

The text has been transformed into a sequence of tree structures, one for each sentence, conforming to the formal specifications of normalized structure. The "leaves" of the trees are English lexical items.

TRANSFER

INPUT = Sequence of tree structures from ANALYSIS conforming to normalized structure.

V. Transfer Dictionary Look-up

Each lexical entry is a lexical procedure which is applied to the tree structure. English lexical items in each tree have been replaced by their French equivalents. According to the French equivalent, some lexical transformations can be applied on the tree structure in accordance with the normalized structure.

VI. Structural Transfer

Some structural adjustments (non-lexical transformations) have been made in the tree structure of French. The trees still conform to the specifications of normalized structure; their leaves are now French lexical items.

GENERATION (OR SYNTHESIS)

INPUT = Sequence of tree structures from TRANSFER conforming to normalized structure and containing French lexical items.

VII. Syntactic Generation

Each tree structure has been transformed into a string of words correctly ordered, but not yet conjugated or put into grammatical accord.

VIII. Morphological Generation

Words have been conjugated, grammatical accord established and rules of elision and contraction applied.

IX. Post-Processing

The French text has been put into readable form and laid out according to the required norms.

2.4.2 NON-SEQUENTIAL PHASES

Up to this point we have assumed that in a modularized system the modules are applied in a fixed order. Since each module has a specific task to perform, our assumption has been that the tasks are best performed sequentially - that the system should not suspend work on one task, undertake another, then return to the one that was interrupted. In our discussion of non-sequential phases that assumption will be dropped.

The tasks mentioned in (49) can be grouped in two different ways such that within each group there seems to be a natural sequence; this is shown in (50) and (51).

(50) Tasks involving only the source language: analysis
Tasks involving both source and target language: transfer
Tasks involving only the target language: generation

(51) Tasks involving a particular linguistic level:
morphological, lexical, syntactic, semantic[8]

(50) and (51) correspond to the major components of a system and their sub-components, respectively. The consequences of departing from the strict order indicated in (50) are somewhat different in the case of (51); the two cases will therefore be examined separately.

A. MAJOR COMPONENTS

Processing a text in the order analysis/transfer/generation has been well-motivated. The basic idea is rather simple:

- extract as much information as possible from the original text;
- use this information in choosing the correct target language equivalents for lexical items in the original text;
- make whatever adjustments are required by the grammar of the target language.

Of course, the execution of this plan is not at all simple and there are many ways of carrying out the details. We will now look at the possibility of handling certain details in ways that depart from the strict order of processing indicated in (49). Consider, for example, the following suggestions:

(i) Substitute lexical items of the target language for all those words in the original text which have only one equivalent in the target language and use local analysis of context, as required, for replacing the remaining words.

Attempts to blend analysis and transfer in this manner have not proved successful. As we saw in section 2.3, this approach inevitably leads to such complexity in the statement of transfer rules that human intervention in the translation process is preferable. In any event, local context analysis too often fails to provide the information needed to choose the correct lexical equivalent.

(ii) Replace idiomatic expressions in the original text with their target language equivalents at the very outset in order to avoid unnecessary analyses based on literal interpretations of the words in those idioms.

Unfortunately, a sequence of words that constitutes an idiom in one context may not do so in another; therefore the possibility of interpreting the words literally may be desirable. But suppose this consideration is unimportant for statistical reasons (perhaps these sequences of words do constitute idioms in the vast majority of their occurrences). It is still not necessary to replace an idiom with its target language equivalent prior to parsing, since it can be treated as a single lexical item of the source language anyway, and so avoid the literal interpretation of its component words. In fact, this is the normal procedure.

(iii) Permit backtracking to take place between, as well as within, major components. This would permit further analysis to take place after transfer has begun, or further transfer operations after generation has started.

Suppose, for example, there are **choice points** at various places in the system, i.e. points where several alternatives are offered. If, after choosing one of these alternatives, failure occurs farther down the line, processing returns to the choice point and another alternative is tried. In one version of backtracking, the return is to the last choice point encountered before failure occurred; if this does not result in success, the return is to the choice point encountered just before the last one; etc.

Backtracking is commonly used in a variety of parsers. It often happens that at a choice point some alternatives are known to have a greater probability of success than others. Backtracking allows the parser to explore the most likely alternative first, then return to try the next most likely, if necessary, etc. This has proved to be an important tool in parsing; the question raised by the suggestion in (iii) is whether it would also be advantageous to backtrack from transfer to analysis or from generation to transfer.

FROM ANALYSIS TO TRANSFER AND FROM TRANSFER TO ANALYSIS

It can be argued that if a wrong choice is made at some point during analysis of the source text, that mistake should be detected before proceeding to the transfer phase. It is, after all, a function of the parser to eliminate any alternatives that do not lead to an acceptable sentence - not to present them to transfer and generation, which have quite different roles to play. The operations of transfer and generation, as generally conceived, are essentially **deterministic processes.** It is convenient, for example, to write transfer algorithms in something like the following form:

if condition C1 holds, **then** replace source lexeme L with target lexeme L'1
if condition C2 holds, **then** replace source lexeme L with target lexeme L'2

...

if condition Cn-1 holds **then** replace source lexeme L with target lexeme L'n-1
otherwise replace source lexeme L with target lexeme L'n.
(Assume that the Ci are mutually exclusive.)

Now **otherwise** guarantees that some replacement (L'n) will be made. Of course, another condition Cn could be used instead of the default option **otherwise**, so that if none of the conditions C1, ... Cn hold, backtracking is initiated and allowed to restart analysis at some point. However, that would appear to be a rather costly procedure. And it raises the question of just what it means to "restart analysis at some point": would the person(s) writing transfer rules have to assume part of the task of analysis as well? Mixing the role of transfer with that of analysis creates problems of its own. It would seem to be preferable to maintain a strict order of processing - completing all analysis before transfer begins.

FROM TRANSFER TO GENERATION AND FROM GENERATION TO TRANSFER

Transfer algorithms are specifically designed to choose the correct target language equivalents for lexical items of the source language. They take into account the total context of each lexical item in a sentence, making use of the morphological, syntactic and semantic information presented in the normalized structure of the sentence in order to make the proper choices. Once the choices are made, the whole package is handed over to generation, which has a different role to play. Generation assumes that what it receives from transfer is correct and proceeds to transform the normalized structure into a grammatical sentence of the target language on the basis of that assumption. This does not favor any backtracking to transfer.

There is perhaps one argument for returning to transfer after generation has begun. If optional transformations are included among the restructurations at transfer mentioned earlier, and if a given choice among these transformations results in a problem at generation, then, in principle, one might use backtracking between these major components.

As an alternative to backtracking in the technical sense, it is also possible to restart the translation process at certain fixed points if failure occurs somewhere along the line, either making a deeper analysis or relaxing certain constraints that were imposed to prevent multiple outputs (e.g., relaxation of selectional restrictions at analysis has been used to obtain an output when parsing otherwise fails).

* * * * * * * * *

A factor that has not been mentioned in the discussion of sequential and non-sequential processing is the effect of using different formal languages (programming languages) for writing rules at different phases. In a study relating to the advantages of using one formal language throughout the entire TAUM-AVIATION system, Gilles Stewart and Robert Gérin-Lajoie concluded in the technical report TAUM/AVIATION 1980 (TAUM, 1980, p. 131):

> "At the present time, only the sequential link is possible. If all phases were written in the same formal language, the order of and links between these phases could be defined within the language. For example, the order: morphological analysis, analysis dictionary and syntactico-semantic analysis is fixed at this time. In other systems, such as the Grenoble MONITeur, this order may change during the process of going through the grammar. A single language would provide the appropriate framework for modeling complex interactions between linguistic components."

In brief, the use of a single language would support more flexibility in relations between phases.

B. SUBCOMPONENTS

The boundaries between linguistic levels are sometimes blurred. Consider, for example, the morphological and syntactic levels. Roughly, morphology deals with the composition of words, syntax with the combination of words to form larger units. A word on the printed page is usually taken to be a string of characters set off by spaces. According to this criterion, the following are words:

(52)	hook-type	single-point	engine-driven
	piston-type	inter-system	gear-driven
	poppet-type	grit-free	motor-operated
	anti-stall	lint-free	nickel-plated
	anti-rust	non-priority	hand-lubricated
	anti-skid	non-pulsating	well-balanced
	pressure-regulating	zero-flow	1000-hour
	quick-acting	two-lobe	10-micron
	self-adjusting	two-spool	220-volt
	air-cooling	three-way	19-cell

flow-control	four-element	11-ampere-hour
quick-release	eighth-stage	110-to-infinite

There are a number of very productive types among these compound words:

(53)	X-type	anti-X
	X-Ving	non-X
	X-Ved	number-X

Obviously, the size of the dictionary is increased enormously if all such items are listed there; the potential number of items of the type number-X alone is infinite. Just as morphological analysis of words reduces the size of the dictionary by enabling us to list only base forms of words (e.g. 'run' but not 'runs', 'ran', 'running'), so the analysis of compound words should have the same effect. In all those cases where the relations between the parts of compound words are predictable[9], only the parts need be listed in the dictionary. Since nearly all of those parts have to be listed anyway, a substantial saving results.

It is easy to see that many of the relations within compound words are the same as those dealt with on the syntactic level:

(54)	gear-driven	(SUBJECT-VERB)
	motor-operated	(SUBJECT-VERB)
	pressure-regulating	(OBJECT-VERB)
	flow-control	(OBJECT-VERB)
	half-circle	(QUANTIFIER-NOUN)
	high-temperature	(ADJECTIVE-NOUN)
	well-balanced	(ADVERB-VERB)
	non-pulsating	(NEGATIVE-VERB)

The analysis of such words (54) should not therefore be confined to the morphological level; it involves the dictionary and the syntactic level as well. This constitutes a strong argument for non-sequential processing of the linguistic levels within a major component - being able to call on various levels to solve a problem, rather than doing all the work on one level without consulting the others.

There are also good reasons for not separating syntactic and semantic analysis. In recent years many linguists have argued for a model of language in which syntax and semantics are inseparable. Within the field of machine translation it is common practice to use semantic criteria during syntactic analysis by checking for semantic compatibility between predicates and their arguments or between modifiers and heads. Such compatibility may be very difficult to establish for the language as a whole, because of metaphorical extensions of words, but it can be used effectively in restricted semantic domains. (This type of semantic constraint is included under the heading selectional restriction in transformational grammars; see section 3.4 for further discussion.)

It is possible to maintain a strict separation of syntactic and semantic processing, assigning the latter to a "higher" level where it would serve to filter out undesirable combinations that emerged from the syntactic level. However, semantic constraints applied at an early stage may eliminate many alternatives that would be tried if only syntactic criteria were used; and if the system employs backtracking, much of it may be avoided by this elimination of alternatives at an early stage.

The above arguments support the use of non-sequential processing within a major component. The use of information from various linguistic levels at a given point may reduce the amount of work to be done beyond that point and avoid building structures that will be carried along for some time, only to be discarded somewhere down the line. This does not imply that the recognition of linguistic levels within a component is impractical; it is rather a question of how to make the best use of information from those levels for more efficient processing. The answer to this question will come only after extensive testing of real systems on a variety of texts. An important step has been taken in that direction at the Linguistic Research Center of the University of Texas; in particular, see Slocum (1981).

2.4.3 ADVANTAGES OF MODULARIZATION

It is generally recognized that modularity is an important feature in the design of a flexible system that can be extended with the least amount of disturbance to the system as a whole. The underlying assumption is that the complex task for which the system was designed consists of independent sub-tasks. As in any large complex organization, each department (module) is responsible for a particular sub-task and there must be well-defined lines of communication between departments. In the case of machine translation, the form of the input and output for each module must be specified in terms of the kinds of structures that are acceptable; there must be a well-defined interface between modules.

Since modularization allows work to proceed independently on each subtask (so long as interface requirements are met), the work is simplified; there is less concern with complex interactions between different types of rules in different components. This has the additional advantage of permitting more effective use of specialists in particular sub-fields: one person may be able to translate a text outright, but one person is not likely to be effective in dealing with all linguistic aspects of the translation process in a machine translation system.

It is easier to see the effects of changing a rule or of adding a rule in a modularized system, since those effects are localized. If it becomes necessary to make changes in the rules to extend the coverage of a system to new texts or to new language pairs, modularization simplifies the task. And because of the localization of the effects of rule changes, errors are easier to isolate and correct.

Of course, a particular problem is not necessarily confined to a submodule. One of the most serious problems, homography, is a case in point. The resolution of homographs requires morphological, lexical, syntactic and semantic information. This underscores an important fact: linguistic **levels**, not particular linguistic problems, are the basis for the submodules we have been discussing. The resolution of homographs can proceed bit by bit as processing moves from one level to another. A **task** (such as morphological analysis or syntactic analysis) should not be confused with a **problem** (such as homography or noun stacking).

At the beginning of **section 2.4** we mentioned the possibility of merging the transfer and generation modules into a single module, as illustrated in (47). However, the essential task of transfer is well-defined: replace lexemes of the source language with those of the target language in the abstract structures representing sentences of the original text. Likewise, the essential task of generation is well-defined: convert the abstract structures containing the target language lexical items into actual sentences - strings of words conforming to the grammar of the target language. Notwithstanding the restructurations subsumed under **structural transfer** in **section 2.3**, transfer and generation involve two essentially different tasks that can be worked on independently within separate modules, resulting in a more flexible system.

The use of modularity in systems designed for multilingual translation is particularly important. Suppose there are n different languages, with translation from any one of these to any of the others to be accomplished by a system incorporating separate modules for analysis, transfer and generation. Since analysis is a unilingual operation, a single analysis module should suffice for translation from a given language to any of the others - provided that a uniform interface structure is specified for communication between modules, no matter what language pair is involved. The same can be said for generation, since it is also a unilingual operation. Consequently there need be just n analysis modules and n generation modules in all. Only the transfer module is inherently bilingual, so that n (n - 1) transfer modules are required (assuming that in the near future no universal pivot language will be used to reduce the number of transfer modules).

The fact that such a large number of transfer modules must be used in multilingual systems means that the size of this module should be kept to a minimum. With only five languages, for example, twenty transfer modules are required compared with five each for analysis and generation, and this numerical disparity increases rapidly with the number of languages involved. In a bilingual system it may prove convenient to perform certain operations at transfer that are normally considered to be the function of generation, but in a multilingual system this could be a costly practice.

2.5 DOMAIN DEPENDENCY

The texts within a given field usually have a restricted vocabulary and, in some cases, a restricted syntax as well. This may result in a significant reduction of the linguistic obstacles to automatic translation in that field - obstacles that abound in the general language. If there is sufficient demand for translation in such a field, it may prove worthwhile to design a computerized translation system specifically to take advantage of these restrictions - a domain dependent system. METEO, the system used to translate weather forecasts from English to French in Canada, is a case in point. In fact, the success of FAMT in the immediate future can be expected to be limited to domain dependent systems. As for HAMT, even if such a system is claimed not to be domain dependent, its performance will depend very much on the domain of application.

Recognition of the importance of domain dependency for computerized translation, and for information retrieval, has spurred interest in the study of sublanguages in recent years, principally in North America and the Soviet Union[10]. These studies provide valuable information about the kinds of problems likely to be encountered in translating specialized texts, and the feasibility of extending the coverage of a system from one domain to another.

There are two important aspects of domain dependency - (1) the lexical, and (2) the syntactic - which affect the extendability of a system to new domains in different ways.

2.5.1 LEXICAL

Restricting texts to a particular subject matter results in (A) a smaller vocabulary, and (B) a reduction in the meaning range of many words in that vocabulary. Domain dependent systems benefit from such lexical simplification in several respects:

(i) Smaller dictionaries. This eases the task of dictionary building and maintenance.

(ii) Fewer ambiguities to resolve in the source text. Often a word in one domain has a homograph in a different domain, and that homograph can be ignored in a system operating only in the first domain.

(iii) Fewer target language equivalents for some of the words in the source language vocabulary.

The following examples illustrate typical domain related lexical restrictions.

- 'Hatch' can be either a noun or a verb in general English; but only the verb belongs to the technical vocabulary of biology (bring forth young from an egg), and only the noun belongs to the technical vocabulary of ship construction (a kind of covered opening).
- The English noun 'bug' refers to an error in computer science, to a kind of insect in biology, to a hidden microphone in the "intelligence" field (where the verb 'bug' means to hide a microphone for eavesdropping); and in popular slang the verb 'bug' means to annoy, while 'bug off' means to stop annoying and leave.

- The French equivalent of English 'line' in mathematics is 'ligne' and in hydraulics (a pipe or tube containing liquid under pressure) it is 'canalisation' or 'conduit'.

The effect of domain restriction in reducing dictionary size, homography, polysemy and the number of target language equivalents is obvious. In order not to lose all the benefits of lexical simplification when extending a domain dependent system to new domains, separate technical dictionaries can be used (or the dictionary can be modularized) so that entries are marked according to their relevance for different domains.

2.5.2 SYNTACTIC

Extending a system to cover a new domain may involve more than just adding entries to the dictionary, since texts from different fields may differ syntactically as well as lexically. For example, the METEO system could not be used to translate aircraft maintenance manuals simply by extending or replacing the dictionary; the syntax in those manuals is far more complex than that in weather forecasts. In fact, METEO could not even be used to translate meteorology textbooks; these not only have a wider range of vocabulary, but a richer syntax as well.

Syntactic differences are of two types: (1) difference in degree of complexity (multiple embedding, lengthy noun sequences, etc.), and (2) differences caused by deviations from standard grammar.

(2) can be illustrated by daily weather reports in the newspaper: 'Rain Thursday', 'High tomorrow 20°C', and 'Becoming cooler in the evening' are legitimate sentences in the sublanguage of weather reports, but not in Standard English. The grammar of the METEO system accounts for this deviant (and relatively simple) syntax.

Changing the syntactic rules of a computerized translation system is complicated and risky; a change in one rule is likely to affect the operation of others. For this reason, extending a domain dependent system to new domains may require a complete overhaul of the syntactic component. This may be true even when the domains are semantically related (e.g., weather reports and meteorology textbooks).

Syntactic differences between texts may be due more to differences in their purpose or function than to differences in subject matter. For example, technical **descriptions** consist mainly of declarative sentences with a high frequency of passives, no imperatives and no direct questions; but technical **instructions** consist mainly of imperative sentences, and direct questions may occur (e.g., in flow charts: "Is the voltage high? **Yes** ⟶ Proceed to step H. **No** ⟶ Proceed to step K."). Consequently, text function is an important factor to consider in choosing a new domain of application for a computerized translation system, or in designing a system for a particular domain.

* * * * * * * * *

Following is a brief summary of the main aspects of domain dependency discussed in this section.

1. <u>Lexical</u>

    - dictionary size
    - extent of homography and polysemy

2. <u>Syntactic</u>

    - degree of syntactic complexity
    - deviations from standard grammar
    - effect of text function

Semantic considerations, implicit in this discussion, are examined in section 3.4.

The effects of extending coverage to a new domain may be classified as follows:

1. Vocabulary extension, with little or no change in syntax

    - Separate dictionaries.

- Increase in homography and polysemy may produce ambiguities not removed by separation of dictionaries alone.

2. Change in syntax as well as vocabulary

A. Common grammar

- Both domains conform to the same general grammar, but one may include some constructions that the other does not (or that the other uses only rarely).

B. Radically different grammars

- Texts in some domains have highly deviant syntax (e.g., extreme use of telegraphic style, as in weather reports[11]).

It will become clear in **CHAPTER 3** that an increase in lexical complexity has important consequences for the syntactic component of a computerized translation system.

3. LINGUISTIC COMPONENTS OF A SYSTEM

In chapter 2 we gave a broad characterization of computerized translation systems in terms of their automaticity, depth of analysis, type of transfer, relations between phases, and dependency on domain of application. Now we turn our attention inward to the characteristics of a system's linguistic components. These components (lexical, morphological, syntactic and semantic) do not necessarily correspond to stages in the translation process, ordered one after another. Different systems not only have different types of rules, but also different ways of applying them. It is not necessary that all the rules dealing with a given linguistic level be applied in a block. And within a single rule there may be information from more than one linguistic level.

An understanding of the individual linguistic components of a system is crucial to the evaluation of the system's limitations and improvability (section 5.3).

3.1 LEXICAL COMPONENT

3.1.1 NUMBER OF DICTIONARIES

A computerized translation system may have only one dictionary or it may have several, depending on the type of system. These dictionaries may be classified as follows:

(1) UNILINGUAL DICTIONARY

a. Language
- source language
- target language

b. Word Form
- only base form of word listed in dictionary
- inflected forms listed also

c. Word Properties
- grammatical categories (noun, verb, adjective, adverb, pronoun, preposition, determiner, quantifier, etc.)
- subcategories, including morphological classes (count, mass, masculine, feminine, abstract, concrete, action, state, etc.)
- complementation (number and types of arguments)
- other information.

(2) BILINGUAL (TRANSFER) DICTIONARY

A transfer dictionary could simply list all target language equivalents, as in (a); or it could list these equivalents along with information about their grammatical categories, syntactic and/or semantic subcategories, complementation, etc., as in (b); or it could also specify which equivalent is appropriate in a given context, as in (c), with the right hand side of each rule consisting of a procedure which permits automatic lexical selection of a particular target language equivalent, depending on context, rather than just listing them all. (Note: The "words" in these entries could be either in the base form or in the inflected form; see comments below.)

(a)

```
[source ]  ───►  [target word W1 + category ]   Note: n =
[word   ]        [..........................]   total number of
                 [target word Wn + category ]   target language
                                                equivalents.
```

(b)

```
                 [target word W1 + category                         ]
                 [               + syntactic/semantic subcategories ]
                 [               + complementation + (etc.)         ]
[source ]  ───►  [........................                          ]
[word   ]        [target word Wn + category                         ]
                 [               + syntactic/semantic subcategories ]
                 [               + complementation + (etc.)         ]
```

```
                          ┌                                                        ┐
                          │in context C1  Target word W1                           │
                          │               + category                               │
                          │               + syntactic/semantic subcategories       │
(c)  ┌source   ┐          │               + complementation + (etc.)               │
     │word     │ ──────►  │........................                                │
     └         ┘          │in context Cn  Target word Wn                           │
                          │               + category                               │
                          │               + syntactic/semantic subcategories       │
                          │               + complementation + (etc.)               │
                          └                                                        ┘
```

COMMENTS:

- Following are some examples of words in base form (boldface) and inflected forms: (English) **run**, runs, ran, running; (French) **bon**, bons, bonne, bonnes. If words are listed in the dictionary only in base form, the system must have a morphological component capable of recognizing inflected forms in the source text and generating the correct inflected forms in the target language (see section 3.2).

- Any grammatical category (**part of speech**) may be subcategorized; the number of subcategories that have been used or proposed is very large and the optimum number for the purpose of automatic translation is not known for any natural language.

- **Complementation** usually refers to arguments of verbs (i.e., subject and objects), but words from other categories may also have complements. For example, the adjective (English) 'acceptable' / (French) 'acceptable' and the noun (English) 'damage' / (French) 'dommage' may take prepositional phrase complements:

  (English) a plan acceptable **to the public** damage **to the motor**
  (French) un plan acceptable **pour le public** des dommages **au moteur**

- Subcategories permit more refined statements of complementation. For example, instead of saying that the arguments of the verb 'drink' are nouns, we can say that the first argument is a noun of the subclass [animate] and the second argument is a noun of the subclass [liquid] (in non-metaphorical usage). Assigning full complementation to dictionary entries requires highly trained specialists, but the resulting system may be capable of very subtle analyses, thus reducing the amount of human assistance needed in the translation process.

- Generally speaking, relatively simple systems of the direct transfer type use only a bilingual (transfer) dictionary, whereas very complex systems with a pivot language have, in addition, a unilingual source language dictionary - and possibly a unilingual target language dictionary. Having only one dictionary may simplify the task of dictionary building, but this must be weighed against the performance of the resulting system and the extent of human interaction required during translation.

- As indicated in (2c), a transfer dictionary may do more than just list the target language equivalents of a source language word; a dictionary entry may specify the context in which each target language equivalent is used. This enables the computer rather than the translator to choose the correct translation equivalent. Of course, identification of relevant contexts may require extensive analysis of the source text, which, in turn, may lead to the incorporation of a unilingual source language dictionary as part of a sophisticated parser.

3.1.2 INFORMATION CONTENT

As suggested in the preceding section, a variety of information about a word can be given in a lexical entry: its grammatical category, the subcategories to which it belongs (semantic [concrete, abstract, motion, physical property, etc.] and syntactic [mass, count, transitive, intransitive, attributive, predicative, etc.]), and the type of complement it takes (if any). Many other kinds of information could also be given: the semantic domain(s) to which the word belongs, social restrictions on its use, etc.

The sum of all the information given in a lexical entry constitutes the definition of the lexical item within the particular system; for our purposes, it is the information content[12] of the dictionary entry. The greater the information content (in this sense), the greater will be the possibilities for analyzing the source text and for stating context sensitive transfer rules within the system - and the greater will be the cost of dictionary building.

3.1.3 FORM OF A LEXICAL ENTRY

If a dictionary stored in a computer is used only to display definitions for use by a human translator, the definitions could take the same form as the ones found in a standard dictionary. But if the computer itself uses the definitions for automatic analysis and automatic lexical replacements during the translation process, the lexical entries may bear little resemblance to those in a standard dictionary. Much of the information in a standard dictionary can be coded for use in automatic processing, but the form of an entry does put certain constraints on the type of information represented.

Although the details of formalizing a lexical entry depend on the software being used, we may consider the "general form" of an entry apart from these details. After presenting the general forms, several examples of dictionary entries will be given as they are written in some real systems.

(3) **UNILINGUAL DICTIONARY ENTRY**

< lexical item >
< grammatical category >
< subcategories >
< complementation >
< other information >

(4) **BILINGUAL DICTIONARY ENTRY**

Let n be the number of target language equivalents for a given source language lexical item ($n \geq 1$).

(a)

SOURCE LANGUAGE	TARGET LANGUAGE		
<lexical item>	<equivalent 1>	...	<equivalent n>
	<grammatical category>		<grammatical category>
	<subcategories>		<subcategories>
	<complementation>		<complementation>
	<other information>		<other information>

(b)

SOURCE LANGUAGE	TARGET LANGUAGE		
<lexical item>	IF context is C1 then <equivalent 1> <grammatical category> <subcategories> <complementation> <other information>	...	IF context is Cn then <equivalent n> <grammatical category> <subcategories> <complementation> <other information>

The information content and the order of presentation may vary. In the simplest case only the lexical item would be listed; in actual practice at least the grammatical category is given in addition to the lexical item. Many "other" types of information could be given.

The contexts Cn in (4b) are usually grammatical environments or particular word environments of the source language lexical item, although they could also be larger environments such as semantic domains (e.g., the English noun 'charge' becomes French 'charge' in electrical theory, but 'frais', 'tarif' or 'droit' in accounting).

The following examples of entries are taken from the dictionaries set up up for a 1982 version of the ALPS system, a 1977 version of the TAUM-METEO system and a 1980 version of the TAUM-AVIATION system. (ALPS is an interactive system and is a proprietary product of Automated Language Processing Systems, Provo, Utah. While the METEO system has been in operation for several years, the AVIATION system is a research prototype. These two systems are the property of the Department of the Secretary of State of Canada.) The entries illustrate possible realizations of the general forms (3), (4a) and (4b). They are presented without comment in (5)-(14), followed by some explanatory discussion on pages 67,68.

UNILINGUAL DICTIONARY ENTRY

- ALPS System: (not applicable)

- TAUM-METEO System: (not applicable)

- TAUM-AVIATION System:

```
(5)     BLEED =F= N         TRAIT DMVT,DNP,DAB,DSG,DNOMF;
        BLEED =F= V         TRAIT DERG,
                            RESTRICT PART  (OFF,FREE,OUT),
                                           1 (GN [DP,DHUM]),
                                           2 (GN [DP,DFL,DNOMF]),
                                           3 (P [DMVT] (OF));

(6)     ACCEPTABLE =F= ADJ RESTRICT  1 (PH [DINF], GN [DAB,DDEFECT,DVAR]),
                                           2 (P (TO));
        ON =F= P            TRAIT DLOC,DTM,DING;
        ANY =F= Q           TRAIT DLQ,DPRECOMPAR;
```

BILINGUAL DICTIONARY WITH NO CONTEXT

- ALPS System:

```
(7)     BLEED                          BLEEDING

        saigner VERB                   saignant ADJ
        gruger VERB                    ensanglanté ADJ
        extorquer VERB                 navré de douleur ADJ
        pleurer VERB                   saignement NOUN
        fuir VERB                      écoulement NOUN
                                       saignée NOUN,FEM
                                       fuite NOUN,FEM
```

- TAUM-METEO System:

```
(8)     BREEZE == NC (/(F,*WC,*WL), BRISE).
        CLIMBING == VT (EN, HAUSSE).
```

```
CLOUDY == ADJ (/(F5,PO,*WC,*ST), NUAGEUX).
ALONG == PL (LE, LONG, DE).
MANY == DET (PLUSIEURS).
```

- TAUM-AVIATION System:

```
(9)  #OBSERVER# == (*MJP, 20 NOV 78*) TRADUIRE FC PAR #OBSERVATEUR# [P1].

(10) #TECHNICAL# == (*FA, 19 FEV 79*) TRADUIRE FC PAR #TECHNIQUE# [P1].

(11) #AFT OF# == (*LB, MB, 16 JANV 79*)
        DEBUT
        SI NATURE (FC) EST P ALORS
            (*DTRANS, DLOC*) (*JUST BELOW AND AFT OF THE ACCUMULATOR*)
            TRADUIRE FC PAR #à# #l'# #arrière# #de#;
        SINON TRADUIRE FC PAR UT (FC)
        FIN.
```

BILINGUAL DICTIONARY WITH CONTEXT

- ALPS System: (not applicable)

- TAUM-METEO System:

```
(12)    EVENING == NI (/(F), soirée).
        EVENING == NT (/, soir).

(13)    INCREASING == ADJ (/(*DT), de, plus, en, plus, grand, AC).
        INCREASING == ADJ (/(*MSR), en, hausse).
        INCREASING == ADJ (/(*ANTE, *PR, *ST, *WL), de, plus, en, plus, de).
        INCREASING == VB (NP, P(TO), NP, /, devenant).
```

- TAUM-AVIATION System:

```
(14) #BLEED# ==      (*F.P.,M.B. 15.01.1980
                      V[DERG] RESTRICT PART (OFF, FREE, OUT),
                          1(GN[DP,DHUM]), 2(GN[DP,DFL,DNOMF]), 3(P[DMVT](OF))

     TRADUCTION GENERALE = EVACUER
     AUTRES TRADUCTIONS  = PURGER,(LAISSER)ECHAPPER,EVACUER,PRELEVER*)
```

(*ALGORITHME DE TRADUCTION DU VERBE :
1. PH NON [APASS] V 1 2[DFL,DNOMF] 3
    1.1 PH [AERG] V 1 2 3 = s'échapper 1 2 3
        a) the air bleeds out. (HYP)
        b) the air bleeding forward...is returned to the gearbox.
        c) the air bleeds overboard. (HYP)
    1.2 PH V 1 2[DFL,DNOMF] 3[DFL] = laisser échapper 1 2 3
        d) bleed all air from fluid. (CP-3114)
    1.3 PH V 1[DOBT] 2 3 = laisser échapper 1 2 3
        e) cover permits bleeding off air. (CP-902)
2. V 1 2[DP] 3 = purger 1 2 3
        a) bleed and fill system. (HYP)
        b) bleed brakes below 2200 PSIG. (CP-32850)
        c) bleed system of air. (L1011)
3. AUTRES CAS = traduction générale
        a) bleed air. (HYP)
        b) bleed all air from the reservoirs. (CP-3220)
        c) bleed off air.(CP-3294) Someone bleeds off air.(HYP)
        d) air is bled from the air/oil separator. (CP-1116)
        e) the value bleeds the air overboard. (HYP)
        f) the value bleeds out air. (HYP) *)

(*Other comments:

- Those sentences (fairly rare in English) where the direct object is DNOMF] and which may be expected in the complementation of the verb BLEED cannot be processed in the lexicon without major restructuring and will therefore have to be dealt with using the "general" translation (i.e., the unmarked or default value).

    ex.: By using X to bleed off pressurization from both reservoirs, ground interflow can be completely eliminated. (CP-770)

- Since for the moment there is no feature to distinguish between nouns in the class [DCONT], the verb BLEED in the expression BLEED ACCUMULATOR will be translated as "évacuer" rather than "dégonfler".

    ex.: Use caution when bleeding off air from accumulator (cf. L1011, ligne 449)

Should the case arise where this class of [DP] is sub-categorized, the feature [DVAR] must be added to the complementation of the verb in OBJD to take account of the above case. Consequently, even if "dégonfler" is the exact translation of BLEED, every time the [DCONT] involved is flexible or connected to a bladder, for the time being BLEED will be translated as "évacuer". *)

```
(*   The algorithm of BLEED may be skewed whenever there  is conjunction
     of V and elision of an argument.
     ex.: Bleed and refill system
          Evacuer et remplir à nouveau le circuit (trans. obtained)
          Purger et remplir à nouveau le circuit  (trans. desired)*)

(*------------------------------------------------------------------------*)

VAR  CHEMIN : BOOLEEN ;   A1,A1 : ARBRELIBRE   FIN

DEBUT
SI NATURE (FC) EST V ALORS
     DEBUT
     TRADUIRE FC PAR #évacuer# [B6]; (*voir en 3 *)
     CHEMIN := FAUX;
     SI PARCOURS /CV /GV $EGV /GOV (OPS $EOPS) $EGOV /PH $EPH
             \SUJ $ESUJ ──→ OBJD $EOBJD ALORS
          DEBUT
          SI PARCOURS EGV (GPREP (CP (P $EP))) ALORS
          TRADUIRE EP PAR #BOF#;  (* OFF,FREE,OUT *)

          SI TRAITS (EOBJD) >= [DP] ALORS
               DEBUT
               TRADUIRE FC PAR #purger#[B8];  (* voir en 2 *)
               SI PARCOURS EOBJD (GPREP (CP (P $EP2 )))
                          ──→ OBJI[1] TELQUE TRAITS(ICI) >= [DFL] $EOBJI
                         \GPREP \CP \P TELQUE UT(ICI) = #OF# $EP3 ALORS
                    DEBUT
                    TRADUIRE EP2 PAR #de# ;
                    TRADUIRE EP3 PAR #BOF# ;
                    A1 := COPIE (EOBJD) ;
                    A2 := COPIE (EOBJI) ;
                    DEPLACER A2 EN OBJD SOUS EPH ;
                    DEPLACER A1 EN OBJI[1] SOUS EPH ;
                    FIN
               FIN
          SINON           (*si l'objet n'est pas un [DP] *)
               DEBUT
               SI PARCOURS EPH TELQUE (NON TRAITS(ICI) >= [APASS])
                         \OBJD TELQUE ((TRAITS(ICI) >= [DFL]) OU
                                       (TRAITS(ICI) >= [DNOMF])) ALORS
                    DEBUT
                    SI TRAITS(EPH) >= [AERG] ALORS
                    CHEMIN := VRAI ;                 (* voir en 1.1 *)
                    SI PARCOURS EPH \OBJI[1]
                              TELQUE TRAITS(ICI) >= [DFL] ALORS
```

```
                        DEBUT
                        CHEMIN := VRAI ;
                        DEPLACER OPS !TRAITS(EOPS)
                                  (VOP UT TRADUITE #laisser# [B6])
                                  EN OPS SOUS EGOV ;     (* voir en 1.2 *)
                        FIN;
                   SI PARCOURS ESUJ TELQUE TRAITS(ICI) >= [DOBT] ALORS
                        DEBUT
                        CHEMIN := VRAI ;
                        DEPLACER OPS !TRAITS(EOPS)
                                  (VOP UT TRADUITE #laisser# [b6]
                                  EN OPS SOUS EGOV ;       (* voir en 1.3 *)
                        FIN;
                   SI CHEMIN ALORS
                        TRADUIRE FC PAR #échapper# [B6] ;
                   FIN
              FIN
         FIN
    FIN
SINON
SI NATURE (FC) EST N ALORS      (* F.PARC 12.02.1979 *)
    DEBUT
    SI PARCOURS  /CN TELQUE TRAITS(ICI) >= [MPRESP] ALORS
         DEBUT   (* traduction de la nominalisation BLEEDING *)
         TRADUIRE FC PAR #purge# [F0,P1] ;
         TRAITS EN FC := TRAITS (FC) + [TFEM] ;
         FIN  (* hydraulic system bleeding is required CP-3162 *)
    SINON         (* J. Blais 15.01.1979 *)
         DEBUT    (* traduction du nom BLEED *)
         SI PARCOURS /CN /GN $EGN
                    /GP TELQUE POSITION(ICI) EST GP[1]
                    (GPREP (CP (P TELQUE UT (ICI) = #OF#)))
                   /GN TELQUE TRAITS(ICI) >= [DFL] ALORS
              DEBUT     (* ex.:  engine bleed air *)
              TRADUIRE FC PAR #prélèvement# [P1] ;
              TRAITS EN EGN := TRAITS(EGN) + [TSTOPDET];
              FIN
         SINON
              DEBUT
              TRADUIRE FC PAR #purge# [p1];
              TRAITS EN FC := TRAITS(FC) + [TFEM];
              FIN
         FIN
    FIN
SINON          (* catégorie lexicale autre que verbe ou nom *)
TRADUIRE FC PAR UT(FC)        (* BLEED traduit par BLEED *)
FIN.
```

The principal aim of examples (5) to (14) is to show that the dictionary of a system does not necessarily contain all the linguistic information listed in (3) and (4). It is also important to make a distinction between a single lexical equivalence rule (7, 8, 9, 10, 11) and a set of rules (12, 13, 14) which allow a system to automatically choose an equivalent from several possible translations.

In the ALPS system, there is a single dictionary with entries containing information from both the source and target languages. For example in (7), the symbols VERB, ADJ, NOUN designate lexical categories of the source language (verb, adjective, common noun). The symbol FEM designates the grammatical gender (feminine) of the target language word. If a word has more than one translation, as in (7), the ALPS system never automatically selects the translation, but rather asks the human translator to choose from the equivalents proposed by the dictionary. In this system, lexical selection is done interactively.

In the TAUM-METEO system, there is only one dictionary. The dictionary is subdivided into three sub-dictionaries: the general dictionary, the dictionary of place names and the dictionary of idioms. Dictionary entries contain information from both the source and target languages. For example in (13), the expression NP P(TO) NP describes the complementation of the English verb 'increasing' and the symbol VB shows the lexical category of this English word. This information is used by the English parsing grammar. In (13), there are four possible translations for the word "increasing". Based on this lexical information and depending on the context of the sentence, the TAUM-METEO system will automatically choose one translation from these four possible choices. In this system lexical selection is done automatically.

In the TAUM-AVIATION system, there are two dictionaries: an analysis dictionary and a transfer dictionary. The analysis dictionary is a unilingual dictionary of the source language (5, 6), while the transfer dictionary is both a bilingual dictionary and a unilingual dictionary of the target language (9, 10, 11, 14). For example in (5), the verb BLEED may appear in an ergative construction (marked by the symbol DERG; see discussion of TRANSITIVE/INTRANSITIVE in section 2.3.1), and the verb + particle forms of the base BLEED are BLEED OFF, BLEED FREE and BLEED OUT. The first argument of the verb BLEED is a noun phrase or "groupe nominal" (GN) belonging either to the class of parts [DP] or to the class of humans [DHUM], while the second argument is a noun phrase belonging to the class of parts [DP], the class of fluids [DFL] or the class of function nominal [DNOMF], and the third argument may be a prepositional phrase introduced by a preposition of motion [DMVT] or by the preposition 'OF'. In (14), the word BLEED exists as an entry in the transfer dictionary of the TAUM-AVIATION system. It is not necessary here to explain the formalism used for the entry of the word BLEED in (14). It is more important to note that, in this system, each dictionary entry is a program (or lexical procedure) which allows a translation to be chosen automatically from a set of possible equivalents and which also performs all the structural transformations entailed by this equivalent (or lexical element of the target language). For more information on the dictionaries of the TAUM-AVIATION system, see Chevalier et al. (1981) and Bourbeau (1981b).

Since each system has its own guide to dictionary-making, it is essential to consult a system's technical manual to obtain all the relevant information. Articles are occasionally published describing the dictionaries of a given system, for example the article by Van Slype and Pigott (1979) which provides a linguistic description of the SYSTRAN system dictionary. Even though the number of examples (5 to 14) has been reduced to a strict minimum, it should be borne in mind that the "intelligence" of a translation system depends heavily on the linguistic information formalized in its dictionaries (or data banks).

3.1.4 IDIOMS

Multiword expressions may be entered in the dictionary as well as single words. Thus idioms are normally listed as single entries since their meanings cannot be determined from the meanings of their component words and they may not follow the usual patterns for combining words in the language. An idiom, like any other dictionary entry, belongs to some grammatical category. For example, 'in spite of' is a complex preposition and should therefore be assigned the category PREPOSITION in the dictionary.

There is a tendency to avoid analyzing many complex expressions which are not idioms by entering them in the dictionary. This sometimes creates more problems than it solves, since the same string of words can function quite differently in different sentences. For example, if 'water pressure' is entered in the dictionary as a noun, then (15) may be correctly analyzed by the computer while (16) and (17) present problems:

(15) **Water pressure is low.**

(16) **In deep water pressure gages should be checked frequently.**

(17) **To lift the well water pressure is obtained from the pump.**

Unless the system is capable of backtracking and re-analysis, 'water pressure' will be treated as a single word, which results in the following French translations:

(15) (a) **La pression d'eau est basse.**

(16) (a) **En pression d'eau profonde les indicateurs doivent être vérifiés fréquemment.**

(but the correct translation is)

En eau profonde les indicateurs de pression doivent être vérifiés fréquemment.

(17) (a) **Pour faire monter le puits la pression d'eau est obtenue à l'aide de la pompe.**

(but the correct translation is)

Pour faire monter l'eau du puits la pression est obtenue à l'aide de la pompe.[13]

The following examples in (18), (19) and (20) taken recently from the English/French dictionary of an interactive system in use illustrate further the tendency to avoid analysis by stacking a dictionary with multiword expressions.

(18) **evidence through work history = antécédents professionnels témoignant de** [MULTIWORD]

(19) **at progressively more responsible levels = acquise à des postes de responsabilités croissantes** [PREPOSITION]

(20) **there are = il y a** [VERB]
there are not = il n'y a pas [VERB]
there can be = il peut y avoir [VERB]
there can not be = il ne peut pas y avoir [VERB]
there could be = il pourrait y avoir [VERB]
there could have been = il aurait pu y avoir [VERB]

there could not be = il ne pourrait pas y avoir [VERB]
there could not have been = il n'aurait pas pu y avoir [VERB]
there had been = il y avait eu [VERB]
there has been = il y a eu [VERB]
there has not been = il n'y a pas eu [VERB]
there have been = il y a eu [VERB]
there have not been = il n'y a pas eu [VERB]
there is = il y a [VERB]
there is not = il n'y a pas [VERB]
there may be = il pourrait y avoir [VERB]
there may not be = il ne pourrait pas y avoir [VERB]
il ne peut pas y avoir [VERB]
there might be = il pourrait y avoir [VERB]
there might not be = il ne peut pas y avoir [VERB]
there should be = il devrait y avoir [VERB]
there should not be = il ne devrait pas y avoir [VERB]
there was = il y avait [VERB]
there were = il y avait [VERB]
there will be = il y aura [VERB]
there will have been = il y aura eu [VERB]
there will not be = il n'y aura pas [VERB]
there will not have been = il n'y aura pas eu [VERB]
there would be = il y aurait [VERB]
there would have been = il y aurait eu [VERB]
there would not be = il n'y aurait pas [VERB]
there would not have been = il n'y aurait pas eu [VERB]

An idiom belongs to some grammatical category; but (18) is marked as a "MULTIWORD", which is not a grammatical category.

Another problem, illustrated by (19), is that some strings are assigned to grammatical categories incorrectly; for example, (19) is marked as a "PREPOSITION" although it would not be considered as a preposition in any normal grammar. On the other hand, listing all the forms of THERE BE as in (20) indicates that the grammar lacks rules for analyzing THERE BE constructions. Furthermore, even the multiple entries in (20) fail totally in expressions such as (21):

(21) there certainly are...
there probably is...
there must surely be...
there can hardly have been...
there should, in any event, be...
etc.

Dictionary builders must exercise control over the entry of idioms in the dictionary; using the dictionary as a wastebasket for unanalyzed expressions can only lead to trouble in the long run.

3.2 MORPHOLOGICAL COMPONENT

In section 3.1 we explained in (3) and (4) that a dictionary entry was made up of a lexical item to which could be joined various types of linguistic information. The written form of a lexical item serves as the access key to a dictionary entry. A lexical item may be a word or an idiomatic expression.

In a text a lexical item may be realized in various forms according to the grammatical category of number, gender, person, tense, etc. Since the written form of a word is the access key to a dictionary entry, we might decide to create an entry in the dictionary for each separate form of a given word. To consult the dictionary, we would then simply establish a direct correspondence between the words in a text and dictionary entries. This method is very simple to program, but it brings with it a number of disadvantages (e.g. rapid increase in the number of entries, redundancy of lexical information between entries, tedious and costly up-dating). To avoid these disadvantages, it would be more economical and more natural to put only the base form of a word in the dictionary and to use a morphological component to establish relations between the various forms of a word present in a text and the base form of this word in the dictionary. A morphological component performs either morphological analysis or morphological generation. The term morphological analysis designates the process by which we can go from the word forms realized in a text to a base form recorded in a dictionary. The term morphological generation designates the reverse process, i.e. generating from a base form the form of the word governed by the grammatical context of this word in a text.

In a machine translation system with a morphological component the base form contained in the dictionary as a lexical item is normally the entry form of a conventional dictionary; e.g. in French the infinitive for the verb, the masculine singular form of a noun, the masculine singular form of a qualifying adjective. The role of the morphological component is then to break the word down into BASE FORM + SUFFIX (or PREFIX + BASE FORM + SUFFIX, BASE FORM + DERIVATIONAL SUFFIX + INFLEXIONAL SUFFIX). The grammar of a morphological component should include the most productive rules specific to the language being treated in order to reduce the number of entries in the dictionary to a minimum (e.g. compositional morphology, derivational morphology).

In this chapter we will simplify our definition of each linguistic component by stating that morphology describes the arrangement of the base units into words, that syntax describes the arrangement of words into a sentence and that semantics deals with the meaning of the words and sentence. In the present section, we will describe the following specific forms of processing: preliminary processing of the text to be translated, inflectional morphology, derivational morphology and compositional morphology.

3.2.1 PRELIMINARY PROCESSING

The physical layout of any typed text is governed by certain conventions, the principal objective of which is to facilitate the reading of the text. These typographic conventions may be specific to a given type of document or even correspond to a given established norm or standard. In general, the complexity and refinement of these conventions depends on the range of distribution of the document. In addition, some typographic standards are general while others are peculiar to a given publisher. For an illustration of this situation, the reader might be interested in consulting the typographic grammar prepared by A. Ramat (1982).

When a text is transcribed onto a computer medium, the transcription conventions particular to a given word-processor or computer system must be followed. This transcription operation would be quite simple if all type styles and all typographical symbols were directly available on the computer. Unfortunately, this is not the case. For historical and economic reasons, a computer is equipped with a base alphabet of only one style and sets of 64, 128 or 256 characters.

Given the variety of typographic standards as well as the many rules governing the entry of texts on computers, a machine translation system must be capable of recognizing these pre-established conventions automatically or else adapt quickly to certain variants in order to be able to read the input text. In a machine translation system, preliminary processing consists in reading the input text, identifying what is to be translated, conserving what is not to be translated and organizing or transforming all this textual information to conform to the internal connections and information representation structure required for subsequent phases of processing. All these pre-processing operations are carried out in the automatic pre-processing phase and then, in the reverse order, in the automatic post-processing phase.

In some MT systems this preliminary processing step is called the pre-editing phase; however, the term 'pre-editing' does not mean the same thing for all MT systems. In certain cases (e.g. controlled-syntax systems) the term pre-editing is taken in a much broader sense to mean human preparation of the input text depending on the state of the system's rules. To avoid this type of confusion we prefer to use the term "automatic pre-processing".

When evaluating a system it is essential to identify what is done automatically as opposed to what is done by the translator. For the time being we will confine ourselves in this chapter to describing the typographic phenomena a system should be capable of processing automatically. For this purpose we have divided typographic phenomena into three sub-sections: automatic identification of the typographic conventions of the input text, automatic segmentation of the text into processing units and automatic identification of word units.

A. AUTOMATIC IDENTIFICATION OF TYPOGRAPHIC CONVENTIONS

In addition to recognizing all the various representation codes for typographic signs a preliminary processing program should also automatically distinguish between the different functions performed by a given typographic sign. For example, in a French text the hyphen may have various functions: joining compound words ('arc-en-ciel'), linking a pronoun to a verb ('dites-moi'), linking the adverbial particles 'ci' and 'là' to nouns or demonstrative pronouns ('cette maison-ci'), marking the breaking of a word at the end of a line, and as the arithmetical sign for subtraction (A - B). The hyphen may also replace the coordinating conjunction 'et' or the preposition 'à' in expressions such as: 'Voir les figures 5-7' (see figures 5-7), or 'lire les pages 21-35 inclusivement' (read pp. 21-35 inclusive). In such a case identifying the different functions of the hyphen is important in order to correctly determine the word boundaries.

In an evaluation it is essential to first examine all the typographic conventions that have been adopted in the texts to be translated. We must next verify and test how the rules of a system process these typographic phenomena. On the basis of the results obtained we must then evaluate the possibilities for correcting, modifying or adapting these rules to the texts to be translated. The principal typographic phenomena that should be taken into consideration are listed in (22), (23), (24) and (25).

(22) Photocomposition, formatting and make-up codes of the source and target texts: for example, photocomposition codes indicate type fount and body, line spacing, type size and spacing.

(23) **Set of characters:**

- space (blank character)
- Latin alphabet (A ... Z, upper and lower case)
- accents or diacritical marks (acute, grave, dieresis, circumflex, cedilla, tilde)
- Latin digraphs (æ , œ)
- low punctuation (period, comma, suspension points, leaders in a table)
- high punctuation (semi-colon, colon, apostrophe, quotation marks, question mark, exclamation mark)
- special characters (plus sign, dash or minus sign, equal sign, less than or open angle sign, greater than or closing angle sign, opening parenthesis, closing parenthesis, opening bracket, closing bracket, opening quotation mark, closing quotation mark, asterisk, diesis, per cent, degree sign, left diagonal, right diagonal, vertical stroke, commercial a or "at" sign, ampersand)
- Greek alphabet, if required (α to Ω)
- other alphabets, as required

(24) **Typography of text:**

- footnotes and footnote references in text
- paragraph numbering
- punctuation of enumerations
- breaking words at the end of a line
- titles of chapters, sections, sub-sections
- quotations in text (not to be translated)
- figures, tables, illustrations, diagrams

(25) **Typography of words:**

- Arabic and Roman numerals, whole numbers, fractions, improper fractions, arithmetical and algebraic formulas, mathematical formulas of sets, chemical and electronic formulas

- reference codes for parts, catalogues, manuals

- abbreviations, acronyms, initials

The photocomposition codes in (22) are control codes which enable one, for example, to select type style or size, set predetermined tabulation stops, jump from page to page or to predetermined lines. Some of these codes may be stated outside the text, while others must be written inside the text. The preliminary processing program or grammar must identify these photocomposition codes in order to distinguish the words to be translated and to determine which codes must be carried through the translation chain and which do not have to be so transported. For example, codes specifying the presentation of titles are transportable codes, while codes prescribing line changes based on a maximum number of characters per line are non-transportable codes.

The set of characters listed in (23) is an example of the variety of characters necessary to process French texts. Since the processing equipment (terminal, printer, computer) has only a limited set of characters, the consequences of these restrictions must be measured, i.e. conventions for coding unavailable characters, decoding and transcoding operations on these characters and possible inadequacies in the mechanisms or equipment used.

For each typographic phenomenon listed in (24) there are specific characters or symbols in the text to be translated. These marker characters must be identified in order to distinguish them from words to be translated. These markers are also indicators of the linguistic context of the utterance. For example, paragraph numbers are arrangements of letters, figures and special characters combined according to the specific rules used to index the paragraphs in order to mark subdivisions in some sort of descending order, as in (26):

(26) I. CHAPTER
    A. Section
        1. Sub-section
            a) Paragraph
                1° Sub-paragraph
                    - further paragraph division

The example in (26) may be used for a work containing six subdivisions. All these subdivisions into paragraphs bear specific names which are given beside a corresponding numbering sign. This example was taken from Ramat (1982, p.16).

Example (25) lists other types of symbols which are not part of the lexicon of a natural language. Some of these symbols belong to artificial languages such as that of Arabic numerals. These artificial language symbols may be recognized and analyzed by a given internal syntax. A preliminary (or morphological) processing grammar should be able to identify such foreign symbols and automatically associate syntactic-semantic properties with them in order to avoid placing them in the dictionary as lexical items. Abbreviations, acronyms and initials should, however, appear in the dictionary as lexical items, since, like the other words of a natural language, they carry linguistic information. In spite of this we have included abbreviations, acronyms and initials in (25), since the pre-processing grammar must in any case identify them in order to conserve their spelling in full (i.e. capital and small letters, punctuation forming part of the symbol). In some systems general rules for the processing of capital letters or punctuation are often erroneously applied to abbreviations, acronyms and initials. In general, this yields faulty word separation, faulty modifying of words, etc. This question will be covered in more detail in the next two sub-sections.

B. AUTOMATIC SEGMENTATION OF TEXT INTO PROCESSING UNITS

The preliminary processing phase consists mainly in reading the input text and laying the groundwork for subsequent linguistic processing. The first linguistic operation of this phase is the breaking down of the text into processing units and then dividing the processing units into word units. This operation is simple if the text contains only sentences ending with a period. A rule where a period followed by a space followed by a capital letter indicates a sentence boundary would then suffice as a rule to distinguish processing units. In most cases, however, processing units are not homogeneous. For example, a text may contain various types of processing units: titles, normal sentences, paragraph numbering, nouns or noun phrases in figures, quantifiers or figures in tables, and so on.

Breaking a text down into processing units has a significant impact on the analysis which may be made of the text. When the notions of processing unit and sentence always coincide, the parser is faced with a simple situation. In addition, even if the processing units differ in nature, this matters little provided the preliminary phase of processing can correctly identify each type.

The notion of normal sentence must, however, be extended when the text contains sentences with enumerative structures. This also implies that the system must be capable of analyzing very long and complex sentences. For example, the text in (27) is a sentence in the linguistic sense, and so too is the text in (28):

(27) This system operates the following:
(a) Surface control boosters
(b) Wing flaps
(c) Right bomb bay door actuating cylinders.

(28) Obtain hydraulic fluid sample as follows:
(a) Prepare bottle from 644-2 Contamination Analysis Kit for obtaining fluid sample (refer to C-12-000-000/RR-005).
(b) Open hydraulic access for F321.
(c) Depress vent valve (reservoir air bleed valve) above reservoir No. 2 and completely relieve reservoir pressure.
...
(k) Analyze and evaluate fluid samples in accordance with instructions contained in Analyzing Hydraulic Fluid Samples paragraph in this Section.

In a technical manual sentences with enumerative structures such as (27) and (28) are very frequent and varied. It is important to be able to distinguish automatically between different types of enumerative structures (for example, the sentence enumerative structure in (28) and the noun phrase enumerative structure in (27)). To illustrate the kind of problem that often arises, take the case where the preliminary processing phase yields undifferentiated processing units for the sentences in (29) and the noun-phrases in (30):

(29) (a) Bleed system.
(b) Bleed pump.
(c) Refill reservoir.
(d) Open electrical load center door.
(e) Drain reservoir.

(30) (a) Bleed valves on reservoir service panel.
(b) Bleed fittings on power brake valves.
(c) Wing flaps.
(d) Drain hose assembly.
(e) Drain tank.

If the type of enumerative structure is not identified, it may be seen that all the examples in (29) may be analyzed not only as sentences, but also as noun phrases, while all those in (30) may be analyzed not only as noun phrases, but also as sentences. We would thus have two readings in each case and consequently two translations for each processing unit.

What these examples show is that, for a text with heterogeneous processing units, it is impossible to correctly break down the more or less arbitrary portions of a text unless these can be identified in the structure of the text. To be efficient, a system must accordingly have an integrated understanding of the typographic structure of a text.

C. AUTOMATIC IDENTIFICATION OF WORD UNITS

A text is made up of a succession of characters. All the characters used in a text form a pre-determined set of characters. These characters combine to make words and sentences. It might thus be said that a word is a succession of characters preceded and followed by a blank space. This statement must, nevertheless, be qualified. Punctuation marks, for example, are not part of the word. This rapidly becomes more complicated when in a given text the same characters performs various functions (e.g. period, dash, comma, capital letter, etc.).

The principal operations of identifying and delimiting the words in a sentence consist in separating the word from punctuation marks, transforming non-significant capitals into small letters and reconstituting character elisions (i.e. processing apostrophes).

As an example of these operations, a system might read the source text in (31) and reproduce it as the text in (32). In the four processing units in (32) we have used the character (#) to show word boundaries and the symbol $$ to identify processing unit boundaries.

(31) HYDRAULIC POWER SYSTEM NO. 1 OPERATION
Set ac hydraulic pump control switch, No. 1, No. 1A or No. 2, as applicable, to ON. Refill hydraulic reservoirs as necessary (refer to C-12-140-000/ML-000). Disconnect tube (13) at dc hydraulic pump No. 1B SUCT port reducer (11).

(32) #hydraulic# #power# #system# #No.# #1# #operation#$$

#set# #ac# #hydraulic# #pump# #control# #switch# #,# #No.# #1# #,# #No.# #1A# #or# #No.# #2# #,# #as# #applicable# #,# #to# #ON# #.# $$

#refill# #hydraulic# #reservoirs# #as# #necessary# #(# #refer# #to# #C-12-140-000/ML-000# #)# #.# $$

#disconnect# #tube# #(# #13# #)# #at# #dc# #hydraulic# #pump# #No.# #1B# #SUCT# #port# #reducer# #(# #11# #)# #.# $$

If we compare (32) to (31), it may be seen that the capital letters of the title, as well as those at the beginning of sentences, have been changed to lower-case letters. Significant capitals have, however, been maintained: the abbreviation NO. has been normalized as #No.#, the words ON and SUCT are legends appearing on a control device, and the word C-12-140-000/ML-000 is a code referring to a manual. Punctuation and parentheses have been separated from words, except for the abbreviation #No.#. The period in the abbreviation No. has not been mistaken for a period at the end of a sentence.

To illustrate some cases of apostrophe treatment, we have selected the examples in (33); the results obtained are shown in (34).

(33) Don't worry, I won't interfere.
Sam'll not miss us.
I've found you a good example.
She didn't have the children's toys.

(34) #do# #not# #worry# #,# #I# #will# #not# #interfere# #.# $$
#Sam# #will# #not# #miss# #us# #.# $$
#I# #have# #found# #you# #a# #good# #example# #.# $$
#she# #did# #not# #have# #the# #children# #'s# #toys# #.# $$

In English the apostrophe may mark the elision of the negation (#not#) or of an auxiliary (#will#, #have#). The apostrophe or 's may also be a mark of the genitive case. In French the article #le# and the pronouns (#je#, #me#, #te#, #se#) must be elided before a word beginning with a vowel or mute h.

Confronted with all these different phenomena and specific usages, a machine translation system designer has two choices: either to impose a strict procedure during codification and transcription of the source text onto the computer medium, or to develop mechanisms which enable the system to adapt rapidly to different typographical conventions. The latter solution is obviously more advantageous than the former. During the evaluation of a system, it is easy to measure how easily the system adapts to the specific typographical conventions of the text to be translated.

Once the text has been segmented into processing units and word units, grammatical analysis may then begin. The first step in grammatical analysis consists in examining each of the words in a sentence and making the necessary morphological breakdowns. Morphological breakdowns (e.g. BASE FORM + SUFFIX) allow the number of dictionary entries to be reduced considerably. Words may be broken down from the standpoint of inflectional morphology, derivational morphology or compositional morphology. Selkirk (1982) gives a very good description of these linguistic phenomena.

3.2.2 INFLECTIONAL MORPHOLOGY

Inflectional morphology (or the morphology of word conjugation) is the body of rules permitting the description of the manner in which a lexical item has a grammatical morpheme joined to it (e.g. the root of a word and its ending). This ending, or grammatical suffix, is strictly a mark of syntactic information, showing a grammatical category of gender, number, person, tense, etc. In English, for example, the grammatical suffix #s# marks the plural of nouns or the third person singular of the present indicative of verbs. In this section we will use the terminology BASE FORM + SUFFIX rather than ROOT + ENDING.

The inflectional suffixes of English are listed in (35). To these must be added the particular forms of irregular verbs and irregular plurals.

(35) S, ING, ED

In English the number of inflectional suffixes is very small compared to French or German. When a language has a highly developed inflectional morphology, it becomes very important that a system contain a morphological grammar. For example, in English this would allow the number of dictionary entries to be reduced by 2.5 times, while for French the reduction factor would be about 7.5. This gain is important not only in terms of reduction of dictionary entries, but above all in terms of the quality and transparency of the work of up-dating and consulting these dictionaries.

There are a number of programming techniques as well as various algorithms for processing this type of linguistic phenomena, as described for example in Harris (1971), Bourbeau and Poulin (1977), and Guilbaud (1980). Although it might have been useful here to present the principal techniques used in carrying out morphological analysis and generation by computer and show the advantages and disadvantages, we have decided not to deal with this question in the present report. In our system evaluation approach we feel it is more important that the evaluator study and determine the relevance and rigour of the linguistic descriptions of each linguistic phenomenon before evaluating the computer mechanics used to obtain the expected results.

It is nevertheless important to give an example of this morphological processing in order to remind the reader of the fundamental relations between the linguistic components of a system. Our simplified example will deal only with the treatment performed by a morphological analyzer of English words.

Words foreign to English in (25) having already been identified by the preliminary processing grammar, the inflectional morphology analysis grammar will be applied only to the remaining words in the source text. These English words will be designated as being the input forms of the inflectional morphology analyzer. When an input form carries one of the endings in (35) it will be broken down into BASE FORM + SUFFIX. In the case of certain breakdowns the morphological rules of English will call for a class of hypothetical base forms. The analyzer then constructs a graph to express these hypotheses. For example, an input such as (36) would be transformed into a graph similar to (37).

(36) . **#this#** → . **#unties#** → . **#our#** → . **#series#** → . **#of#** → . **#supplies#** → .

(37)

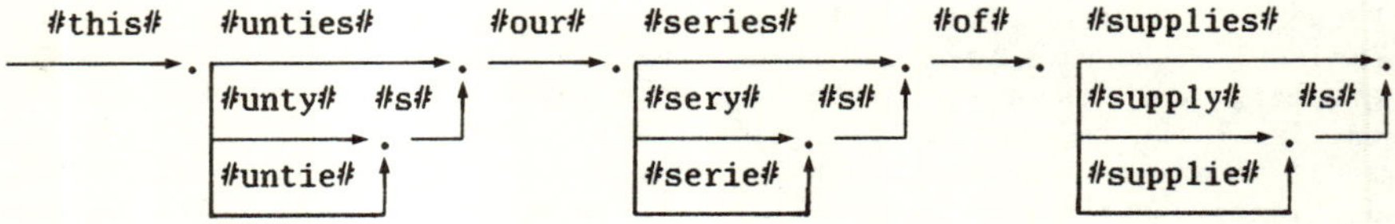

A string **ΩIES** may be the realization of **ΩY** + S or **ΩIE** + S. The suffix #s# is detached from the base form and will be entered in the memory as the mark of a grammatical category. Note that the input form is always maintained in the output graph (37). Next, the English dictionary is searched for entries that correspond to the written form of the base forms shown in the graph (37). The presence or absence of these base forms in the dictionary will serve to verify the graphic hypotheses formulated by the morphological analyzer. In the case of (37) the English dictionary accepts as hypotheses the forms UNTIE, SERIES and SUPPLY and eliminates from graph (37) all other hypotheses, to yield graph (38).

(38)

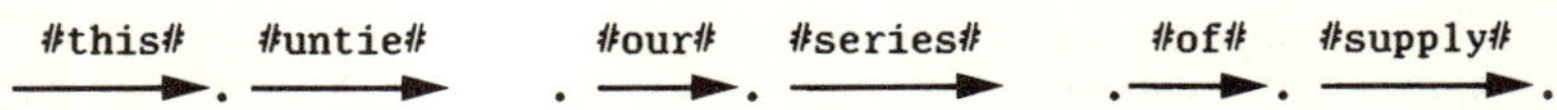

To each base form of graph (38) is then associated all the linguistic information (see Section 3.1) presented in the lexical item corresponding to each of these base forms. Next, the syntactic component (see Section 3.3) determines if SUPPLY in (38) is realized as a verb or a noun and, with the aid of the semantic component (see Section 3.4), produces the linguistic structure of the sentence.

It should be emphasized that the morphological analyzer may also contain the rules necessary to associate the appropriate base forms in cases of irregular realization of suffixes: SAW becomes SEE + ED, LEAVES becomes LEAF + S and LEAVE + S, FROZEN becomes FREEZE + ED, etc.

When making an evaluation, to determine whether a system includes a morphological grammar, we only have to examine the written form of dictionary entries. Testing of a morphological grammar may be done in three stages. The first stage consists in selecting several examples for each morphological class of all lexical categories and submitting this list of examples to the system. The second step consists in choosing examples that are homographic forms: for example, in English, TESTS is either a plural noun or a verb in the third person singular present indicative, while in French, the word AVIONS is either the verb AVOIR in the first person plural of the imperfect tense, or the noun AVIONS in the plural. Once a list of various homographic forms has been drawn up we have the system process this second list of examples. The third step consists in submitting to the system sentences that are representative of texts to be translated in order to observe the interactions between the various linguistic components.

3.2.3 DERIVATIONAL MORPHOLOGY

Derivational morphology (or the morphology of the formation of lexical items) is the body of rules that enable us to describe the manner in which a lexical morpheme is joined to a lexical item to produce a new lexical item. This lexical morpheme is a semantic information marker. In our study of derivational morphology the lexical morpheme will be either a prefix or a suffix.

Contrary to what happens in inflectional morphology, when a suffix is joined to a base lexical item the new lexical item resulting from this operation may have a different lexical category than the base item. For example, the English adjective #electrical# joined to the suffix #ly# produces the adverb #electrically#. In French, the verb #admettre# joined to the lexical morpheme #ion# gives the noun #admission#. When a prefix is attached to a lexical item, the lexical category of the derived lexical item is normally the same in French or English: for example, the verb #admettre# joined to the prefix #re# produces the verb #réadmettre#. In this section, we will use the terminology BASE FORM + SUFFIX and PREFIX + BASE FORM rather than the terms ROOT + LEXICAL MORPHEME or LEXICAL MORPHEME + ROOT.

To illustrate this morphological phenomenon, we have shown below several English examples taken mainly from Selkirk's (1982) classification. Examples (39), (40) and (41) illustrate noun-forming suffixes; (42), (43) and (44) illustrate adjective-forming suffixes; (45) and (46) illustrate verb-forming suffixes. Examples of prefixes are given in (47), (48) and (49).

	BASE FORM	+	SUFFIX	=	DERIVED FORM
(39)	Noun	+	Suffix	=	Noun
	sister		hood		sisterhood

	favorite		ism		favoritism
	village		er		villager

(40)	Adjective	+	Suffix	=	Noun
	national		ist		nationalist
	scarce		ity		scarcity
	wide		th		width

(41)	Verb	+	Suffix	=	Noun
	converse		ation		conversation
	confuse		ion		confusion
	amuse		ment		amusement

(42)	Noun	+	Suffix	=	Adjective
	inflation		ary		inflationary
	adventure		ous		adventurous
	accident		al		accidental

(43)	Adjective	+	Suffix	=	Adjective
	near		er		nearer
	near		est		nearest
	green		ish		greenish

(44)	Verb	+	Suffix	=	Adjective
	prefer		able		preferable
	create		ive		creative
	fidget		y		fidgety

(45)	Noun	+	Suffix	=	Verb
	code		ify		codify
	agony		ize		agonize
	winter		ize		winterize

(46)

Adjective	+	Suffix	=	Verb
pretty		ify		prettify
active		ate		activate
hard		en		harden

(47)

Prefix	+	Noun	=	Verb
de		bug		debug
en		slave		enslave
be		cloud		becloud

(48)

Prefix	+	Adjective	=	Verb
en		noble		ennoble
be		calm		becalm

(49)

Prefix	+	Verb	=	Verb
re		assemble		reassemble
de		centralize		decentralize
un		tie		untie

Derivational morphology is a much more complex phenomenon than inflectional morphology. A number of studies in the field of theoretical linguistics deal explicitly with this phenomenon of word formation and derivation, e.g. Chomsky (1967), Esau (1973), Jackendoff (1975), Aronoff (1976), Bourbeau (1976), Lieber (1980), Selkirk (1982).

Most MT systems do not have the appropriate mechanisms to process derivational morphology phenomena. The base form of a word and its derived forms are accordingly recorded in the dictionary as separate entries and no connection is established between these entries. It should nevertheless be mentioned that, in certain cases, there is partial treatment of some derivational suffixes (for example, in English, the formation of adverbs in #ly#, or the formation of the comparative and superlative forms of adjectives using the suffixes #er# and #est#).

3.2.4 COMPOSITIONAL MORPHOLOGY

Compositional morphology (or the morphology of compound words) is a body of rules that enable us to describe the manner in which two or more lexical items are joined to produce a new lexical item.

From the viewpoint of typography compound words may be divided into three distinct types: lexical items separated by a hyphen or diagonal (e.g. pilot-static, 110-to-infinite, air/oil, 7/32-inch), lexical items separated by a blank (e.g. apron string, living room, state of the art, off year), and lexical items agglutinated (e.g. smallpox, overdose, overdo).

Some examples of compound-word structure, taken mostly from Selkirk (1982), provide an interesting illustration of this linguistic phenomenon. Example (50) shows compound nouns and (51) compound adjectives.

	HYPHENATED	SEPARATED	AGGLUTINATED
(50) (a)	Noun + Noun = Noun		
	self-assertion	apron string	sunshine
	bull's-eye	mill wheel	hubcap
(b)	Adjective + Noun = Noun		
	well-wisher	high school	smallpox
(c)	Preposition + Noun = Noun		
	by-product	off year	overdose
			underdog
(d)	Verb + Noun = Noun		
	go-cart	frying pan	swearword
		slip ring	rattlesnake

(51) (a) Noun + Adjective = Adjective

honey-sweet	sky blue	headstrong
skin-deep		nationwide

(b) Adjective + Adjective = Adjective

white-hot	icy cold	easygoing
worldly-wise		highborn

(c) Preposition + Adjective = Adjective

off-white		overwide
		overabundant

In this report, as opposed to the above examples from Selkirk, a compound word is designated as a lexical item in which lexical units are separated by a hyphen or diagonal stroke. In speaking of a lexical item where the units are separated by a blank we use the term complex nominal group (cf. Section 3.3.3 and Section 3.4.2). Compound words in which the elements are agglutinated will be considered as autonomous and independent lexical items.

In Section 2.4.2 of Chapter 2 some typical English compound words are presented (e.g. (52), (53) and (54)). These examples showed us that, in English, there are highly productive mechanisms for producing compound words. A machine translation system should be able to automatically analyze at least such compound words as those in (53) and (54). This automatic analysis of the units making up a compound word eliminates the need to place in the dictionary all compound words or all groups containing a compound word. If a system does not have rules for dealing with the principal mechanisms of compound word production, up-dating the dictionaries runs the risk of being a constant, never-ending task.

Most of the types of compound words described in Chapter 2 in (52) are normally translated in French not by French compound words, but by multiword expressions with various syntactic structures. This type of translation is illustrated by the following examples of French equivalents of English compound words:

(52) (a) lock-bolt

(a') boulon de blocage

(b) motor-pump combination
(b') ensemble moteur-pompe

(c) line-type X
(c') X à canalisation

(d) 42-pin X
(d') X à 42 pôles

(e) motor-driven X
(e') X entraîné par moteur

(f) pressure-regulating flow-control valve
(f') soupape de régulation de débit et de pression

(g) reusable 10-micron corrugated stainless-steel wire cloth element
(g') élément filtrant réutilisable en acier inoxydable ondulé de 10 microns

(h) spring-loaded flexible fluid level indicator cable
(h') câble souple à rappel de l'indicateur de niveau du liquide

(i) slip ring-to-pump hydraulic tube
(i') tube hydraulique reliant la pompe au collier de contact

(j) converging-diverging nozzle
(j') tuyère convergente divergente

(k) two-position four-way manually operated selector valve
(k') robinet sélecteur manuel à quatre voies, à deux positions

(l) identical three-position four-way solenoid-operated selector valve
(l') robinet sélecteur identique à solénoïde, à quatre voies, à trois positions.

The examples in (52) are not exceptional cases. On the contrary, they are regularly encountered in technical texts. Analyzing and translating the internal structure of examples (c) to (l) in (52) without recourse to idiomatic dictionary entries (see in this connection Section 3.1.4) implies an interrelation between morphological, lexical, syntactic and semantic components. For example, the morphological component could filter compound words through dictionary look-up. If a word such as (52a) did appear as a lexical item in a dictionary entry, the morphological component would not break this word down into units. But if a compound did not appear in the dictionary, the morphological component would break the compound word into lexical units (e.g. line-type in (52c) would be transformed as #line# #-# #type#). The lexical elements #line# and #type# would then be searched in the dictionary. Based on the linguistic information shown in the entries for #line# and #type#, the syntactic and semantic components would then analyze the internal structure of the compound word. The translation process would then translate this internal English structure into a French internal structure, and the syntactic and morphological components of the target language would generate the appropriate surface structure.

This example of machine processing of the word #line-type# is obviously quite simplified. The aim of this example of compositional morphology was basically to justify the necessity of having the appropriate mechanisms in an MT system to integrate productive rules for the formation of new words. In addition, we wished to show through this example that compositional morphology is not independent from syntax and semantics.

3.3 SYNTACTIC COMPONENT

The function of the syntactic component is to analyze sentences and their constituents in the source language and to generate syntactically correct sentences in the target language. Its effectiveness depends very much on information coded in dictionary entries. Human translators draw on a huge store of knowledge about individual words in making syntactic judgments about sentences and their constituents; the syntactic component of a computerized translation system looks to the dictionary stored in the computer for that information. In fact, there can be a considerable amount of trade off between components. It is important to bear this in mind when assessing the possibilities for making improvements to a system by altering its components and in determining the limitations of the system.

3.3.1 SIMPLE SENTENCE

Let us define a simple sentence as one in which there is no embedding, no conjunction and no modification within a constituent except by determiners or verb auxiliaries; a simple sentence may not contain more than one (non-auxiliary) verb[14].

Other definitions of simple sentence can be found in the literature[15], but this one is well suited for our discussion of the syntactic component of a computerized translation system. Linguists have been fairly successful in writing computer programs for automatic parsing and generation of simple sentences, in the above sense. Therefore, for such sentences, it is reasonable to expect the syntactic component of a system to be able to identify the verb and its arguments, establish grammatical agreement where necessary and solve certain types of homography problems - without human intervention. Examples (53) and (54) illustrate the use of syntactic rules to resolve homographs.

(53)	**Remove filter from motor.** (N) (V)	The syntactic rules can be used to reject the interpretation of 'filter' as a verb by not permitting a sequence of non-auxiliary verbs in a simple sentence.
(54)	**The filter must be clean.** (N) (ADJ) (V) (V)	The syntactic rules can be used, to reject the interpretation of 'filter' and 'clean' as verbs by not accepting a constituent of the form article + verb and by not accepting a predicate of the form copula + verb, where the verb form is neither present participle nor past participle.

In (53) and (54) the only dictionary information needed in order to apply the syntactic rules is the set of grammatical categories for each word. In the following examples (55) it is necessary to have information about subcategories and complementation as well.

(55) (a) **He installed the bearing.**
(a') **Il a installé le roulement à bille.**

(b) **The bearing is heavy.**
(b') **Le roulement à bille est lourd.**

(c) **He calculated the bearing.**
(c') **Il a calculé la position.**

(d) **The bearing is computable.**
(d') **La position est calculable.**

If the dictionary provides the information that the noun 'bearing' can be either abstract or concrete, that the verbs 'install' and 'calculate' take concrete and abstract second arguments (direct objects) respectively, and that the adjectives 'heavy' and 'computable' take concrete and abstract arguments[16] respectively in a particular domain, then selectional restrictions between verbs or adjectives and their arguments enable the computer to make the correct interpretation of each sentence in (55). Otherwise, the computer will produce, in addition to the correct translations, the following "garbage" (in French):

(56) (a) * Il a installé la position.
(b) * La position est lourde.
(c) * Il a calculé le roulement à bille.
(d) * Le roulement à bille est calculable.

We do not mean to imply that all such potential ambiguities can be resolved automatically within simple sentences, nor that none can be resolved automatically within complex sentences; but the number of problems and the difficulty of isolating them are much greater in the case of complex sentences.

3.3.2 COMPLEX SENTENCE

Automatic analysis of complex sentences requires a very sophisticated syntactic component:

- If a sentence contains more than one verb, the arguments of each verb must be identified as well as the relations between clauses.

- Nominalized sentences must be identified and their role in the matrix sentence determined.

- If conjunctions are present, the scope of each must be determined; the conjoined elements may be noun phrases, verb phrases, prepositional phrases, adjective phrases, sentences, or even segments that do not belong to any category officially recognized in the analysis grammar.

- Deletions associated with conjunction and embedding must be taken into account.

- Relations of modification must be identified; modifiers and modified elements may be either single words or phrases.

- Constituent boundaries must be determined and the constituents themselves analyzed; this can be extremely difficult in the case of complex constituents.

The following examples (57) taken from a corpus (aircraft maintenance manuals) used in a machine translation experiment illustrate some of the problems posed.

(57)	(a)	**Rotate disc to lock nut.**	Is 'lock nut' a kind of nut and 'to' a movement preposition? Or is 'to lock' a verb in the infinitive with 'nut' as direct object?
	(b)	**Insert selector lever actuating arm in slot of selector lever.**	Is 'actuating' a modifier of arm' in a noun phrase 'selector lever actuating arm'? Or is 'actuating' the verb in a reduced relative clause modifying 'selector lever'?
	(c)	**Disconnect pressure inlet port and drain lines.**	Is this a conjunction of sentences or of noun phrases?
	(d)	**The function of the priority valve is to restrict fluid flow to the secondary sub-systems and to supply fluid on a priority basis for operation of the flight controls.**	Is this a conjunction of predicates ('to restrict ... and to supply ...')? Or is it a conjunction of prepositional phrases ('to the secondary sub-systems and to supply fluid'), where 'supply fluid' is a noun-noun compound?
	(e)	**The other system will maintain fluid pressure for flight control at a reduced rate of flow.**	Is 'at a reduced rate of flow' a modifier of 'flight control'? Or is it a modifier of 'fluid pressure'? I.e., [fluid pressure for (flight control at a reduced rate of flow)] or [(fluid pressure for flight control) at a reduced rate of flow].

Of course, a human translator can usually disambiguate such sentences by using his knowledge of the subject matter, the situational context and the preceding text already translated. But the machine must rely on information coded in its dictionary and on the programs that make use of this information. There are practical limits on how much "knowledge of the subject matter" can be coded in the dictionary; attempting to make the computer sensitive to "situational context" leads the system's designer into an unexplored area; and making use of the "preceding text" in the analysis of a sentence (i.e., writing a formal text grammar) poses problems of a very high order of difficulty.

3.3.3 COMPLEX CONSTITUENT

Sentence constituents are as complex as sentences themselves. In fact, a constituent may even be a sentence ('Be sure the valve is open'). We will use the same criteria for defining simple and complex constituents as we used for simple and complex sentences:

> **A simple constituent** is one in which there is no embedding, no conjunction and no modification except by determiners or verb auxiliaries; a simple sentence is one type of simple constituent.
>
> **A complex constituent** is one which is not simple.

It is necessary to distinguish constituent **functions** (subject of a verb, object of a preposition, sentence adverbial, etc.) from constituent **types** (noun phrase, verb phrase, adjective phrase, prepositional phrase, etc.). A given type may function in different ways, depending on the context, and this is one source of problems for the automatic analysis of sentences. Thus in searching for an argument of a verb in a complex sentence there may be many potential candidates of the required type; the candidates may be quite complex in themselves and, of course, the presence of homographs (which is the normal situation) makes identification even more difficult. We will look at some of these problems in detail, but first it is important to call attention to the enormous variety of structures possible within a single constituent type.

Noun phrases have a number of syntactic functions in a sentence, including subject or object of a verb, object of a preposition and modifier of a noun. In addition to their pervasiveness, their internal structure exhibits endless variety, as shown by the examples in (58).

(58) (a) a big new red wooden barn
(a') une nouvelle et grande grange rouge en bois

(b) all of those new books
(b') tous ces nouveaux livres

(c) not a single one of the many participants
(c') pas un seul des nombreux participants

(d) the slowly drifting white sand
(d') le sable blanc qui s'entassait lentement

(e) the most eagerly sought prize
(e') le prix le plus âprement convoité

(f) the wisest, boldest, most decisive and, without doubt, the best candidate
(f') le candidat le plus sage, le plus audacieux, le plus déterminé, bref le meilleur sans aucun doute

(g) the poor
(g') le pauvre

(h) John's hat
(h') le chapeau de Jean

(i) the King of England's hat
(i') le chapeau du roi d'Angleterre

(j) John's older brother's second wife's lover
(j') l'amant de la deuxième femme du frère aîné de Jean

(k) pump pressure control valve setting
(k') la pose de la soupape régulatrice de pression de la pompe

(l) No. 2 and 3 nacelle main landing gear door forward left fireshield lower panel assemblies
(l') les ensembles Nos 2 et 3 du panneau inférieur du pare-feu gauche avant de la trappe du train d'atterrissage principal de la nacelle

(m) the signing of the treaty
(m') la signature du traité

(n) the people here
(n') les gens d'ici

(o) all those present
(o') toutes les personnes présentes

(p) the books on the shelf behind the metal filing cabinet
(p') les livres sur l'étagère derrière le classeur en métal

(q) books we like to read
(q') les livres que nous aimons lire

(r) books that the people who lived here left behind
(r') les livres que les gens qui vivaient ici ont laissés

(s) the book of which I am speaking
(s') le livre dont je parle

(t) the books on top of which the manuscript was found
(t') les livres sur lesquels on a trouvé le manuscrit

(u) the fact that it happened
(u') le fait que cela soit arrivé

(v) the thing to do
(v') ce qu'il faut faire

(w) the man running from the police
(w') l'homme qui se sauvait de la police

(x) the car the fender of which was dented
(x') la voiture dont le garde-boue était bosselé

(y) people young and old alike
(y') aussi bien les jeunes que les vieux

(z) eating and drinking in moderation
(z') manger et boire avec modération

(A) a good many of the previously mentioned benefits derived from walking, jogging, swimming and dancing
(A') un grand nombre des avantages déjà mentionnés que l'on tire de la marche, du jogging, de la natation et de la danse

(B) the increasing number of utterly fascinating new books and plays that have been written about computers and how they affect our daily lives

(B') le nombre croissant de nouveaux livres et de nouvelles pièces vraiment fascinants qui ont été écrits au sujet des ordinateurs et de leur influence sur notre vie quotidienne

Finally, consider the noun phrase beginning with 'the action....' in the following toast from a Hungarian short story by G. Fehér (English translation):

(59) I wish that true love would bind this company in the same manner as for centuries the material of the bridge is bound by the action of the binding force of the nails protruding from the draw-bridge of the brigand feudal castle illuminated by the moonlight being reflected in the tears that dropped from the protruding eye of the tick that clung in the hair of the sheep-dog excited by the terrifying scraping of the cart-wheels striving to break from the embraces of the mud.

It should not be assumed that because a text contains many long lists of sentence fragments it is a better candidate for automatic translation than one which consists almost entirely of full sentences in connected discourse. If those lists are made up of complex nominal groups they may prove intractable to automatic analysis. For example, (58-1) was taken from a long list of similar nominal groups in a table of wing and nacelle components that extends over many pages in an aircraft maintenance manual. As is well-known, this phenomenon of noun stacking is one of the most difficult problems for automatic analysis and it has not yet been adequately dealt with. We will discuss it further in section 3.4.

Another example of the regular use of extremely complex nominal groups is found in the description of patents. W. Moskovich, who played an active role in the study of the structure of patent descriptions in the Soviet Union, gives the following example in Kittredge and Lehrberger (1982, p. 196):

(60) A manually usable convertible implement comprising a handle having head means at the leading end of the handle, said head means embodying a fixed hook and a projectible and retractable pike, said pike having selectively usable pointed prongs ...

In general, texts that contain detailed descriptions of complex devices and processes are likely to employ complex noun phrases in those descriptions. A small part in a large machine may be precisely identified by a noun phrase incorporating information about the location of that part with respect to other parts and the way it functions in the machine. This can be seen in (58-1), (60) and in the following examples (61), (62).

(61) (a) vertical stabilizer lower spar attachment fittings
(a') ferrures de fixation du longeron inférieur du plan fixe vertical

(b) engine-driven variable-displacement pressure-compensated pump
(b') pompe-moteur à pression régulée et à déplacement variable

(c) nose wheel steering shut-off valve pressure line
(c') canalisation de refoulement du robinet d'arrêt d'orientation de la roue avant

(62) (a) aft fuselage right and left upper attach bolt receptacle
(a') logement du boulon de fixation supérieur des parties droite et gauche du fuselage arrière

(b) upper, lower, and corner longerons to frame attachment
(b') raccordement supérieur, inférieur et de coin des longerons au cadre

(c) fuselage aft section flight control and utility hydraulic system filter elements
(c') la commande de vol de la section arrière du fuselage et les éléments filtrants du circuit hydraulique des servitudes

Keeping in mind the potential complexity of noun phrases, let us return to a problem that was mentioned earlier: identification of the arguments of a verb. This is absolutely essential in order to parse a sentence and build a representation of its structure that is adequate for the needs of transfer. There are two problems involved:

(A) The boundary problem: Isolate potential arguments; find out where they begin and end in the sentence.

(B) The internal problem: By examining the internal structure of a potential argument, find out whether it satisfies the conditions specified for the given verb in the dictionary. (Of course, it is also necessary to know the internal structure in order to be able to translate the argument after it has been found.)

The boundary problem is well-illustrated by the examples in (57) and example (59) above. The computer examines many possibilities, as indicated by the partial list of candidates for direct object of the boldfaced verb in each sentence of (63).

(63) (a) **Rotate** disc to lock nut.

disc disc to lock nut	(The computer must consider the possibility that 'disc to lock nut' is a noun phrase like 'road to Rome'.)

(b) **Insert** selector lever actuating arm in slot of selector lever.

selector lever
selector lever actuating arm
selector lever actuating arm in slot of selector lever

(c) **Disconnect** pressure inlet port and drain lines.

pressure inlet port
pressure inlet port and drain lines

(d) The function of the priority valve is to **restrict** fluid flow to the secondary sub-systems and to supply fluid on a priority basis for operation of the flight controls.

fluid flow
fluid flow to the secondary sub-systems
fluid flow to the secondary sub-systems and to supply fluid
fluid flow to ... and to supply fluid on a priority basis
fluid flow to ... on a priority basis for operation of the flight controls

(e) The other system will **maintain** fluid pressure for flight control at a reduced rate of flow.

fluid pressure

fluid pressure for flight control
fluid pressure for flight control at a reduced rate of flow

(f) Camper killed fighting bear.

fighting bear
camper

In (63-f), because of the telegraphic style, it is not clear (at least, not to the computer) whether 'killed' is in the active or passive, hence whether its direct object is to the right or left.

The kind of ambiguity created by 'fighting' in (63-f) and 'actuating' in (63-b) is a frequent source of trouble in parsing. The syntactic component needs a strategy for dealing with the form Ving N, some means of deciding whether

(i) Ving is a present participle modifying N like an adjective

or whether

(ii) it is the progressive aspect of the verb V taking N as its direct object.

This case raises the question of internal structure (see (B) above); in fact, the **boundary problem** (see (A) above) cannot, in general, be solved without knowing the internal structure of the proposed candidates. In order for (ii) to hold, V must be a transitive verb and N must be an acceptable second argument of V. It is easy to verify the transitivity of V, but checking the second argument may involve another round of constituent analysis at a different level, as in the case of example (64).

(64) leading or trailing edge flap actuator support and attachment

We cannot pursue the extremely difficult problem of -ing forms here, but only note that a very sophisticated syntactic component is needed to deal with it. The ambiguous expressions in (65) give some idea of the problem.

(65)	moving parts	furniture moving	[In N Ving, Ving may
	checking accounts	student teaching	introduce a reduced
	matching socks	cattle stampeding	relative clause.]

flying planes	information leaking
mounting plates	dust collecting
sticking doors	police searching

In order to verify the selectional restrictions between a verb and a potential noun phrase argument it is necessary to identify the head noun of the noun phrase, since it is the features of the head noun that are relevant for that purpose. But the head noun may be premodified, postmodified or both. Furthermore, the modifiers are of arbitrary complexity. The result is that just to identify the head noun a very detailed analysis of the internal structure of the noun phrase is required.

Prepositional phrases may also be very complex since a prepositional phrase consists of a preposition followed by a noun phrase. And the noun phrase may contain other prepositional phrases, etc. When a string of prepositional phrases occurs in a sentence it may be difficult to decide which element of the sentence each one modifies. This is sometimes referred to as the problem of **prepositional attachment**. In the classic example 'John saw the man in the park with the telescope' the computer will not know whether John, the man, or the park has the telescope. In any English sentence containing a string which has the form ... V N1 P N2 ... the parser must decide whether N1 is the object of V (with P N2 functioning as an adverbial in the sentence) or N1 P N2 is the object of V (with P N2 functioning as a postmodifier of N1). The corresponding normalized structure built by the parser will be quite different in these two cases and it cannot be assumed that the same ambiguity holds in the target language - even though the ambiguity often carries over from English into French, as in the above example («Jean a vu l'homme dans le parc avec le télescope»).

Another problem concerning prepositional attachment arises when a preposition is followed by two or more nouns: does the preposition govern the first noun only, the first two nouns, ...? The parser must decide whether a string of the form P N1 N2 is to be bracketed as ((P N1) N2 ...) or as (P (N1 N2)), where (N1 N2) is an instance of noun stacking (e.g., 'In winter conditions change frequently').

Coordinate conjunctions create a particularly serious problem for any machine translation system. At the heart of the problem is the fact that elements of almost any category or phrase type can be joined by a coordinate conjunction. This means that when a coordinate conjunction is encountered in a sentence, a thorough analysis of the entire sentence is usually required to determine what is being conjoined with what. Unfortunately, 'and' and 'or' have a very high frequency of occurrence in most texts. Their repeated use gives rise to long sentences containing many complex constituents. The examples (66) and (67) are from technical writing which went through the usual processes of editing and revision before being printed.

(66) After the pressure checks of the transmitter and gauge have been completed, and the actual pump output pressure is found to be greater than 3100 PSI or less than 3000 PSI at zero flow, or greater than 3000 PSI or less than 2900 PSI at maximum flow, remove pump and install replacement.

(67) Corrosion is often aggravated and accelerated by mechanical factors that are either within the metal or applied to such as residual, static or cyclic stresses, erosion or poor heat treatment techniques.

To find the scope of each conjunction the parser tries many combinations on the word level, phrase level and sentence level. It should also be noted that commas are often interpreted as coordinate conjunctions.

A syntactic constraint that is useful in determining the scope of a conjunction is the fact that the conjuncts are normally of the same syntactic type (noun phrases, verb phrases, sentences, etc.). However, there are exceptions, as can be seen in (67): 'either within the metal or applied to such as ...'. Sometimes the conjuncts are sentence fragments that are not recognized as phrase types within the grammar used by the parser; it is easy to imagine, for example, that some grammars might not give official status to the conjuncts in (68).

(68) Interconnect emergency down and normal down lines.

Of course, one may argue that the "real" conjuncts in (68) are 'emergency down lines' and 'normal down lines', which are noun phrases. This problem of recovering zeroed (ellipted) elements and "filling out" the surface structure gives further emphasis to the importance of depth of analysis in parsing sentences with complex constituents: from the actual arrangements of words that occur, the parser must be able to discover relations that are implicit in the sentence.

Ellipsis occurs frequently within the scope of conjunctions. The ability to infer that a certain element has been ellipted is vital to the understanding of a sentence. In the presence of a conjunction nearly any sentence element can be ellipted, including the verb, its subject and object, as in (69).

(69) Customers may demand a rebate and probably will.

Ambiguity is rife in the neighborhood of conjunctions, sometimes due to ellipsis ('old men and women') and sometimes to homography ('Connect inlet and drain lines').

Much more could be said about conjunction-related problems. Attempts to solve these problems by purely syntactic means have not proved very successful and the use of semantic criteria (see **section 3.4.2**) has not improved matters greatly as far as practical parsing is concerned. We are still faced with the **combinatorial explosion** that results when the parser tries out all possible candidates for conjuncts in a sentence with coordinate conjunctions. The proper treatment of this subject remains an important goal of research in machine translation.

* * * * * * * * *

Clearly, the difficulty of parsing complex constituents is on a par with that of parsing whole sentences. Just the identification of constituents that perform given functions (subject, object, etc.) requires syntactic analysis of the entire sentence. Any claim that adequate parsing can be accomplished by means of **local analysis** must be viewed with skepticism, even in limited domains. To the extent that the syntactic component is unable to deal with the problems mentioned above, there will be ample work for human translators and revisers. Many researchers are looking to the field of semantics for solutions to these problems - and other problems as well. In the next section we will see how semantic criteria might be used to complement syntactic analysis.

3.4 SEMANTIC COMPONENT

There has been significant progress in semantic theory within the field of linguistics, but considerably less progress in making effective use of semantic theory in practical machine translation systems. The need for semantic analysis is generally recognized; the big question is how to do it. Before examining that question, it should be pointed out that those systems which are purported to have a "semantic component" do not necessarily contain a semantic module. It is convenient to talk about the semantic component of a system even if there is no phase where only semantic analysis takes place. In fact, it may be convenient to talk about a semantic component even if there are no **semantic rules** as such, provided the system has some device that enables it to perform semantic analysis.

3.4.1 WORD LEVEL

To find the meaning of a word one usually looks in the dictionary. The same is true in a machine translation system: a dictionary entry provides a definition of a word for the system. These definitions usually contain more syntactic and morphological information than semantic. One way to give the definition more semantic content is to assign **semantic features** to the word. Features may be of a very general nature (CONCRETE, ABSTRACT, PHYSICAL OBJECT, ACTION, etc.) or they may be highly specific for use in translating texts from a narrow domain (e.g., in chemistry, ORGANIC, INORGANIC, SOLVENT, BASE, etc.). They are commonly used in the statement of selectional restrictions (between verbs and their arguments or between modifiers and modified elements) and in signalling different meanings of a polysemous word so that transfer algorithms can use the information in choosing appropriate target language equivalents.

As an example of semantic features used in stating selectional restrictions, the verb 'drink' might have the feature LIQUID assigned as a constraint on its second argument (object) so that only a noun with that feature will be accepted as second argument of 'drink'. If the parser encounters the sentence (70), it will not interpret 'day and night' as the object of 'drank', but as a circumstantial element. If the parser encounters the sentence (71), 'liquid drunk' will not be interpreted as a noun phrase, provided that the adjective 'liquid' is incompatible with nouns carrying the feature HUMAN.

(70) (a) **John drank day and night.**
(a') **Jean buvait jour et nuit.**

(71) (a) **There was no liquid drunk at the meeting.**
(a') **On n'a rien bu à la réunion.**

To make use of semantic features in this way, there must be a convention for rejecting combinations of words having incompatible feature sets. This convention, which can also be applied to syntactic features (COUNT, MASS, PLURAL, etc.) is not itself a semantic rule.

(70) and (71) illustrate the importance of semantic analysis at the word level in helping to determine the correct syntagmatic combinations (see section 3.4.2). Word level semantics needs further clarification since it too involves complex relations as well as problems of representation and terminology.

HOMOGRAPHY

Word ambiguity can result from homographs belonging to different grammatical categories ('walk' as a noun or verb; 'well' as a noun or adverb) or from homographs within the same category ('play' a game, a role, a record; 'attachment' as the act of attaching something or as the thing attached). Semantic features can be used to identify different senses of a word within the same category. Thus, instead of having two dictionary entries, attachment1 and attachment2, we can have just one entry with the features ACTION and PHYSICAL OBJECT. Since these two features are incompatible with each other, whenever one is selected at any stage of processing the other can be eliminated from further consideration. This prevents confusion at a later stage of analysis and it also signals which meaning is to be used at the transfer phase for choosing the correct target language equivalent. The choice of 'attachement' or 'accessoire' as the French equivalent of the English word 'attachment' would, for example, depend on which feature is present on the English word at the output of the analysis phase.

Language users make incredibly subtle distinctions between word senses; we would like to have the computer do the same. Suppose a machine translation system recognizes that a word of a given category has more than one sense by the fact that the word has been assigned at least two incompatible features. Since different senses of a single word in the source language may correspond to different translation equivalents in the target language (as in the preceding example), it is hoped that the set of semantic features in the system will suffice to detect all such differences. The content of that set may be difficult to determine. Features such as CONCRETE and ABSTRACT are fairly obvious candidates for membership, but the optimum set depends on differences in vocabulary structure of the two languages and on the domains of the texts that are to be translated by the system. Also, in addition to theoretical considerations, there are practical limits on the number of features used; for example, the people who make dictionary entries must decide, for each entry, which of the features should be assigned and how they are to be used in formulating selectional restrictions in the dictionary.

Fortunately, the number of features actually listed in a dictionary entry can be reduced by means of **redundancy** rules: the presence of some features can be **predicted** by the presence of others, as illustrated in (72).

(72) **HUMAN ⟶ ANIMATE ⟶ PHYSICAL-OBJECT ⟶ CONCRETE**

This can be read "if a word has the feature HUMAN, it also has the feature ANIMATE; if it has the feature ANIMATE, it also has the feature PHYSICAL-OBJECT; etc." There are various hierarchies of features like (72); another example is COLOR ⟶ PROPERTY ⟶ ABSTRACT. If any feature in one of these hierarchies is assigned as an inherent feature of a word in the dictionary, then all features to the right of it in the hierarchy can be filled in by a redundancy rule.

Given a set of semantic features, let us define the hierarchical relation '⟶' and the incompatibility relation 'i' as follows:

(73) (a) A ⟶ B — if and only if every word having A as an inherent feature must also have B as an inherent feature, where A is not the same as B. (The last condition simply excludes A ⟶ A as a matter of convenience; hence '⟶' is an irreflexive relation.)

(b) A i B — if and only if a word, in a given sense, cannot have both A and B as inherent features. (The presence of incompatible features on a word therefore indicates a sense difference.)

For illustrative purposes a small set of semantic features is given in (74), together with a few nouns bearing those features.

(74) **ABSTRACT:** idea, truth, thought, action, flight, attachment
ACTION: movement, vibration, battle, fusion, flight, attachment

CHEMICAL-COMPOUND: sodium chloride, vitamin C, benzene, laughing gas
CONCRETE: water, air, child, attachment, Plato, galaxy, motor, molecule
FORM: circle, sphere, square, ellipse, cylinder, cone
HUMAN: man, child, sister, Plato, chairperson
MALE: man, Plato, uncle, rooster, king
MEASURE-UNIT: centimeter, mile, kilogram, liter, second, °C, light year
PHYSICAL-OBJECT: flower, motor, Plato, galaxy, molecule, attachment
VERTEBRATE: man, fish, salmon, bird, Plato

The hierarchical relation '→' and the incompatibility relation 'i' are shown in Table 1 for these ten features; the numbers in the table refer to the features, as indicated in the LEGEND on page 107. A relation symbol is placed at the intersection of a row labeled A and a column labeled B if the feature A bears that relation to the feature B, otherwise not. Note that since incompatibility is a symmetric relation (i.e., A i B implies B i A), each pair of incompatibles results in two instances of i in the table. Also, since '→' is transitive and irreflexive by (73a), it is a partial order[17] on the set of semantic features.

	1	2	3	4	5	6	7	8	9	10
1			i	i		i	i		i	i
2	→		i	i	i	i	i	i	i	i
3	i	i		→	i	i	i	i	i	i
4	i	i			i			i		
5	→	i	i	i		i	i	i	i	i
6	i	i	i	→	i			i	→	→
7	i	i	i	→	i			i	→	
8	→	i	i	i	i	i	i		i	i
9	i	i	i	→	i			i		
10	i	i	i	→	i			i	→	

TABLE 1

LEGEND
1 = ABSTRACT
2 = ACTION
3 = CHEMICAL-COMPOUND
4 = CONCRETE
5 = FORM
6 = HUMAN
7 = MALE
8 = MEASURE-UNIT
9 = PHYSICAL-OBJECT
10 = VERTEBRATE

Semantic features subcategorize the grammatical categories: corresponding to each feature is the set of words which bear that feature. Statements about semantic features can therefore be interpreted as statements about semantic classes of words. To say that the noun 'idea' bears the feature ABSTRACT is equivalent to saying that 'idea' is a member of the set of ABSTRACT nouns. The relation ACTION ⟶ ABSTRACT can be stated as: the set of ACTION nouns is a proper subset of the set of ABSTRACT nouns ("proper" since definition (73-a) excludes A ⟶ A). The relations between the features MALE, HUMAN, VERTEBRATE, PHYSICAL-OBJECT and CONCRETE can be represented by a Venn diagram of the corresponding semantic classes of words, as in (75).

(75)

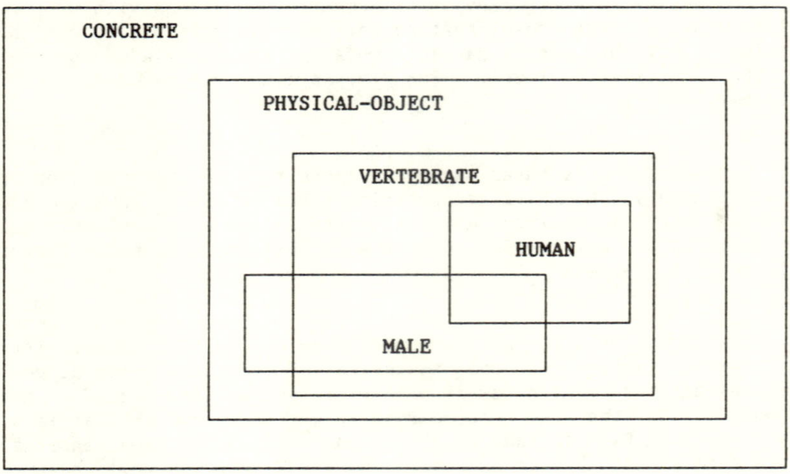

Our examples so far have involved features assigned to nouns since the semantic subcategorization of the noun class plays such an important role in the statement of selectional restrictions between verbs and their arguments. However, semantic features are assigned to words in other grammatical categories as well. A few examples are listed in (76).

(76)	Prepositions:	LOCATIVE (at, in, in front of, on, under, ...) MOVEMENT (by way of, into, onto, toward, via, ...) TIME (after, at, before, during, prior to, ...)
	Adjectives:	DEGREE (bright, happy, large, useful, young, ...) DEFECT (bad, corrosive, defective, rusty, sick, ...) FORM (angular, circular, oblong, polygonal, round, ...)
	Adverbs:	LOCATIVE (afar, centrally, here, nearby, there, ...) TIME (now, soon, today, tomorrow, yesterday, ...) DEGREE (extremely, quite, rather, too, very, ...) DEFECT (badly, excessively, harmfully, poorly, ...)
	Verbs:	CAUSATIVE (blow up, break, kill, open, put, ...) FACTIVE (ascertain, discover, know, realize, regret, ...) INCHOATIVE (break, grow, mature, rise, stop, ...) DEFECT (crack, deteriorate, rot, rust, scar, ...)

Obviously there are many other semantic subclasses within the grammatical categories, but these suffice for our discussion. It will be shown in section 3.4.2 that such semantic subcategorization plays an important role on the syntagmatic level. For the present we may note a few points of interest.

Some semantic features may be assigned to words in more than one grammatical category (LOCATIVE prepositions and adverbs; DEGREE adjectives and adverbs; DEFECT adjectives, adverbs, verbs and nouns). In such cases it is necessary to be very careful about the criteria for assigning features within different categories.

The choice of a set of semantic features is, of course, influenced by the subject matter of the texts to be analyzed. Now suppose a set of features has been chosen for a domain D1 and another set for a domain D2. Suppose further that the feature F is in both sets and that it is assigned to a word used in D1. If that word is used in D2 in the same sense as in D1 it would seem reasonable to expect it to bear F in D2 as well; however, this is not always the case. The noun 'dirt' may bear the feature DEFECT in texts on engine maintenance, but not in agriculture texts, and the verb 'freeze' may belong to the DEFECT class in texts on the cultivation of tropical plants, but not in texts on cryogenics. In other words, the subject matter can affect both the choice of features to be used and the assignment of those features to individual words. In most theoretical discussions of semantic features it is tacitly assumed that each feature subcategorizes the vocabulary of the whole language. The foregoing discussion suggests that semantic subclasses have greater relevance within particular sublanguages; experience in machine translation seems to bear this out.

The features CAUSATIVE, FACTIVE and INCHOATIVE tell us something about the nature of and relations between the arguments of the verbs that bear them. The subject of a causative verb brings about a change in the condition or location of the direct object; a sentence which forms the complement of a factive verb is taken to be true; the subject of an inchoative verb undergoes a change in condition or location. Furthermore, there is an important syntactic relation between certain verbs used causatively and inchoatively, as in (77) and (78).

(77) (a) John grows flowers.
(a') Jean cultive les fleurs.

(b) Flowers grow.
(b') Les fleurs poussent.

(78) (a) Someone broke the glass.
(a') Quelqu'un a brisé le verre.

(b) The glass broke.
(b') Le verre s'est brisé.

The direct object in (77-a) and (78-a) is the same as the subject in (77-b) and (78-b). This was discussed at some length in section 2.3.1 (see examples (9) to (14) and the following paragraph in section 2.3.1) with reference to dictionary entries and the statement of selectional restrictions.

* * * * * * * * *

We have looked at a particular way of using semantic features on words; there are other methods and notations in the literature. Some linguists prefer a strictly binary notation (i.e. plus or minus notation) e.g. + - CONCRETE, + - HUMAN, etc. On the theoretical plane there is the idea that the meanings of the words in any natural language can be represented by means of a set of **universal semantic components** (= semantic features or semantic markers); this is the goal of **componential analysis** (see Lyons 1968, for a brief discussion). If such a goal could be realized, it would lend support to the idea of a universal pivot language for multilingual translation (cf. section 2.3.2). The actual use of semantic features in machine translation systems reveals a more modest goal at present: to provide a tool that facilitates the statement of word co-occurrences and to provide adequate information on word senses for use at transfer in choosing target language equivalents.

Word meanings can also be analyzed by means of semantic rules called **meaning postulates** (cf. Carnap 1956). These are language specific. For example, to specify the meaning of the noun 'man' in English we might give the set of entailments :

> **whatever is a man is a male**
> **whatever is a man is an adult**
> **whatever is a man is a human being**
> etc.

Briefly, we may write these as: man ⟶ male, man ⟶ adult, man ⟶ human being, etc. Each such relation is part of the meaning of 'man'. The set of all meaning postulates in which a given lexical item occurs in the language specifies the meaning of the lexical item; if some postulates are missing, a **partial meaning** is obtained. The set of meaning postulates for a language is obviously very large; it would hardly be feasible to list all of them in the dictionary. However, the transitivity of the relation '⟶' makes possible the use of redundancy rules to reduce the total number. For example, it is not necessary to list 'man ⟶ animal' since it can be obtained from 'man ⟶ human' and 'human ⟶ animal'.

Word-level relations such as synonymy, antonymy, polysemy, hyponymy and incompatibility can be defined within the framework of either componential analysis or meaning postulates. Meaning postulates have been criticized on the ground that there is no mechanism within the theory for relating the meaning postulates in one language to the corresponding ones in another language. Componential analysis has been criticized on theoretical grounds for attempting to specify lexical meaning by a simple set of features (semantic components). Kempson (1977, pp. 89-90) points out that 'give' and 'take' would have the same set of components (e.g., + [CAUSE], + [CHANGE OF POSSESS-ION]) although they differ in meaning. An alternative suggested to overcome this defect makes use of a predicate notation. Letting [CAUSE], [CHANGE OF POSSESSION] and [HAVE] be predicates, 'give' is then represented by (79) whereas 'take' is represented by (80).

(79) [CAUSE] X ([HAVE] Y Z)
[CAUSE] X (¬ [HAVE] X Z)

(80) [CAUSE] X ([HAVE] X Z)
[CAUSE] X (¬ [HAVE] Y Z)

The number and types of arguments are specified for each predicate and the meaning representation takes on more structure than a mere set of semantic features. Also, this type of representation is obviously well-suited for making inferences if it is properly formalized.

Meaning representation will undoubtedly play an increasingly important role in machine translation in the future as systems are designed to incorporate more semantics. Whatever devices are used for meaning representation at the word level, they must be integrated with parsing rules at the syntagmatic level. And finally, on a more mundane level, certain practical matters must be taken into account such as the cost of building a system and the ease of building and updating dictionaries.

3.4.2 SYNTAGMATIC LEVEL

It has been customary in machine translation to assign semantic features to lexical items - but not with the intention of making a complete componential analysis of word meaning. The most common use of these features on the syntagmatic level is to verify selectional restrictions between verbs and their arguments (81).

(81)	(a)	Perform the check.	[ACTION]	The direct object of 'perform' is an action noun.
	(a')	Vérifier.		
	(b)	Deposit the check.	[CONCRETE]	The direct object of 'deposit' is a concrete noun.
	(b')	Déposer le chèque.		

In like manner, an adjective may "select" a given sense of the noun that it modifies (82).

(82)	(a)	a sudden stop	[ACTION]	'sudden' modifies action nouns;
	(a')	un arrêt brusque		
	(b)	an apico-alveolar stop	[CONSONANT]	'apico-alveolar' is applied to certain classes of consonants in articulatory phonetics.
	(b')	une occlusive apico-alvéolaire		

If the past participle of a verb is used as an adjectival modifier, the argument restrictions of the verb may still apply as if the modified noun were the object of the verb in a simple sentence (83).

(83)	(a)	the wounded coach	[ANIMATE]	(= Someone wounded the coach.)
	(a')	le cocher blessé		
	(b)	the refurbished coach	[INANIMATE]	(= Someone refurbished the coach.)
	(b')	la diligence rénovée		

And just as verbs and adjectives select certain nouns (or noun senses), so the noun sometimes selects a particular sense of a verb (84) or adjective (85):

(84)	(a)	we will integrate this school.	(= admit people of all types)
	(a')	nous les intégrerons à cette école.	
	(b)	we will integrate this logarithmic function.	(= mathematical operation)
	(b')	nous calculerons l'intégrale de cette fonction logarithmique.	

(85)	(a)	a hard problem	(= difficult)
	(a')	un problème difficile	
	(b)	a hard mineral	(= physical property of solids)
	(b')	un minéral dur	
	(c)	a hard blow	(= powerful, delivered with great force)
	(c')	un coup solide	

(d)	hard cider	(= fermented)
(d')	un cidre sec	
(e)	hard feelings	(= hostile)
(e')	un ressentiment	
(f)	hard X-rays	(= highly penetrating)
(f')	des rayons X pénétrants	

Examples (81) to (85) illustrate cases where one word selects the appropriate sense of another (polysemous) word. Such selection is not possible in all cases; a verb or adjective may apply to more than one sense of a polysemous word. Thus in (86) 'cancel' and 'faulty' are compatible with either sense of 'check', and 'wear out' and 'new' are compatible with either sense of 'coach'.

(86) (a) Cancel the check.
(a') Contremander la vérification.
(a'') Annuler le chèque.

(b) a faulty check
(b') un chèque incorrect
(b'') une vérification imparfaite

(c) The coach was worn out.
(c') L'entraîneur était épuisé.
(c'') La diligence était délabrée.

(d) a new coach
(d') un nouvel entraîneur
(d'') une diligence neuve

No amount of semantic subclassification will guarantee the selection of the proper word or word sense in all cases. The use of semantic features for verifying selectional restrictions does not, in itself, remove all the problems due to multiple word senses; it does, however, become more effective as the subject matter is narrowed down. Thus only a few of the many senses of 'hard' in (85) are likely to occur in a given sublanguage.

There are some instances where semantic features can be used to select the appropriate word sense of the object of a preposition:

(87) (a) during the mounting [ACTION]
(a') pendant l'assemblage

(b) beneath the mounting [PHYSICAL-OBJECT]
(b') sous l'ensemble

For texts where there is potential ambiguity between the action of mounting things (machinery, etc.) and the device which serves as the support, 'during' could be marked to accept noun objects with features like [ACTION], while 'beneath' would accept those with the feature [PHYSICAL-OBJECT].

In spite of examples like (87), the practicality of making full use of selectional restrictions on prepositions in the same manner as for verbs and adjectives is questionable. The problem is that most prepositions have many different senses and each sense might require different selectional restrictions. Consider the various senses of 'on' in (88).

(88) (a) the book on the shelf
(a') le livre sur le rayon

(b) the book on mathematics
(b') le livre de mathématiques

(c) the book on sale
(c') le livre en solde

(d) the duty on alcoholic beverages
(d') les droits sur les boissons alcooliques

(e) payment on delivery
(e') paiement à la livraison

(f) on penalty of death
(f') sous peine de mort

(g) on the wing
(g') sur l'aile
(g'') au vol
(g''') à la volée

(h) on the run
(h') en fuite

(i) He is on his feet.
(i') Il se tient debout.

(j) He is on his own.
(j') Il est à son compte.

(k) He is on his best behavior.
(k') Il se conduit le mieux qu'il peut.

(l) He is on a trip.
(l') Il est en voyage.
(l'') Il est drogué.

(m) He is on drugs.
(m') Il prend des médicaments.

(n) She lived on vegetables.
(n') Elle vivait de légumes.

(o) She served on the jury.
(o') Elle faisait partie du jury.

(p) She sat on his left.
(p') Elle était assise à sa gauche.

(q) She saw it on television.
(q') Elle l'a vu à la télévision.

(r) She talked on the phone.
(r') Elle a parlé au téléphone.

(s) She said it on leaving.
(s') Elle l'a dit en partant.

(t) She left on Monday.
(t') Elle est partie lundi.

(u) We got on the subject of politics.
(u') Nous en sommes venus à parler de politique.

(v) We can leave on a moment's notice.
(v') Nous pourrions partir à l'instant.

(w) On seeing the police, he left.
(w') Lorsqu'il vit la police, il partit.

(x) On further reflection, he decided to stay.
(x') Après y avoir réfléchi, il décida de rester.

(y) They were on time.
(y') Ils étaient à l'heure.

(z) They were on call.
(z') Ils étaient en service commandé.

(A) The car runs on propane.
(A') La voiture fonctionne au propane.

(B) The teachers are on strike.
(B') Les enseignants sont en grève.

(C) The joke is on him.
(C') C'est le dindon de la farce.

(D) The building is on fire.
(D') La maison est en feu.

The problem of multiple senses is further compounded by the occurrence of prepositions in close construction with many verbs, leading to ambiguities like 'He decided on Sunday' and 'He insisted on the train'.

There are many ambiguities involving prepositional attachment. One type occurs with strings of the form **N1 P N2**, as in 'John saw the man in the park with the telescope'; P N2 might be a complement of N1 or it might be a sentence adverbial. Another type occurs with strings of the form **P N1 N2**. In this case, it is necessary to decide whether the object of P is N1 alone or **N1 N2**:

(89) (a) In winter additives prevent freezing of external lines.
(a') En hiver, des additifs préviennent le gel des canalisations extérieures.

(b) In winter conditions prevent freezing of external lines.
(b') Par temps froid, prévenir le gel des canalisations.

Ambiguity could have been avoided in (89) by using commas, but they are often omitted in texts employing telegraphic style (e.g., in maintenance manuals). Most readers would take 'winter' as object of 'in' in (89-a) and 'additives' as subject of 'prevent', and they would take 'winter conditions' as object of 'in' in (89-b) with 'prevent' introducing an imperative sentence. But how is the parser to arrive at these conclusions? What train of inferences would be required to establish the inconsistency of the imperative interpretation of 'prevent freezing of external lines' in (89-a) and an initial sentence adverbial 'In winter additives'?

Purely syntactic analysis of the problem of prepositional attachment has just about been pushed to the limit; further progress most likely depends on semantic analysis. An approach based on the use of semantic features to establish selectional restrictions between prepositions and their "arguments" faces many unknowns. At present there is no use of selectional features with prepositions comparable to that with verbs and adjectives. It is not clear whether such a strategy is feasible for some sublanguages or whether a deeper form of semantic analysis is required. Also, the cost of implementing such a scheme in terms of dictionary construction and updating must be taken into account as well as the effect on parsing time.

RAISING FEATURES FROM MODIFIERS

If a noun phrase has the form **N1 P N2**, where **P N2** is a complement of **N1**, then the features of **N1** (the head of the noun phrase) normally determine whether the noun phrase is an acceptable argument of a verb or adjective. For example, in (90) the head noun 'wine' could be assigned the feature [LIQUID] and 'drink' could be marked to accept a noun with that feature as direct object - or a noun phrase having a head noun with that feature. This is normal practice. But certain classes of nouns have a special property that interferes with this straightforward application of selectional restrictions. The classes are listed in (91).

(90) John drank the wine from France

(91)	(a)	**GENERAL PARTITIVES:**	piece, part, bit, layer
	(b)	**CONTAINERS:**	can, bottle, tank, glass
	(c)	**ZONES:**	surface, end, top, midsection
	(d)	**MEASURE UNITS:**	pound, liter, centimeter, quart

If **N1** is one of these nouns and **N1** of **N2** [18] is a noun phrase with **N1** as its head, then **N2** may assume the role of head in determining the semantic subclass of the whole noun phrase; i.e., it may be necessary to use the features of **N2** (in the complement) rather than those of **N1** (the head) when verifying selectional restrictions between the noun phrase and a verb or adjective.

Thus in 'John drank the glass of wine' it is 'wine' not 'glass' that satisfies the selectional restriction on the second argument of 'drink'. And you may find 'Pour a can of oil', but not *'Pour a can': the verb 'pour' accepts 'a can of oil' as argument on the basis of 'oil' in the complement, not on the basis of the head 'can'. Of course, number agreement still depends on the head noun: 'Two cans of oil are on the shelf.' Examples involving zones and measure units are given in (92).

(92) (a) **Wipe the surface of the plate.** [ZONE]
*** Wipe the surface of the water.**

(b) **Lubricate with a pint of oil.** [MEASURE-UNIT]
*** Lubricate with a pint of paint.**

To account for this phenomenon the parser can "raise" the features from the noun in the complement to the node dominating the entire noun phrase so that a verb or adjective can easily use those features to accept or reject the noun phrase as a possible argument.

In some cases a noun modifier is equivalent to the prepositional phrase complement (e.g., plate surface = surface of plate). Here, too, it may be necessary to raise the features from the modifier since it, rather than the head noun, determines whether the noun phrase is a possible argument of a verb or adjective in the sentence (assuming the head noun is one of the types listed in (91)). Thus in 'oxygen supply' the parser must know that a gas is involved whereas 'clothing supply' involves solids (or physical objects). The modifiers, not the head nouns, furnish this information.

The strategy of raising features from the complement or modifying noun, as discussed above, works quite well in many cases, but there are exceptions:

(93) (a) **Open a can of oil.** *** Open the oil.**
(b) **Stack the oil cans.** *** Stack the oil.**

Raising the feature of 'oil' in (93) (say [LIQUID]) would give the wrong result. (93-b) can be handled by the rule that if the head noun N2 in a noun phrase N1 N2 bears the feature [CONTAINER] then features are not raised from N1, but the problem remains in (93-a). Further research is needed to determine exactly when the modifier plays the dominant role in verifying selectional restrictions involving noun phrases of the type N1 of N2 or N1 N2.

Another case where the semantic features of the modifier play a leading role is that of nouns modified by adjectives bearing the feature [DEFECT]. In the sentence (94)

(94) (a) **Replace all defective components before installation in the aircraft.**
(a') **Remplacer toutes les pièces défectueuses avant l'installation dans l'avion.**

the verb 'replace' should be interpreted as 'substitute (new components)', not as 'put back in place (defective components)'. In French the former sense of 'replace' is translated by 'remplacer', the latter by 'replacer'. The feature [DEFECT] on the adjective 'defective' becomes a feature of the noun phrase which is the direct object of 'replace', and this can be used to signal the correct translation of the verb.

If an adjectival modifier is derived from a verb which bears the inherent feature [DEFECT], this feature can be retained on the derived adjective which is then treated as any other DEFECT adjective. Examples of such derived adjectives are: broken, damaged, contaminated, malfunctioning, cavitating, deteriorating. Furthermore, if an adverb with the feature [DEFECT] modifies an adjective (or a participle used as an adjective), the feature can be passed along from adverb to adjective (or participle) to the node dominating the whole noun phrase. The adjective (or participle) by itself may not indicate any defect: dangerously high, improperly adjusted, inadequately prepared, wildly fluctuating, poorly fitting, etc.

These examples in which semantic features from a modifier take precedence over those of the head noun in a noun phrase show that the application of selectional restrictions in parsing real texts is more complicated than some theoretical accounts might lead one to believe.

NOUN-NOUN COMPOUNDING

Complex nominals consisting of sequences of nouns constitute one of the most difficult problems in parsing. Such sequences are common in technical writing and many are quite long. In order to translate them the parser must be able to bracket them correctly. But the number of possible bracketings increases rapidly as the number of words increases: a three-word string can be bracketed in two ways, a four-word string can be bracketed in five ways and a seven-word string can be bracketed in 132 ways! If the correct bracketing cannot be determined, either the parser runs a considerable risk of misinterpreting the string (with consequent mistranslation) or it produces as many outputs as there are possible bracketings (an unacceptable result). The situation is far worse when several of these noun strings occur in the same sentence, which happens frequently.

In addition to bracketing noun sequences correctly the parser must also provide information about the syntactic-semantic relations between the resulting constituents so that transfer can build up the correct target language equivalents, insert the correct prepositions where needed, etc. Researchers at the University of Montreal (TAUM), after a lengthy empirical study of these relations, devised a scheme for assigning complementation to nouns in such a way that the parser might use the relations between nouns to obtain the correct bracketing and assign a semantic interpretation (in terms of those relations). This would entail much more complicated noun entries in the analysis dictionary than is customary; for example, an entry would specify all the predictable semantic relations that could hold between the given noun and others in a noun-noun compound. Since a noun may enter into many different relations with other nouns, the cost of dictionary building and updating could be increased considerably - especially considering the fact that nouns form the largest class of words in the dictionary.

The network of relations between nouns in a noun sequence is complicated by the fact that a given noun may enter into different relations with various others in the same context, as in (95) and (96).

(95) (a) Check for **wing damage**. (damage is done to the wing)
(a') Vérifier **les dommages à l'aile**.

(b) Check for **particle damage**. (damage is caused by particles)
(b') Vérifier s'il n'y a pas de **dommages causés par des particules**.

(96) (a) Drain **fuel tank**. (tank contains fuel)
(a') Vidanger **le réservoir de carburant**.

(b) Drain **wing tank**. (tank is located in wing)
(b') Vidanger **le réservoir de l'aile**.

Also, a given noun may enter into different relations with the same noun in different contexts, as in (97).

(97)	(a)	end fitting	(= fitting which is at the end)
	(a')	raccord de bout	
	(b)	fitting end	(= end of fitting)
	(b')	bout du raccord	

('fitting' in this example denotes a physical object: a part used to join or adapt other parts.)

Polysemy adds to the complexity of the network of relations, since each sense of a noun determines its own set of relations with other nouns (or noun senses).

Leaving aside the question of polysemy, there is the further problem of establishing semantic subclasses of nouns (= semantic features) on which to base the semantic relations. If the fact that a noun N can bear a relation R to other nouns is to be of any use in parsing, we must be able to say with some precision what those "other" nouns are; i.e., we must be able to specify the domain and range of each relation.

The problem of specifying the relevant subclasses for stating syntactic-semantic relations between nouns is similar in certain respects to the problem of specifying the subclasses needed for stating selectional restrictions for verbs and adjectives. Just as a verb "selects" a certain type of noun as its subject or object, so a noun "selects" a certain type of noun to which it bears a particular relation. In either case the relevant subclasses of nouns can be specified by assigning features to each noun entry in the analysis dictionary.

Given these two bases for subcategorizing the class of nouns, an interesting question arises: will the same subclasses (set of features) used for stating selectional restrictions between verbs or adjectives and nouns also suffice for stating noun-noun relations? In the case of nominalizations we might expect an affirmative answer; for example:

(98)	(a)	bicycle repair	repair the bicycle
	(a')	réparation de bicyclette	réparer la bicyclette
	(b)	machine translation	the machine translates
	(b')	traduction mécanique	la machine traduit

(c)	oil leakage	oil leaks
(c')	fuite d'huile	l'huile fuit
(d)	rust removal	remove the rust
(d')	enlèvement de la rouille	enlever la rouille
(e)	business manager	manage the business
(e')	directeur commercial	diriger l'entreprise
(f)	delivery man	the man delivers
(f')	livreur	l'homme fait la livraison

Now consider the noun 'operation' as it occurs in 'pump operation', 'engine operation', 'automobile operation' and 'high-speed drill operation'. Whenever the preceding noun N could be taken as object of the verb 'operate' then 'N operation' can be understood as 'operation of N' and is therefore related to 'X operates N'. In order to relate possible noun modifiers of 'operation' to possible objects of the verb 'operate' we can either refer back to the verb entry in the dictionary or we can put the relevant information into the noun entry in the form of noun complementation resembling verb complementation. There would seem to be greater economy in using the information already present in the verb entry, but both methods need to be evaluated. Note also that 'operation' can enter into different relations with other sets of modifying nouns: hospital operation, field operation, heart operation, permutation operation, group operation, police operation, etc.

Apart from nominalizations, there are many other types of nouns that participate in noun-noun relations: war story, pipe organ, trouser leg, lake water, grape wine, motor noise, voice quality, scout knife, north wind, television components, tennis ball, etc. It would be impossible to list all such combinations as idioms, hence information about predictable semantic relations involving many nouns would have to form an integral part of the dictionary entries for those nouns.

Finally, it would be necessary to work out the syntax of the semantic relations specified in the complementation of nouns: whether a noun N bears a relation R to another noun preceding or following N in a noun sequence, what restrictions there are on combinations of relations in a noun sequence, and so on. An example of the representation of the syntactic-semantic relations in a noun string, as proposed by researchers at the University of Montreal (Project TAUM) in the late 1970s, is given in (99).

(99)

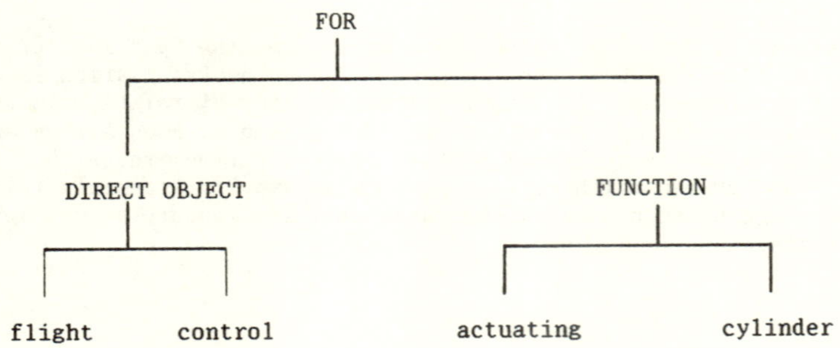

This interpretation, derived from properties of the nouns themselves, is read as follows: 'flight' is the direct object of 'control', the function of the 'cylinder' is to actuate something, the 'actuating cylinder' is for the 'flight control'.

Finin (1980) proposed a frame-based approach to the analysis of nominal compounds in his thesis "The Semantic Interpretation of Nominal Compounds". A concept is represented by a frame (the basic data type) which lists a number of roles such as A KIND OF (the frame's super-concepts), INSTANCE (sub-concepts), AGENT, INSTRUMENT, etc., each role having an internal structure as well. The frames are organized in an abstraction hierarchy, which is a directed graph with no cycles (not a rooted tree, since a frame can have more than one immediate ancestor). Finin's approach involves the mapping of words into concepts, bracketing strings of more than two nouns and interpreting the modification of one concept by another. Recently Finin (1986) has refined this approach, taking discourse context into account and treating some nominal compounds as referring expressions in that context ('a short-term naming device' p.163). He proposes (p.172) that

> "Candidate interpretations for a nominal compound with constituents denoting CONCEPT1 and CONCEPT2 can be found by considering all potential relationships between CONCEPT1 and its generalizations and specializations and CONCEPT2 and its generalizations and specializations."

Scores are to be assigned to candidate interpretations «by adding a characteristic scoring function for the value facet. Furthermore, we can adjust this function to give more or less weight to the "discourse-bases" interpretations». The use of such discourse constraints may be practicable for processing texts within a particular sublanguage.

Whether either of the above approaches to the parsing of nominal compounds is adequate for the purpose of machine translation is an open question. A noun can enter into an incredible number of relations with other nouns; determining the appropriate relations within a noun string and correctly bracketing the string remains a problem for further research. We can expect that any system which makes a serious attempt to translate texts with a high percentage of such nominal compounds will incorporate a very powerful semantic component.

COORDINATE CONJUNCTIONS

Coordinate conjunctions usually join constituents of the same grammatical category. However, it is well known that the "like-category" constraint on conjuncts is not sufficient to resolve the ambiguities associated with conjunctions (see, e.g., (57-c) (57-d) and (66) to (69) in section 3.3). Even with the choice of conjuncts limited to pairs having the same category, the number of potential candidates may still be very large. Ellipsis, which so often accompanies coordination, adds to the difficulty of determining what elements are conjoined.

Selectional restrictions can, in certain cases, help to eliminate some of the candidates for conjunction. If two noun phrases are conjoined, the semantic features of the conjuncts must satisfy the selectional restrictions of any verb or adjective that is presumed to take the resulting noun phrase as an argument. Likewise, if verbs, adjectives or adverbs are conjoined, their selectional restrictions must be satisfied by any phrase that is presumed to be an argument of the conjoined elements. Unfortunately, the semantic constraints that have been applied so far have not proved adequate to eliminate the conjunction problem. Nonetheless, the main hope for progress in this area lies in improved semantic analysis of the sentence. Coordinate conjunctions pervade most texts and the problem they present remains one of the most serious for automatic analysis.

PARENTHETICAL INSERTIONS

Comments enclosed in parentheses may be inserted almost anywhere in a sentence. It is often difficult to determine which constituent the parenthetical expression is "attached" to since there is no like-category constraint between the sentence constituent and the associated parenthetical expression. In fact, the parenthetical expression may not belong to any established category (i.e., any category recognized by the parser). As for the semantic link, this may range from synonymy to supplementary information or reference to other parts of the text where further information can be obtained. Consider the following examples (100) to (107) taken from aircraft maintenance manuals.

(100)(a) Reservoir No. 1 has a full (total) capacity of 5.6 U.S. (4.56 IMP.) gallons of fluid.

(a') Le réservoir no. 1 a une pleine capacité (totale) de 5,6 gallons E.-U. (4,56 imp.) de liquide.

(101)(a) Install and torque (refer to Part 1) the 12 retaining bolts.

(a') Poser et serrer les 12 boulons de retenue (voir Partie I).

(102)(a) Disconnect plug connector (15, Figure 2-2-1) from ac hydraulic pump motor.

(a') Débrancher le raccord de fiche (15, Figure 2-2-1) du moteur de la pompe hydraulique ca.

(103)(a) Fluid flows through the check valves (provided to prevent reverse flow in the event of single ac hydraulic pump operation) by the system relief valves and to the filters.

(a') Le liquide circule à travers les clapets de retenue (destinés à prévenir l'inversion du débit advenant le fonctionnement d'une seule pompe hydraulique ca), puis par les soupapes de sûreté jusqu'aux filtres.

(104)(a) A visual indicator actuates (extends) when fluid flow is restricted.

(a') Un indicateur visuel s'actionne (apparaît) lorsque le débit du liquide est entravé.

(105)(a) The ac hydraulic pump weighs 31.25 pounds (dry).

(a') La pompe hydraulique ca pèse 31,25 livres (à sec).

(106)(a) Fluid is drawn into the pump through a suction (or inlet) port.

(a') Le liquide est aspiré dans la pompe au moyen d'un orifice de suction (ou d'entrée).

(107)(a) Two hydraulic system service center packages (No. 1 and No. 2) (service center assembly), commonly referred to as manifolds, are located on either side of the hydraulic service center access door.

(a') Deux ensembles bloc collecteur (no. 1 et no. 2) du circuit hydraulique (bloc collecteur), communément appelés collecteurs, sont situés de chaque côté de la porte d'accès du compartiment hydraulique.

Since the order of constituents may differ in a source language sentence and its target language equivalent, it is necessary to discover, during analysis, which constituent a parenthetical expression is associated with; otherwise, even if the expression is translated correctly, it may not be properly placed in the target language sentence.

Parenthetical expressions are not usually integrated into the sentence structure in the same way as normal sentence constituents. The syntactic links may be weak or non-existent. In order to establish the relation between a parenthetic expression and other parts of the sentence it is necessary to understand the semantic role of that expression in the sentence. This entails more than the use of semantic features to establish selectional restrictions since it is often the case that no selectional restrictions are applicable between the words inside and outside the parentheses (see, e.g., (101), (102) and (107)).

* * * * * * * * *

There are many constructions in complex sentences that demonstrate further the need for semantic analysis. We will mention three of them briefly:

(108) **NOUN + V-ing CLAUSE**

(a) Determine silting index of samples using appropriate equipment.

(a') Déterminer l'indice d'ensablement des échantillons à l'aide de l'équipement approprié.

(b) Install rotor with part number facing aft.

(b') Poser le rotor de manière que le numéro de la pièce soit face à l'arrière.

(109) **NOUN + V-ed CLAUSE**

(a) We saw the celebrity seated at the table.
(a') Nous avons vu la personnalité assise à la table.

(b) They read many recent works influenced by the new movement.
(b') Ils ont lu plusieurs ouvrages récents inspirés par le nouveau mouvement.

(110) **NOUN + INFINITIVE CLAUSE**

(a) He designed the first plane to break the sound barrier.
(a') Il a conçu le premier avion à franchir le mur du son.

(b) Place container under fittings to catch fluid from disconnected hoses.
(b') Disposer le contenant sous les raccords pour recevoir le liquide provenant des conduits déconnectés.

There is a potential ambiguity between the use of these clauses as post modifiers of the noun and as sentence adverbials. The intended use is normally obvious to the reader, but not to the parser. One may adopt ad hoc strategies such as not accepting these clauses as sentence adverbials unless they are sentence initial (assuming that in most texts sentence adverbials occur more frequently in that position), but this will obviously cause many incorrect translations. Selectional restrictions will disambiguate only a very small percentage of these cases. A general solution will require a more subtle semantic analysis of the sentence (or text).

4. BUILDING A SYSTEM

Machine translation systems incorporate grammars, in one form or another, of the source and target languages. These grammars may be designed to fit a particular type of text or they may be designed on the basis of some model of the standard language, independent of any particular texts. In the former case the builders of the system are likely to adopt a corpus-based approach, while in the latter they are likely to be guided more by a standard grammar than by a collection of sentences from outside sources (i.e., outside the grammar books and outside their own minds). A system built by the standard grammar approach aims for generality, but that does not mean that a system which is tailored to particular texts is simply a mini-version of the other (more general) system. In fact, given the present state of the art, a system that is not limited in its coverage may, of necessity, be highly interactive, while one which does limit its coverage sufficiently may be fully automatic. Also, one tends to think of a corpus-based approach as leading to a lot of ad hoc rules that are not firmly anchored in any general theory; this is certainly possible, but it is quite possible, too, that the rules may be principled and the whole system theoretically tight.

4.1 CORPUS-BASED APPROACH

Following this approach, the linguists collect representative texts to form a corpus, they read the texts and note any grammatical peculiarities, and they study the terminology to discover any special word usage in the given domain. An essential tool in building the dictionaries is a KWIC (Key Word In Context) based on the corpus. As work on the dictionaries and grammars proceeds there is constant testing of components and finally of the entire translation chain. Test sentences should be taken not only from the corpus, but from other texts in the same field (at least in the later stages of testing).

A corpus-based approach does not imply that only information found in the corpus should be used in the dictionaries and grammars of the system. As linguists and terminologists become better acquainted with the texts, it usually becomes apparent that certain words and syntactic structures not found in the corpus could very well occur in texts from the same field. Such information would normally be incorporated in the system. In other words, the corpus is a guide, not a strait-jacket.

This is, of course, an oversimplified account of the activity of building the linguistic components of a system, but it gives a rough idea of what is meant by a corpus-based approach. Clearly, this path is more likely to be followed when the system is to be used for translation in limited domains. The effects of domain restriction have been discussed in detail in section 2.5 ("Domain Dependency"); what needs to be emphasized here is that a system built by the standard grammar approach, aiming for generality, cannot be applied successfully to all types of texts. The problem is that sublanguage grammars are not simply subgrammars of the standard grammar. That is, the structures found in certain texts are not just a subset of the structures described in a standard grammar. Particular sublanguages employ radically different structures. The example of METEO has already been given: a standard grammar would simply reject many of the "sentences" in a weather report.

Generally speaking, the more restricted the domain, the simpler will be the task of stating selectional restrictions. Using a corpus as a guide, the relevant semantic subclasses are more readily identified.

A corpus-based approach may result in some radical departures from standard practice, even on the level of major components. For example, we would normally consider a morphological component to be an essential part of any parser of English; however, in the case of METEO this component was eliminated since the small vocabulary and absence of certain inflectional forms suggested that it would be more economical to simply list all morphological variants as separate entries in the dictionary. Furthermore, it was found that because of the similarities between English and French weather reports using telegraphic style in this highly restricted domain, it was usually sufficient to look at the immediate environment of the English word to determine its French equivalent. Consequently, a separate transfer phase was not considered necessary.

We have seen that a corpus-based approach offers a number of advantages in building a system for use in a restricted domain. The disadvantage is that the resulting system may not be generalizable: if the user decides to translate texts from another domain, he may find that much more is needed than an increase in the size of the dictionary.

4.2 STANDARD GRAMMAR APPROACH

A system built by using a standard grammar as a guide should, ideally, be able to handle all the major syntactic structures of the source language. If this can be accomplished the system will have the advantage of very wide applicability. The parsing of texts with deviant (i.e., non-standard) structures would present a serious problem, but the parsing of those domain restricted texts in which there is simply an absence of certain standard structures should not pose any problem. A "general" grammar would handle the special cases.

Most of us have been exposed to a standard grammar of some sort in school and we would certainly be surprised if a school grammar did not cover the major syntactic structures of the language. However, as we saw in the sections on complex constituents (3.3.3) and semantics at the syntagmatic level (3.4.2), this is a herculean task for a grammar in the form of an automatic parser. There are still a number of formidable barriers to the parsing of complex sentences. Gradual improvements will undoubtedly be made, but in the near future we can expect continued heavy reliance on post-editing and interactive processing (HAMT).

One of the advantages claimed for the corpus-based approach was that it enabled the designer to produce a system that could deal successfully with highly deviant texts. But a system depending on a standard grammar can also be designed to cope with grammatical deviation. One method for accepting deviant combinations is to relax selectional restrictions when parsing fails. For example, a verb or adjective might be permitted to accept a certain noun as an argument even though the noun was at first rejected as a result of not having the required features. Other constraints imposed by the standard grammar can be relaxed in order to accept "ungrammatical" constructions involving the deletion of articles or prepositions (as occurs in texts using telegraphic style). The whole question of relaxing grammatical constraints in parsing is under active investigation and has already been shown to be of practical value. Some of the motivation for this work has come from the desire to accept sentences which contain actual errors; on the other hand, the deviations we have been discussing are not the result of mistakes, but constitute normal usage in some fields. In texts where departures from the standard language are the norm it is questionable whether the relaxation of grammatical constraints is an effective way to deal with non-standard usage, or even whether it is feasible.

On the lexical level a general purpose system can be adapted to texts from various fields by having separate dictionaries for those fields or in some way marking dictionary entries according to the fields for which they are relevant. We would also expect a common core of frequently used words with wide distribution, especially the so-called grammatical words such as articles, conjunctions and prepositions. If a dictionary is "compartmentalized" for use in various fields it is necessary to take into account the fact that selectional restrictions may not be the same for a word in two different domains and the inherent semantic features assigned to a word in one domain may be inappropriate in another. This affects both analysis and transfer dictionaries. Consequently, it should not be assumed that the only dictionary change needed to translate texts from a new domain is the addition of new terms from that domain.

* * * * * * * * *

The standard grammar approach does not try to discover the grammar of the texts it will translate; rather it assumes a grammar and tries to formalize it in the computer. Given the complexity of a natural language, the task is extremely difficult; in the long run the reward is great, if the job can be done. The corpus-based approach, with its more modest goal, is more likely to yield practical results in the short run - for limited domains. The grammar it "discovers" describes only a sublanguage, not the whole language[19]. Each approach has its advantages and disadvantages, and these must be considered in the light of the user's needs.

5. LINGUISTIC EVALUATION BY THE USER

Given the principal technical characteristics of a system (see **Chapter 2**), it is possible for a specialist to predict the performance of the linguistic components of the system. In **CHAPTER 3** we attempted, using various linguistic phenomena, to explain the content and role of each of the linguistic components of a translation system. If the anticipated performance is positive, we then go on to make a more detailed evaluation.

Before proceeding with the more detailed evaluation, it is most important to look specifically at the following elements:

(1) the type of texts to be translated,
(2) the linguistic processing model,
(3) the planned level of automation,
(4) constraints on the quality of translation of the raw output,
(5) constraints on the quality of translation of the final version,
(6) mechanisms for dealing with errors,
(7) word processing system used.

In each case, the objectives must be described exhaustively in order to determine in advance what one wishes to measure. This work must therefore be carried out before starting the evaluation. In this chapter, we will deal briefly with each of these elements.

Once the user's requirements and expectations have been clearly identified, we may proceed with the detailed evaluation. There are three approaches to this evaluation: an evaluation by the system designer, a cost/benefit evaluation and a linguistic evaluation by the user. **Table 2** gives a general outline of a translation system evaluation that illustrates these three approaches. Before explaining the details, however, we would advise the reader to refer to the **Appendix A**, where a synthesis of evaluations of various machine translation systems is given.

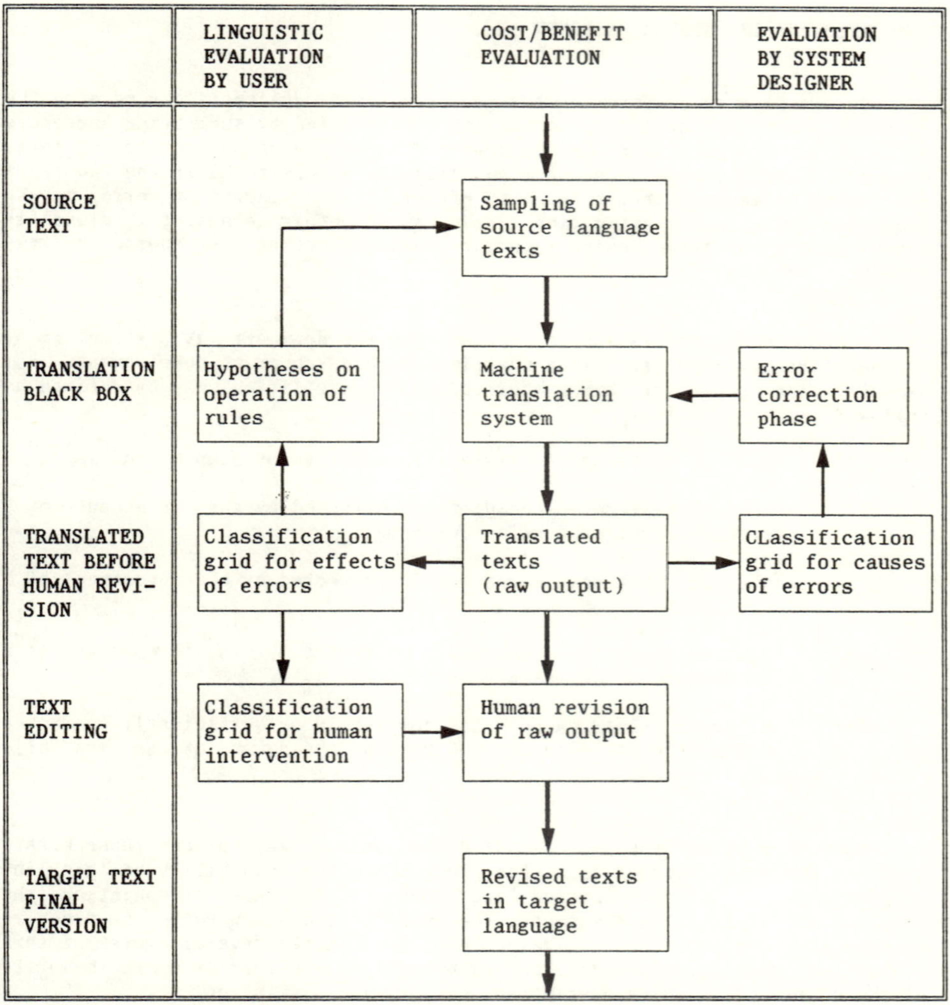

GENERAL OUTLINE OF TRANSLATION SYSTEM EVALUATION

TABLE 2

EVALUATION BY THE SYSTEM DESIGNER

Before placing a system on the market a system designer may measure the operating capacity of its grammars and dictionaries by submitting sentences or texts to the system. Since the designer knows the actual nature and power of his linguistic model, he may thus classify errors found in the raw translation as to cause rather than as to effect. These causes of error may be tabulated using a classification grid. Among other things, this classification grid enables the designer to more easily pinpoint the source and frequency of errors.

Based on a tabulation of this type the designer may next determine whether correcting an error is a question of research or of development. For example, the scale of error correction possibilities may be defined as follows:

(1) an error that may be completely corrected by simple updating,

(2) an error that may be completely corrected by the investment of a certain amount of development time,

(3) an error that may be partially corrected by the investment of a certain amount of development time,

(4) an error that may be partially corrected by the investment of a certain amount of research time,

(5) an error that cannot be completely or sufficiently corrected because the solution is not within the power of the linguistic model chosen.

Once this first stage is completed the designer may correct those errors that are the most frequent and that are within the capability of his linguistic model. Having carried out this first cycle of operations the designer may resubmit to the system the same text or new texts in order to measure the consequences of the corrections. After several cycles of this evaluation process the designer should normally have corrected the majority of those errors for which development can provide a solution.

The TAUM Report (1980) and Lehrberger (1981-b) are examples of system designer evaluation.

COST/BENEFIT EVALUATION

Before investing in a machine translation system a potential customer should make a cost/benefit evaluation. This is done by submitting texts to the system and monitoring and measuring all production costs up to the final version of translated texts. Once all direct and indirect production costs have been identified and measured a comparison may be made between these costs and those for human translation of the same quality. To carry out this type of evaluation it is necessary to monitor a fairly large body of parameters if truly reliable results and figures are to be obtained.

Ideally, to make a comparative evaluation of the costs of human translation as compared to the costs of machine translation, the same texts should be translated using different methods. For example, the following methods may be compared:

(1) human translation and human revision,
(2) machine translation and human revision.

In addition, it is possible to add a number of variants to the above by using other instruments (e.g., typewriter, dictaphone, word processor). Since the same texts are translated using different methods or instruments, an objective comparison may be made between the results obtained.

The following reports are examples of cost/benefit evaluations: Pierce, Carroll et al. (1966), Van Slype (1978), Gervais (1980), Van Slype (1982), Secretary of State of Canada (1985).

LINGUISTIC EVALUATION BY THE USER

As opposed to the system designer, the users or potential purchasers of a commercial system do not have access to the grammars or programs of a system. The user does not have direct access to the linguistic model simulated by the grammar rules of a system but sees only the results. How then can the user, who has access only to the effects and not to the causes, evaluate a system in anything but a superficial way? How can he determine if a given linguistic phenomenon is within the capacity of a system if he can only analyze the effects?

Since a potential purchaser normally finds himself in a situation where he sees only part of a system, we have attempted to develop an evaluation methodology that would allow the future user to understand the nature of the problem and formulate his own evaluation instruments.

In this third approach, the only practical means of evaluating the grammars of a system consists in submitting to the system representative texts and making a detailed examination of the raw translation results. The next step is to classify the results obtained according to the linguistic phenomena they represent. Using a linguistic phenomena classification we may begin to formulate various hypotheses on the way rules function, and, on the basis of such hypotheses, we may construct other examples or counter-examples and submit these to the translation system. We can thus confirm or modify the hypotheses we have formulated on the nature and operation of the grammatical rules contained in the system programs. This will enable the user to set up a grid to classify the effects of errors.

Reconstituting rules by their effects is a rather laborious process, but it does enable the user to arrive at the following results:

(1) make an inventory of those linguistic phenomena that are satisfactorily processed as opposed to those that are not;

(2) determine precisely which phenomena are not processed at all;

(3) explain good translations as well as poor translations, and good grammatical analyses as well as poor ones;

(4) determine the nature and content of the linguistic components of the system;

(5) determine the processing model used, i.e. how the various components of the system are structured and organized in relation to one another;

(6) understand the underlying linguistic model of the system components.

When an evaluator is able to predict the results a system will give when confronted with a given linguistic phenomenon, he has a very good intuition of the system. Once all the linguistic characteristics of a system have been evaluated in this way, we can compare the linguistic model of this system to a reference model in order to determine its strong and weak points.

Once all these steps have been completed the user should be in a position to make an informed judgement of the true possibilities for improving a system. As a guide to evaluating the potential of a system, Section 5.3 gives various criteria which may be used in judging the limitations and improvability of a system. The report by Tellier and Bourbeau (1982) is an example of the kind of evaluation by the user suggested above.

It is interesting to note that there are also complementary applications of this strategy for the classification of the effects of errors (see Table 2). For example, Loffler-Laurian (1983) proposed a typology for machine translation errors in order to use this information as criteria for the selection of texts to be submitted to a machine translation system. These text selection criteria would allow the weaknesses or deficiencies of a given system to be circumvented, since texts would be chosen to fit the performance of a particular system. The text selection criteria described by Loffler-Laurian (1983) are applicable to the SYSTRAN system and indirectly reflect the state of linguistic rules in that system. This approach may be extended to other systems, but it should be noted that the selection criteria developed will in most cases be specific to each system.

Van Slype (1982) proposed a grid to classify the action that a human translator must take to correct the effects of errors in a machine translation system. This would enable us to qualify and quantify intervention by a human reviser on the raw output to obtain a final version that would satisfy pre-established translation quality standards. This approach may be extended to other systems, but it should be remembered that the classification grid for human intervention will reflect the linguistic performance of a given system and the translation quality criteria of a given organization.

In the following sections we will give a more detailed explanation of the principal steps of a linguistic evaluation made by the user.

5.1 IDENTIFICATION OF USER'S NEEDS AND CONSTRAINTS

The potential user of a computerized translation system has certain needs and must operate under certain constraints. The evaluation of a system by the user is made in the light of these needs and constraints, therefore it is important to identify them at the outset and to formulate them explicitly. Three factors that play a key role are

(i) the characteristics of the texts that are to be translated,
(ii) the desired level of automation of the translation process,
(iii) the quality of translation acceptable to the user.

5.1.1 CHARACTERISTICS OF TEXTS TO BE TRANSLATED

It is customary for readers to characterize a text impressionistically as consisting of technical jargon, as containing an extensive or a restricted vocabulary, as using formal or informal style, as smooth and flowing, marked by awkward or convoluted syntax, concise, rambling, etc. For the purpose of objective linguistic evaluation it is necessary to establish a framework for characterizing texts in terms of specific structures, transformations, linking devices (for textual cohesion) and semantic range. The form that the description takes will, of course, depend on the theoretical leaning of the analyst, but this should not obscure the facts.

In addition to determining the linguistic characteristics of the texts to be translated, there are questions about the domain and volume of texts that should be answered during the preparatory phase of an evaluation.

A) DOMAIN OF TEXTS TO BE TRANSLATED

- What fields are the texts to be taken from?
- What subject matter is covered?
- Are the texts intended for specialists in these subjects or for a more general audience? (This is important in determining the acceptable quality of translation.)
- Are there terminological dictionaries for these fields?
- How much terminological research is likely to be needed in each domain?

B) VOLUME OF TEXTS TO BE TRANSLATED

How many words per year are expected

- in each domain?

- for the first year and for the following years?

Estimating the size of vocabulary in a domain requires a very careful choice of representative texts. Furthermore, estimates of vocabulary size should specify what constitutes a vocabulary item - what inflectional forms are subsumed in a vocabulary item (see section 3.1 and section 3.2 for a discussion of morphological variants and dictionary entries).

C) LINGUISTIC CHARACTERISTICS OF TEXTS

- Vocabulary size in each domain

- Homography

  cross-categorial (involves more than one part of speech)
  inner-categorial (within the same part of speech)

- Structures and Processes

  declarative sentences
  interrogative sentences
  imperative sentences
  active voice
  passive voice
  subjunctive
  tense and aspect
  compound words (3-phase, pressure-regulating)
  multi-word verbs (turn on, apply for)
  nominalization (of verb, sentences, etc.)
  pro-forms (pronouns, pro-verbs, pro- (verb phrase), etc.)
  ellipsis
  extraposition
  embedding
  conjunction (coordinate, subordinate)
  modification (by adjectives, adverbs, nouns, prepositional phrases, present participle, past participle, etc.)
  stylistic inversion
  quotation
  parenthetical insertion (sentence "fragments" as well as constituents)
  lists and tables
  abbreviations
  symbols with multiple functions (. - : ' ,)
  special symbols (% < > α Ω Σ = +)

special uses of capitalization or boldface type

- Deviations from Standard Grammar

  These deviations do not include errors, but constructions reflecting normal usage in the given domain. Non-standard constructions frequently result from deletions where telegraphic style is used as in (1).

(1) (a) **Arrive Montreal Friday.**
(a') (= I will arrive in Montreal Friday.)

(b) **Add two teaspoons salt.**
(b') (= Add two teaspoons of salt.)

(c) **Check reservoir full.**
(c') (= Check the reservoir to be sure that it is full.)

The list of structures and processes given above is merely suggestive. Analysts involved in the preliminary survey of texts should make a detailed list appropriate for their own circumstances. They will want to pay particular attention to those constructions known to be troublesome for machine translation in the language of the texts; for example, the modification of nouns by nouns will be of special interest in English texts, but not in French. Finally, it should be kept in mind that such a list is for the purpose of a preliminary survey of texts to be translated, not for evaluation of the grammaticality of the translated texts (see section 5.2.3).

5.1.2 PROJECTED LEVEL OF AUTOMATION

Computerized translation systems were classified according to their degree of automation in section 2.1. That classification serves as a broad frame of reference for the projected level of automation of the translation operation.

FAMT: Fully automatic in the sense that there is no human intervention between the input of the original text and the raw machine output of the translated text.

HAMT: Human translator supplies limited information during translation by the machine, but the machine has control.

MAHT: Basically human translation with limited assistance from the machine; the human translator has control.

As pointed out in section 2.1.3, FAMT does not entail the complete elimination of any human component, but limits it to post-editing and revision of the raw machine output.

There are a number of factors that the user must take into account in determining the projected level of automation. These include:

- acceptable cost of revising raw output;
- acceptable cost of personnel employed in interactive mode;
- acceptable time for producing final text ready for use;
- acceptable cost of dictionary maintenance;
- expected increase in productivity;
- expected decrease in costs;
- acceptable reliance on system's designers after acquisition of system;
- expected improvements in the system;
- acceptable period of amortization;
- acceptable quality of raw output:
    - percentage of sentences needing no revision;
    - percentage of sentences needing revision
        - major errors
        - minor errors;
- percentage of sentences that must be retranslated (not revisable);
- percentage of sentences not translated at all;
- minimum level of quality of raw output considered tolerable for a human reviser.

5.1.3 CONSTRAINTS ON QUALITY OF TRANSLATION

The user of a computerized translation system will demand a certain minimum level of quality in the translated text after human revision. It cannot be assumed that the same quality will result from revised machine translation as from revised human translation; the reviser may not be able to bring all translations, however garbled, to the same level of quality, given the time constraints on revision. Likewise, the quality of the raw output from different machine translation systems may have different effects on the quality of the final revised translations.

Constraints on the quality of the final product depend very much on the intended readers and the type of use:

- General distribution to a wide audience;
- Limited distribution to specialists in the subject matter of the texts;
- Reading for full information content;
- Scanning for particular information;
- Instructions for carrying out specific tasks (e.g., maintenance manuals).

Stylistic constraints include:

- Acceptable types of deletions (definite article, copula, use of sentence fragments):
  - in headings;
  - in the body of the text;
- Use of subjunctive (only a remnant in English; more important in French or Spanish);
- Use of punctuation (freedom in use of commas, etc.);
- Forms used for commands or negation, as in (2):

(2) (a) **Open control valve and purge for at least 5 seconds.**
(a') **Ouvrir le régulateur et purger pendant au moins 5 secondes.**

(b) No smoking.
(b') Défense de fumer.

We have been discussing constraints on quality; as for the actual evaluation of the quality of translation, that may be divided into three sub-tasks:

- fidelity (extent to which translated text contains same information as original);
- intelligibility;
- style.

The methods for evaluating these sub-tasks are discussed in APPENDIX A, and in Van Slype (1982).

5.2 EVALUATION OF PERFORMANCE OF LINGUISTIC COMPONENTS

Once all translation needs and constraints have been explicitly identified the potential user must determine whether a given system is capable of satisfying his requirements. In making this linguistic evaluation the user may proceed as follows:

1° Construct test sentences and have the system translate them;

2° Select sample texts and have the system translate them;

3° Classify and interpret the results of the translations thus obtained;

4° Formulate hypotheses on the operation of rules in order to be able to explain unsatisfactory translations produced by the system;

5° Confirm these hypotheses by having the system translate appropriate sentences.

Support for this approach may be found in Billmeier (1982), which shows the importance of examining the structure of information representation in order to discover the precise underlying linguistic principles of a system. He quotes a number of publications dealing with the SYSTRAN machine translation system: Toma (1977), Van Slype (1979), Arthern (1980), Haller (1980), Rolling (1980), Bruderer (1978) and Freigang (1979). We might also add the study by Lawson (1982) to this list. Bruderer (1978) and Freigang (1979) do not deal exclusively with the SYSTRAN system, but also with several other machine translation systems. Billmeier notes that these various studies look almost exclusively at the quality of machine translation. Translation is considered as a black box, and the focus is rather on the relation that exists between input (i.e. the source text) and output (i.e. the target text). Such descriptions of machine translation are important and necessary, but they do not go far enough. Billmeier points out the marked paucity of studies that explain or evaluate the internal structure of the black box, although he does note that the articles by Van Slype (1978), Arthern (1980) and Rolling (1980) refer to the internal structure of the SYSTRAN system.

When a study does deal with the internal structure of SYSTRAN, for example Haller (1980), Billmeier observes that great emphasis is placed on computer technique when such matters as programming problems, design and the nature of the various system components are examined. It is, of course, important to evaluate the computer characteristics (hardware and software) of a machine translation system, but it is also important to emphasize the technical limitation of a system; for example:

(1) the maximum number of entries in the dictionary,

(2) the maximum size of a dictionary entry,

(3) the set of characters or the alphabet available to transcribe the words in the dictionary,

(4) the maximum length of a word in the dictionary,

(5) the maximum length of sentences that can be processed,

(6) the maximum length of texts that can be processed at a time,

(7) the parsing strategy used and the resulting processing time,

(8) the minimum memory space required for all the programs of the system,

(9) the number of disk accesses necessary to consult the dictionary,

(10) the programming language(s) used.

These types of computer limitations are much more tangible than the linguistic limitations of a system. We reiterate, with Billmeier, that "any realistic evaluation of the capacity of a machine translation system should include an understanding of its linguistic principles and its capability to adequately process the various linguistic phenomena".

5.2.1. BUILDING TEST SENTENCES

After studying the linguistic characteristics of the texts to be translated (see Section 5.1.1.), the user should choose and extract from these texts sentences representative of the various linguistic phenomena they contain. These test sentences should constitute a representative set of sentences from a given domain which is itself represented by the texts. We may successively identify four sets that would constitute the input of a machine translation system, each of which is a sub-set of the set which precedes it. In descending order, these sets are as follows:

1° the set of all source language texts,

2° the set of all texts in a given domain,

3° the set of sample texts in a given domain,

4° the set of test sentences in a given domain.

The test sentences should include enough examples so that all the linguistic phenomena in the texts in a given domain are represented.

Once the set of test sentences from a given domain has been prepared these must be submitted to a translation system. The point of this exercise is mainly to study how the system processes and represents the various linguistic phenomena. We must therefore have at our disposal the raw output and, occasionally, the "execution trace" of certain test sentences. An execution trace is a copy of the progress of a sentence through the various processing phases of the system. This might, for example, be limited to a print-out of the input and output of each of the phases as a test sentence is processed.

As an illustration of this idea of execution trace we have shown below a few examples of English sentences followed by a listing of the output of the English parsing phase of the TAUM-AVIATION MT system. These examples (3, 4,

5 and 6) are taken as is from Stanton (1981). The result of the parsing is a tree structure in the form of a bracketed expression.

(3) **The panel contains four pump control switches.**

ROOT (PH (GOV (GV (CV (V [MTERS, DSTAT] (**CONTAIN**))), OPS [APRS], GP [DC, DHENS, DOBT, DP, DSG] (GPREP (CP (P [XX] (BOF))), GN [DC, DHENS, DOBT, DP, DSG] (CN (N (**PANEL**)), DET (CART (ART [DDEF] (THE))))), GP [MTERS, DC, DHBUNIT, DP, DPL] (GPREP (CP (P [XX] (BOF))), GN [MTERS, DC, DHBUNIT, DP, DPL] (CN (N (**SWITCH**)), DET (GQ [ENUM, DPL] (CQ (Q [ENUM, XX, DSPELL] (4)))), GP [DAB, DMSS, DNOMF, DNP, APRENOM] (GPREP (CP (P (OF))), GN [DAB, DMSS, DNOMF, DNP] (CN (N (**CONTROL**)), GP [DC, DHEQUIP, DP, DSG, APRENOM] (GPREP (CP (P (OF))), GN [DC, DHEQUIP, DP, DSG] (CN (N (**PUMP**)))))))), GP), PONC [XX] (.))

(4) **The flaps are operated by a hydraulic motor.**

ROOT (PH [APASS] (GOV (GV (CV (V [MPAST, MPASTP, DERG, DPP, DPR] (**OPERATE**))), OPS [APRS]), GP [DC, DHEQUIP, DP, DSG] (GPREP (CP (P [XX] (BOF))), GN [DC, DHEQUIP, DP, DSG] (CN (N (**MOTOR**)), DET (CART (ART [DINDEF] (A))), PH [DATRIB, AADJ, APRENOM] (TRANSFERT (COPIETRAIT), GOV (GV (CADJ (ADJ [DATRIB] (**HYDRAULIC**))), OPS (COP [XX] (BOF))), GP [DCOMPART, DDEFECT, DFL, DP, DVAR, AADJ]))), GP [MTERS, DC, DHENS, DP, DPL] (GPREP (CP (P[XX] (BOF))), GN [MTERS, DC, DHENS, DP, DPL] (CN (N (**FLAP**)), DET (CART (ART [DDEF] (THE))))), GP), PONC[XX] (.))

(5) **A hydraulic motor operates the flaps.**

ROOT (PH (GOV (GV (CV (V [MTERS, DERG, DPP, DPR] (**OPERATE**))), OPS [APRS]), GP [DC, DHEQUIP, DP, DSG] (GPREP (CP (P[XX] (BOF))), GN [DC, DHEQUIP, DP, DSG] (CN (N (**MOTOR**)), DET (CART (ART [DINDEF] (A))), PH [DATRIB, AADJ, APRENOM] (TRANSFERT (COPIETRAIT), GOV (GV (CADJ (ADJ [DATRIB] (**HYDRAULIC**))), OPS (COP[XX] (BOF))), GP [DCOMPART, DDEFECT, DFL, DP, DVAR, AADJ]))), GP [MTERS, DC, DHENS, DP, DPL] (GPREP (CP (P[XX] (BOF))), GN [MTERS, DC, DHENS, DP, DPL] (CN (N (**FLAP**)), DET (CART (ART [DDEF] (THE))))), GP), PONC [XX] (.))

(6) **As pressure builds up or decreases, packing moves in its groove.**

ROOT (PH [AERG] (GOV (GV (CV (V [MTERS, DERG, DPR] (**MOVE**))), OPS [APRS]), GP, GP [DC, DHPART, DMSS, DP, DSG] (GPREP (CP (P[XX] (BOF))), GN [DC, DHPART, DMSS, DP, DSG] (CN (N (**PACKING**)))), GP, CIRC [AINIT] (GP (GPREP (CP (P (**AS**))), PH [AERG] (CC (**OR**), PH [AERG] (GOV (GV (CV (V

[MTERS, DERG, DPP] (BUILD)), GPREP (CP (P [DDEG, DLOC, DMVT] (UP)))), OPS [APRS]), GP, GP [DC, DFL, DMSS, DNP, DSG, DVAR] (GPREP (CP (P[XX] (BOF))), GN [DC, DFL, DMSS, DNP, DSG, DVAR] (CN (N (PRESSURE)))), GP), PH [AERG] (GOV (GV (CV (V [MTERS, DERG] (DECREASE))), OPS [APRS]), GP, GP [DAB, DC, DFL, DMSS, DNOMF, DNP, DSG, DVAR], GP)))), CIRC (GP [DC, DNP, DOUV, DSG, DZ] (GPREP (CP (P [DING, DLOC, DTM] (IN))), GN [DC, DNP, DOUV, DSG, DZ] (CN (N (GROOVE)), DET (CART (ART [DPOSS] (ITS))))))), PONC [XX] (.))

The list below gives the meaning of some of the labels used in the trees in (3) to (6).

ROOT	=	Starting point	MTERS	=	S ending
PH	=	Sentence	DSTAT	=	Stative verb
GOV	=	Governor	DSG	=	Singular
GV	=	Verb phrase	DPL	=	Plural
CV	=	Conjunction of V	DMSS	=	Mass
V	=	Verb	DAB	=	Abstract
OPS	=	Operator	DC	=	Concrete
MDL	=	Modal	DFL	=	Fluid
GP	=	Prepositional phrase	DHBUNIT	=	Basic unit
GPREP	=	Preposition group	DHENS	=	Set (French: <u>ens</u>emble)
CP	=	Conjunction of P	DHEQUIP	=	Equipment
P	=	Preposition	DHPART	=	Part
GN	=	Noun phrase	DNOMF	=	Function nominal
CN	=	Conjunction of N	DNP	=	Non-part
N	=	Noun	DOBT	=	Obturation
CADJ	=	Conjunction of ADJ	DOUV	=	Opening
ADJ	=	Adjective	DP	=	Part
DET	=	Determiner	DVAR	=	Variable
CART	=	Conjunction of ART	DZ	=	Zone
ART	=	Article	DERG	=	Ergative
GQ	=	Quantifier phrase	DATRIB	=	Attributive adjective
CQ	=	Conjunction of Q	DLOC	=	Locative
Q	=	Quantifier	DTM	=	Tense
GADV	=	Adverbial phrase	DDEF	=	Definite article
CADV	=	Conjunction of ADV	DPOSS	=	Possessive
ADV	=	Adverb	APASS	=	Passive voice
CIRC	=	Circumstantial	APRENOM	=	Prenominal adjective
PONC	=	Punctuation	APRS	=	Present tense

In the trees in (3, 4, 5, 6) the labels between square brackets are syntactico-semantic features associated with a node of the tree, while the other labels identify the nodes. For example, V [MTERS, DSTAT] identifies the node V, signifying Verb, with which are associated the features MTERS and

DSTAT. Parentheses indicate the various levels of nodes in the tree. For the purposes of this study it is not really necessary to know the definition of these labels; what we wish to show is that all systems have structures for the representation of linguistic information. This structure varies from one system to another. For a given system it is very useful to be able to study its information representation structure from one processing phase to another.

It would be a good idea to compare the various formalisms used in MT systems to represent the structure of linguistic information. What, for example, are the methods and techniques of representing such information, both internally (for the machine) and externally (for the user)? What communication structures exist between the various linguistic components of a system? What are the advantages, disadvantages or deficiencies of a given formalism? These are important questions that have not yet been adequately dealt with.

Once all test sentences have been submitted to the translation system we must then examine the translation of each sentence. If a sentence contains one or more translation errors, the user might ask the system designer to print out the execution trace of this sentence. Using this information, the user may follow each step of the processing of each linguistic phenomenon present in the test sentence(s) in order to identify the nature of the problem.

This first stage in the linguistic evaluation, using test sentences, is thus a very important stage. It allows the user to examine individually the linguistic phenomena particular to the texts to be translated, to identify the various linguistic principles underlying the grammars of the system, to see the treatment proposed for each of these linguistic phenomena and to understand why the system produces a given quality of translation.

5.2.2. SELECTION OF SAMPLE TEXTS

The second stage in our method of evaluating linguistic components consists in choosing sample texts and submitting them to the system. The first stage enabled us, through the use of test sentences, to examine each linguistic phenomenon individually. The second stage will enable us to examine the overall quality of translation of sample texts.

How can we determine whether a text is truly representative of the domain to which it belongs? In our opinion, there are no scientific criteria that will absolutely guarantee that a text is a representative sample of a body of texts. Sample texts are generally chosen on the basis of intuitive criteria, that is, on the basis of thorough knowledge of the domain and several years of experience translating texts in this domain. To provide a valid corpus, we feel that sample texts should contain at least 10,000 words (depending on the domain, it could be much higher).

The volume of the sample text corpus is important since it will enable us to observe the frequency of occurrence of the various linguistic phenomena. We can then establish an order of priority among these phenomena. Once we have tabulated all the translation errors this will also enable us to determine the relative importance of one linguistic phenomenon compared to another.

It should be emphasized that the user should normally follow this sample text translation process very closely. In this way he will be able to actually observe the principal stages of the production of a computer-assisted translation; for example:

(1) transcription of the sample text corpus onto a computer medium,
(2) searching for words missing from dictionaries,
(3) up-dating of dictionaries,
(4) submitting texts to the translation system,
(5) human interaction, if provided for,
(6) recovering and editing of translated texts,
(7) production and printing of texts.

Once the sample texts have been translated, the user may proceed with the examination and analysis of the results. To do this, he should have the following documents:

(1) a copy of the original corpus that was transcribed onto the computer,

(2) a copy of the machine translation,

(3) a copy of all entries in the dictionary or dictionaries used by the system to translate the words in the corpus,

(4) if required, execution traces of certain sentences translated by the system,

(5) a copy of the human revision of the machine translation,

(6) a copy of the translation made of the original corpus by a human translator.

With all this documentation the user-evaluator will be well equipped to make a thorough analysis of the results obtained. It should be ensured that the human translation of the original corpus as well as the human revision of the machine translation satisfy pre-established translation quality criteria. These two translations of the original text will allow the evaluator to obtain a concrete sample of translation quality constraints.

5.2.3. CLASSIFICATION AND INTERPRETATION OF RESULTS

The third stage in the evaluation of linguistic components consists in analyzing the results of the translation of test sentences and sample texts. The user must consequently make a painstaking count of all translation errors he finds in the machine translation. He must then establish a typology of these errors by linguistic phenomenon. It should be borne in mind that a given translation error may be the manifestation of various interrelated linguistic phenomena.

Based on the typology of errors by linguistic phenomenon the evaluator may qualify and quantify the performance of the linguistic components of the system. The main objective of this step is to describe the linguistic performance of the system. After processing one sample we form a certain idea of the capability of the system. We repeat this step with other samples, each time improving our understanding of the system's capability. The evaluator will then make use of these results to formulate projections, i.e. an evaluation of the system's potential. This type of evaluation will be dealt with in Section 5.3.

CLASSIFICATION BY LINGUISTIC PHENOMENON

In a translation context, when the various linguistic phenomena must be identified with a view to evaluating linguistic components, a distinction must be made between source language phenomena and target language phenomena. It is necessary, on the one hand, to identify those phenomena specific to the comprehension of the source language and, on the other, to identify those that are specific to the transfer of this comprehension into the target language, i.e. to translation.

Faulty analysis or incomplete comprehension of the source sentence generally means a translation error. Good analysis and satisfactory comprehension of the source sentence do not necessarily mean error-free translation. There are thus operations that are performed by the source language analysis component, and there are operations that are dealt with by the target language transfer and synthesis component. A typology of errors by linguistic phenomenon must, insofar as is possible, take this latter distinction into consideration.

We show below an inventory of the principal linguistic phenomena of translation into a given target language (here from English to French). This inventory is not exhaustive and the number of examples has been kept to a strict minimum. The reader-translator may nevertheless get a fairly exact idea of the distinction we are trying to establish between a problem in the comprehension of an English sentence and a problem of translation per se.

PARTIAL INVENTORY OF LINGUISTIC TRANSLATION PHENOMENA

(7) **Translation and generation of the order of sentence constituents:**

(a) Main clause and subordinate clauses
(b) Verb and arguments
(c) Placement of modifiers
(d) Placement of constituents in parentheses
(e) Ellipsis
(f) Repetition of the preposition in an enumeration.

(8) **Translation of sentence structure:**

(a) An English passive may be translated into French by:
- a passive construction
- an active construction
- an active construction with an impersonal subject
- an infinitive.

(b) An English gerund may be translated into French by:
- a gerund introduced by 'en'
- an infinitive

- a clause with a finite verb introduced by a conjunction
- a nominalization.

(c) An English infinitive may be translated into French by:
- a finite clause
- an infinitive introduced by 'à'
- an infinitive introduced by 'de'
- an infinitive without an introducing preposition.

(d) An English imperative may be translated into French by:
- an imperative
- an infinitive.

(e) A reduced relative clause may be translated by either a full or a reduced relative clause.

(f) A full relative clause may be translated by a reduced relative clause.

(9) **Translation of tense sequence.**

(10) **Translation of intra-categorial homographs.**

(11) **Translation of grammatical words:**

- particles, prepositions, subordinating conjunctions
- pronouns, determiners
- quantifiers, ordinal numbers

(12) **Translation and creation of articles.**

(13) **Generation of contractions and elision in French.**

(14) Presence of multiword expressions in the dictionary which are not true idioms.

(15) Syntagmatic transformation required by the translation of a lexical item, e.g. translation of verbs:

(a) **Syntagmatic development operations**

- **Insertion of an operator noun after the verb**

+ PREPOSITION NOUN +

X contact Y ⟶ X entrer + en contact + avec Y
X vary with Y ⟶ X varier + en fonction + de Y
X design Y for Z ⟶ X concevoir Y + en fonction + de Z

+ NOUN +

X begin ⟶ il y a + début + de X
X build up ⟶ il y a + formation + de X
X consider Y ⟶ X + tenir + compte + de Y
X override Y ⟶ X + avoir + priorité + sur Y

+ DETERMINER NOUN +

X act as Y ⟶ X jouer + le rôle + de Y
X service Y ⟶ X faire + l'entretien + de Y
X deenergize Y ⟶ X couper + l'alimentation + de Y

+ PREPOSITION DETERMINER NOUN +

X appear as Y ⟶ X se présenter + sous la forme + de Y
X lead to Y ⟶ X conduire + à l'apparition + de Y

- Insertion of new argument

+ PREPOSITION NOUN +

X cantilever Y ⟶ X monter Y + en porte-à-faux +
X backflush Y ⟶ X rincer Y + à contre-courant +
X level Y ⟶ X mettre Y + de niveau +

+ PREPOSITION DETERMINER NOUN +

X ground Y ⟶ X mettre Y + à la terre +
X reseat Y ⟶ X ramener Y + sur (son/leur) siège +
X push up Y ⟶ X ouvrir Y + vers le haut +

+ PREPOSITION DETERMINER NOUN COMPLEMENT +

X service Y ⟶ X soumettre Y + à l'entretien d'escale +
X lockwire Y ⟶ fixer Y + au moyen d'un fil frein +
X feel Y for Z ⟶ X vérifier Y + au toucher pour voir s'il y a Z +

+ OTHER CASES +

X hold Y ⟶ X retenir Y + **ensemble** +
Y hold Y ⟶ X tenir Y + **enfoncé** +
X join Y ⟶ X relier Y + **l'un à l'autre** +
X minimize Y ⟶ X réduire Y + **le plus possible** +

- **Insertion of an operator verb**

X run Y ⟶ X + **faire** + fonctionner Y

(b) **Operations changing lexical category**

- **From verb to adjective**

needed part ⟶ pièce + **nécessaire** +
adhering material ⟶ matière + **adhérente** +
X meet Y ⟶ X être + **conforme** + à Y

- **From verb to prepositional phrase complement**

identifying mark ⟶ marque + **d'identification** +
protruding N ⟶ N + **en saillie** +
involved N ⟶ N + **en question** +

- **From verb in prenominal adjective position to verb in a full relative clause**

leaking reservoir ⟶ réservoir + **qui fuit** +
disturbed N ⟶ N + **qui a été déplacé** +
improperly functioning unit ⟶ unité + **qui fonctionne mal** +

- **From verb to + nominalization +**

X ground Y ⟶ X effectuer + **la mise à la terre** + de Y

(c) **Operation on arguments of verb**

- **From a passive sentence having no subject (agent) to an active sentence**

make → The valve is made of two hoses.
Le clapet comprend deux boyaux.

cause → The displacement is caused when...
Le déplacement survient lorsque...

- From an intransitive verb to a verb with an impersonal subject

miss → If a fastener is missing,...
S'il manque une attache,...

- Verb of perception requiring insertion of 'il y a':

indicate → X indicates Y
X indique + qu'il y a + Y

- Subject / object permutation:

arise → Leakage arises from low pressure.
Une baisse de pression produit la fuite.

- Direct object / indirect object permutation

apply → X apply suction to Z
X mettre Z en suction

supply → X supply Y with Z
X fournir Z à Y

bleed → X bleed system of air
X purger l'air du système

(d) Particular or idiomatic operations

fail → The pump fails to work
La pompe ne fonctionne pas

make sure → X makes sure that
X s'assure que

permit → X permit Y to be connected
X permet de brancher Y

keep out	→	Keep out all sand Empêcher le sable de pénétrer
persist	→	If sticking valve persists, ... Si la valve continue de coller, ...

This typology and the examples in (15) of verbs requiring syntagmatic transformation are taken from Labelle (forthcoming).

Even though the user does not have direct access to the grammars of a system, he may nevertheless, through the machine translation of test sentences and sample texts, determine whether the system possesses the mechanisms adequate to deal with the translation phenomena listed in (7) to (15). By studying the sentences translated by the system, comparing structures used to represent the various linguistic phenomena and knowing the content of dictionary entries, the evaluator may determine, for example:

(1) whether the system makes a local or complete analysis of the sentence,

(2) whether the system analyses both the surface and "deep" structures of the sentence,

(3) whether the system translates by direct transfer from the source language to the target language,

(4) whether the system translates by transferring from the source structure to the target structure by means of a pivot structure,

(5) how the system interprets the linguistic information from the dictionary or dictionaries,

(6) the principal linguistic operations of each component,

(7) the degree of comprehension of the various linguistic relations between each of the sentence constituents,

(8) linguistic phenomena not processed by the grammars of the system,

(9) the linguistic phenomena for which processing or the proposed description is incomplete or inadequate,

(10) the boundaries between the source language analysis phase, transfer from source language to target language, and synthesis of the target language.

EXAMPLE OF A HYPOTHESIS ON HOW THE RULES OF A SYSTEM OPERATE
(See **TABLE** 2 at the beginning of this chapter)

In order to give a concrete explanation of our proposed linguistic evaluation method (i.e. test sentences and sample texts) we will limit ourselves to the presentation of a single linguistic phenomenon. This phenomenon is the processing of complex nominals and, more specifically, the translation of noun sequences from English to French.

English frequently uses noun sequences which can generally be paraphrased by a reversed sequence of noun complements with 'of' (or some other preposition). For example, the sequence N3 N2 N1 may be paraphrased as N1 of N2 of N3 (book cover color = color of cover of book). In French the noun sequence structure does not exist; only the noun complement sequence is allowed. Sequences of English nouns must therefore be transformed in French into noun complement sequences.

Let us first look, in (16), at noun sequences as they were translated by a system:

(16) (a) **the installation configuration**
N2 N1

(a') **la configuration d'installation**
N1 de N2

(b) **service center assembly bowl**
N3 N2 N1

(b') **la cuve d'assemblage du bloc collecteur**
N1 de N2 de N3

(c) **service center assembly filter retainer**
N4 N3 N2 N1

```
(c')  le dispositif de retenue de filtre d'assemblage de bloc collecteur
                N1             de   N2   de   N3      de        N4
```

What hypotheses can be formulated on the basis of the examples in (16)? We may first deduce that the system included a rule that transformed any sequences of English nouns Nj ... N1 into French in the following manner: N1 de N2 ... de Nj-1 de Nj. This rule applied even when a noun sub-sequence was coded as a nominal idiom in the dictionary. For example, 'service centre' translated as 'bloc collecteur' was a single noun, as was 'retainer' translated as 'dispositif de retenue'. This hypothesis may be confirmed by examining all occurrences of noun sequences in the sample texts. If no counter-example is found to this rule, we may conclude that our hypothesis is correct.

Before transforming a noun sequence using the rule postulated above the English parser must first determine the boundaries of the noun sequence. To understand how this is done, we must examine other examples. From examples such as (17), it may be seen that the parser used immediate constituent contexts as in (18) to define the boundaries of a noun sequence.

```
(17) (a)   the facsimile reception  of  weather charts
                 N2        N1      PREP   ADJ     N

     (a')  la réception de facsimilé  de  cartes météorologiques
                 N1          N2      PREP   N         ADJ

     (b)   system functional checkout
             N       ADJ        N

     (b')  le système vérification fonctionnelle
               N          N            ADJ

     (c)*  in the secretaries office
                     Ns        N

     (c')  dans les secrétaires le bureau
                      Ns           N
```

Note that (17c) contains an error (lack of possessive marker). The system did not reject this ungrammatical phrase but translated it as in (17c'). Ideally a system would only translate grammatical sentences and block in the process of parsing ungrammatical ones.

The determination of constituent boundaries in (a), (b) and (c), before translating into French, is shown in (18); the rule concerning noun sequences was applied within these constituents.

(18)	(a)	N N PREP N	⟶	(N2 N1) (PREP N1)
	(b)	N ADJ N	⟶	(N1) (ADJ 1 N1)
	(c)	Ns N	⟶	(N1s) (N1)

It may be concluded from these examples that the parser used the preposition (18 a), the adjective (18 b) and the plural of a noun (18 c) as boundaries of the noun sequence. These hypotheses on constituent-boundary rules must also be tested on other examples from the corpus of texts translated by the system or on examples formulated for the occasion. Again, if no counter-example is found to these rules, the evaluator may conclude that his hypotheses are correct.

Once a certain number of the rules of the system have been deduced through examination of translated sentences, the evaluator may look for examples that will contradict the rules of the system. For example, in (19) it may be seen that, if the head noun N1 was listed in the dictionary as an idiom, the result of the transformation was always a faulty translation.

(19) (a) reservoir air bleed valve
N3 N2 N1
(a') l'air **purgeur** de réservoir
N2 N1 N3

After identifying counter-examples for the basic rules of the system the evaluator may look more closely at the consequences of these rules by adding a complementary structure to the linguistic phenomenon studied. To make a more thorough examination of the treatment of noun sequences we might, for example, look at the treatment of conjunctions in noun sequences.

In (20), we give seven examples of sequences of compound nouns in which more or less the same English words occur. These seven examples were obviously constructed by the evaluator. The lexical category of each of the nouns in (20) has been numbered in order to identify their surface order, and the symbol CC signifies "coordinating conjunction".

```
(20) (a)    aircraft aileron or rudder cables or engine lines
               N6       N5   CC   N4     N3   CC   N2     N1

     (b)    wing surface or cockpit cover or engine nacelle
             N6    N5    CC   N4     N3   CC   N2       N1

     (c)    aircraft engine lines or aileron or rudder cables
               N6      N5     N4   CC     N3   CC   N2     N1

     (d)    aircraft aileron or rudder cables or engine or brake lines
               N7       N6   CC   N5     N4   CC   N3   CC   N2   N1

     (e)    aileron or rudder cables and engine or brake lines and cockpit
               N8    CC    N7     N6    CC   N5   CC   N4    N3  CC    N2
            wires
               N1

     (f)    aircraft right or left  wing or engine nacelle
               N4    ADJ2  CC  ADJ1   N3   CC   N2      N1

     (g)    process control computer and education control computer
               N6      N5      N4     CC     N3        N2       N1
```

In (21), we have used numbered brackets to show the proper arrangement of the conjoined elements. A rather literal translation allows us to visualize the noun movements that must be made to go from English to French. The numbered lexical categories in (20) are arranged in (21) in the surface order they would take in French.

```
(21) (a)    aircraft (((aileron or rudder) cables) or (engine lines))
                     123                    3       2  2            21

     (a')   les canalisations  du moteur  ou les  câbles du  gouvernail ou de
            l'aileron de l'avion
            ((N1 de N2) CC (N3 (de N4 CC de N5))) de N6

     (b)    (wing surface) or (cockpit cover) or (engine nacelle)
            1            1    1             1    1              1

     (b')   la surface  de l'aile  ou le couvercle de la cabine ou la nacelle
            du  moteur
            (N5 de N6) CC (N3 de N4) CC (N1 de N2)

     (c)    aircraft ((engine lines) or ((aileron or rudder) cables))
                     12            2   23                  3       21
```

(c') les câbles du gouvernail ou de l'aileron ou les canalisations du moteur de l'avion
((N1 (de N2 CC de N3)) CC (N4 de N5)) de N6

(d)
```
aircraft (((aileron or rudder) cables) or ((engine or brake)
         123                 3       2    23                3
lines))
     21
```

(d') les canalisations de freinage ou du moteur ou les câbles du gouvernail ou de l'aileron de l'avion
((N1 (de N2 CC de N3)) CC (N4 (de N5 CC de N6))) de N7

(e)
```
((aileron or rudder) cables) and ((engines or brake) lines)
12                 2       1     12                2      1
and (cockpit wires)
    1             1
```

(e') les câbles du gouvernail ou de l'aileron et les canalisations de freinage ou du moteur et les câbles de la cabine
(N6 (de N7 CC de N8)) CC (N3(de N4 CC de N5)) CC (N1 de N2)

(f)
```
aircraft ((right or left) wing) or (engine nacelle)
         12             2     1    1              1
```

(f') la nacelle du moteur ou l'aile droite ou gauche de l'avion
(N1 de N2) CC (N3 (ADJ2 CC ADJ1)) de N4

(g)
```
(process control computer) and (education control computer)
1                        1     1                          1
```

(g') l'ordinateur de contrôle du traitement et l'ordinateur de contrôle d'enseignement
(N4 de N5 de N6) CC (N1 de N2 de N3)

The seven examples in (20) were translated by an MT system, and the resulting translation is shown in (22).

(22) (a) les canalisations de câbles ou de moteur d'aileron ou de gouvernail d'avion

(b) la nacelle de couvercle ou de moteur de surface de cabine d'aile

(c) les câbles de canalisation ou d'aileron ou de gouvernail de moteur d'avion

(d) les canalisations de câbles ou de moteur ou de frein ou d'aileron ou de gouvernail d'avion

(e) les câbles de canalisations ou de cabine de câbles et de moteur ou de frein d'aileron ou de gouvernail

(f) la nacelle droite ou gauche d'aile ou de moteur d'avion

(g) l'ordinateur de contrôle d'ordinateur et d'enseignement de contrôle de traitement

In view of the translations in (22), how can we discover the system rules that produced this result? If we compare the correct translation in (21) to the machine translation in (22), the result is confusing. Before making any hypotheses we might compare the series of English lexical categories (20) and the series of French lexical categories illustrated by the examples in (22). For each of the examples we obtain the series of lexical categories in (23).

(23) (a) N6 N5 CC N4 N3 CC N2 N1
(a') N1 de N3 CC de N2 de N5 CC de N4 N6

(b) N6 N5 CC N4 N3 CC N2 N1
(b') N1 de N3 CC de N2 de N5 CC de N4 N6

(c) N6 N5 N4 CC N3 CC N2 N1
(c') N1 de N4 CC de N3 CC de N2 de N5 de N6

(d) N7 N6 CC N5 N4 CC N3 CC N2 N1
(d') N1 de N4 CC de N3 CC de N2 de N6 CC de N5 de N7

(e) N8 CC N7 N6 CC N5 CC N4 N3 CC N2 N1
(e') N1 de N3 CC de N2 de N6 CC de N5 CC de N4 de N8 CC de N7

(f) N4 ADJ2 CC ADJ1 N3 CC N2 N1
(f') N1 ADJ2 CC ADJ1 de N3 CC de N2 de N4

(g) N6 N5 N4 CC N3 N2 N1
(g') N1 de N2 de N4 CC de N3 de N5 de N6

If we examine the French sequences in (23) the first thing we observe is that N1 is always the first element. After having delimited a noun sequence using rules such as those in (18) the English parser considered the last noun in the noun sequence (i.e. N1) as the head noun of that sequence. How, then, did the program arrange the associated elements starting with noun N1?

A second observation may be made from the examination of the English sequences in (23). Starting from head noun N1, the program scanned the sequence of lexical categories from right to left to group connected elements together. It may thus be seen that the program identified conjoined elements with the same lexical category and, when it met either another lexical category or a sequence N N, it immediately formed a group of connected elements. For example, the sequence N4 N3 CC N2 N1 would be analyzed as N4 (N3 CC N2) N1. The program formed the group of conjoined elements (N3 CC N2) because it had the series N4 N3 at its left. The program then continued scanning from right to left in attempt to form other connected groups. The sequence N N thus served as a boundary for connected elements. The sequences of lexical categories in (20) were analyzed by the English parser as shown in (24).

(24) (a) N6 N5 CC N4 N3 CC N2 N1
N6 (N5 CC N4) (N3 CC N2) N1

(b) N6 N5 CC N4 N3 CC N2 N1
N6 (N5 CC N4) (N3 CC N2) N1

(c) N6 N5 N4 CC N3 CC N2 N1
N6 N5 (N4 CC N3 CC N2) N1

(d) N7 N6 CC N5 N4 CC N3 CC N2 N1
N7 (N6 CC N5) (N4 CC N3 CC N2) N1

(e) N8 CC N7 N6 CC N5 CC N4 N3 CC N2 N1
(N8 CC N7) (N6 CC N5 CC N4) (N3 CC N2) N1

(f) N4 ADJ2 CC ADJ1 N3 CC N2 N1
N4 (ADJ2 CC ADJ1) (N3 CC N2) N1

(g) N6 N5 N4 CC N3 N2 N1
N6 N5 (N4 CC N3) N2 N1

Examples (24a) and (24b) were analyzed (or bracketed) in the same manner. Once the examples in (24) had been analyzed, how did the program transform these sequences of English categories into a sequence of French categories? In examining the translation in (22), we can deduce that the program first moved the associated adjectives to the right of N1 (22f). Then it moved to the right of N1 each group of connected elements lying to the left of N1.

For example, (24a) is transformed into (22a). If necessary the program then moved non-conjoined nouns following the general order explained in (16), i.e. N1 de ... Nj-1 de Nj. We may summarize the changes by comparing the bracketed groups in (25) with the machine translations in (22).

(25) (a) N6 (N5 CC N4) (N3 CC N2) N1
(a') N1 (de N3 CC de N2) (de N5 CC de N4) de N6

(b) N6 (N5 CC N4) (N3 CC N2) N1
(b') N1 (de N3 CC de N2) (de N5 CC de N4) de N6

(c) N6 N5 (N4 CC N3 CC N2) N1
(c') N1 (de N4 CC de N3 Cc de N2) de N5 de N6

(d) N7 (N6 CC N5) (N4 CC N3 CC N2) N1
(d') N1 (de N4 CC de N3 de N2) (de N6 CC de N5) de N7

(e) (N8 CC N7) (N6 CC N5 CC N4) (N3 CC N2) N1
(e') N1 (de N3 CC de N2) (de N6 CC de N5 CC de N4) (de N8 CC de N7)

(f) N4 (ADJ2 CC ADJ1) (N3 CC N2) N1
(f') N1 (ADJ2 CC ADJ1) (de N3 CC de N2) de N4

(g) N6 N5 (N4 CC N3) N2 N1
(g') N1 de N2 (de N4 CC de N3) de N5 de N6

If the evaluator finds no counter-examples for these rules for processing conjunction in noun sequences, he may conclude that his hypotheses about these rules were correct.

It is not necessary to take this example of noun sequence processing any further. Our main objective was to illustrate our method of examining the translation of test sentences and sample texts and making examples and counter-examples that would allow us to formulate hypotheses on the operation of the rules of a system. The last example enables the evaluator to make the following observations:

1° This system makes only a local analysis of the English sentence.

2° This system does not analyze the deep structure of the sentence.

3° This system makes a translation using direct transfer.

4° This system does not translate through a pivot structure.

5° This system does not satisfactorily process noun sequences and gives even less satisfactory treatment to conjunctions of noun sequences.

To get a thorough understanding of the rules of a system the evaluator is obliged to apply this example/counter-example method to all the linguistic phenomena of translation from (7) to (15). Once he has made an inventory of the rules of a system the evaluator may go on to evaluate the potential of a system. This will be dealt with in the next section.

5.3 EVALUATION OF SYSTEM'S POTENTIAL

Before acquiring a computerized translation system the user should, ideally, know (A) whether the system can perform the work at hand in a satisfactory manner, (B) what the limitations of the system are, and (C) what improvements can be expected without changing the system's basic design. (A) can be determined by submitting representative texts for translation under operating conditions and evaluating the results in terms of cost, time and quality. (B) and (C) require knowledge about the type of system, its design features, the nature of the linguistic components - in short, knowledge about the interior of the black box. CHAPTER 2 and CHAPTER 3 provide background for gaining this kind of insight. The following assessment of factors determining the limitations and improvability of a system is based on the arguments presented in chapters 2 and 3.

5.3.1 LIMITATIONS OF THE SYSTEM

A) COMPLETENESS OF GRAMMATICAL COVERAGE

- Direct transfer systems (see section 2.3.1):

These are almost totally dependent on human assistance. Most grammatical phenomena require an analysis of the sentence for their treatment. Ad hoc rules that look only at the immediate environment of a word do not offer solutions to grammatical problems. And what is the "immediate environment" of a word anyway? One word to the right and left? Two words? Three? ...? The important factor is not the number of words, but the constituent boundaries. It was shown in the discussion of complex constituents (section 3.3.3) that constituent boundaries can not, in general, be determined without analyzing the whole sentence. Direct transfer is not a suitable framework for dealing with the host of grammatical problems that beset machine translation; it is not a feasible approach to automatic translation and it places too heavy a burden on the translator/reviser who has to patch up its output.

- Pivot language systems (see section 2.3.2):

Analysis of the whole sentence and representation of its structure in some normalized form (the "pivot language") that makes syntactic-semantic information available for transfer and generation phases is the minimum requirement for a system to obtain full grammatical coverage. Systems of this type now in operation are still plagued by many grammatical problems and this is likely to be the situation for some time to come. However, in principle, the grammatical coverage of a pivot type system is limited only by the sophistication of its components; unlike the case of direct transfer, there are no inherent limitations on the grammaticality of the raw output from pivot type systems.

- Dictionary entries (see section 3.1):

Grammatical analysis depends on information about the grammatical category, morphological type, contextual constraints and semantic properties of lexical items. Consequently, dictionary entries give a good indication of the grammatical limitations of a system. We can not say that a certain level of dictionary information ensures a particular level of grammatical analysis; that depends on how well the parser is designed. What we can say is that if certain information is not present in the dictionary, grammatical coverage will be limited in predictable ways. For example:

(i) If only the grammatical category is given, there will be no grammatical analysis worth mentioning and ambiguity will abound.

(ii) If syntactic complementation is given (e.g., the number of arguments of a verb, whether an argument is a noun phrase, a prepositional phrase or a sentence with a certain complementizer, whether the verb can be passivised or used in the imperative, etc.), but no semantic information is given (neither inherent features nor semantic constraints on possible arguments), we may expect the following limitations:

1) Inability to deal with inner-categorial homography.
2) Limited treatment of cross-categorial homography.
3) Inadequate treatment of complex sentences.

4) High percentage of multiple analyses if the system is nondeterministic.
5) High percentage of incorrect analyses if the system is deterministic.

(iii) If syntactic complementation, inherent semantic features and semantic constraints on arguments of verbs and adjectives are given, but the system makes no other use of semantics (such as semantic relations between nouns or logical inference), some major problems are likely to remain:

1) Noun sequences (proper bracketing and identification of noun-noun relations sufficient for translation of these sequences). (See section 3.4.2.)

2) Coordinate conjunctions (scope of conjunction, identification of ellipted elements). (See section 3.3.3. and section 3.4.2.)

3) Prepositional attachment (identification of a prepositional phrase as complement of a noun, argument of a verb or as a sentence adverbial; identification of a preposition as part of a multiword verb or as part of a prepositional phrase). (See section 3.3.3. and section 3.4.2.)

4) Parenthetical insertions (relation of the expression in parentheses to the constituents of the sentence). (See section 3.4.2.)

Of course, these problems are much more serious under the conditions described in (ii), where they are subsumed under 'Inadequate treatment of complex sentences'. The use of inherent features and selectional restrictions in (iii) offers the possibility of a solution in many instances where parsing would fail in (ii), but a general solution is likely to require additional forms of semantic analysis.

- Maximum unit of treatment = sentence:

If each sentence is treated in isolation, with no analysis extending beyond the sentence boundary, then clearly intersentential anaphora will give rise to certain problems that can not be solved within that framework (e.g., translating a pronoun which has more than one equivalent in the target language when the antecedent of the pronoun is in the preceding sentence). These problems receive a good deal of attention in discussions of text grammar and are often used to argue against the feasibility of FAMT. However, intersentential anaphora may be less of an obstacle to successful automatic translation than the problems that exist **within** the sentence boundary. This was indicated, for example, by analysis of the errors that occurred in translations produced by the TAUM system at the University of Montreal during tests conducted in 1980 for hydraulics texts (see TAUM (1980) and Gervais (1980)) and in 1981 for electronics texts (see Lehrberger (1981)).

B) EXTENDABILITY TO NEW DOMAINS AND TO NEW LANGUAGE PAIRS

(i) DOMAIN EXTENSION

- **Corpus-based system with sublanguage grammar** (see section 4.1):

Extension is limited to related domains where texts have the same grammatical peculiarities. Problems caused by increases in homography can be reduced to some extent by using separate dictionaries for specialized terminology in different domains, in addition to a "core" dictionary of common words; of course, selectional restrictions may vary from one domain to another even for words in the core vocabulary. To account for grammatical differences, major changes in the system are likely to be required.

- **"General" system with standard grammar** (see section 4.2):

These systems are not extendable to domains in which texts do not conform to standard grammar (i.e., where the grammar of the sublanguage is not simply a subgrammar of the standard grammar). It is doubtful that selective relaxation of grammatical constraints will prove adequate for adjusting to such domains. Systems that aim for general coverage will also require specialized dictionaries for particular domains in order to deal with such problems as homography, and they will also have to take into account the changes in selectional restrictions that accompany changes in domain.

- **Non-modular design** (see section 2.4):

Failure to modularize the processing on different linguistic levels, or at the level of major components (analysis, transfer, generation), makes it difficult to adjust the system to meet the requirements of different domains. Changes at one point in the system are likely to produce undesirable effects in other parts.

(ii) **EXTENSION TO NEW LANGUAGE PAIRS**

- **No pivot language** (see section 2.3.2):

This is impractical in a multilingual environment. A pivot language is essential if transfer modules for different target languages are to be plugged in to one analysis module for a given source language.

- **Partial analysis** (see section 2.2):

Assuming that partial analysis of a language L1 is adequate for translation into another language L2 (perhaps because of strong structural similarities between L1 and L2), it is not likely to prove adequate for translation into languages other than L2. Full analysis is essential for extension to different target languages.

- **Non-modular design** (see section 2.4):

Not suitable for use in a multilingual environment. Modularity permits separation of the work of transfer (the bilingual aspect of machine translation) from analysis and generation (both unilingual). Work can then proceed independently on these modules, constrained by the requirements of the common interface structure rather than the details of the other phases of all the other languages. Without modularity the task of coordinating the work of all the groups involved in a multilingual system would be much more difficult.

C) **LIMITATIONS ON SPEED OF TRANSLATION**

- **Interactive systems** (see section 2.1.1 and section 2.1.2):

Interactivity slows down the machine translation process drastically. The problem is that the phenomena which require the machine to stop and wait for the translator's assistance occur with very high frequency in nearly all texts: homography, conjunction, prepositional attachment, nominal compounding, sentence embedding, etc. Interruptions may occupy so much time that computerized translation with interactive processing becomes slower than straight human translation.

It is no simple matter to program the computer so that it can make effective use of human assistance. The underlying assumption is that the machine will ask relevant questions (and not too many - otherwise the translator who answers them does all the work), will know when to ask them and will be able to apply the information obtained to solve the problem at hand. This is, in fact, a big assumption. We have seen (section 3.3.3) that it is extremely difficult just to identify the boundaries of complex constituents that are likely to cause problems. The machine needs to recognize such constituents and ask the right questions about them. In order to use the information supplied by the translator the machine must know the grammatical functions of the constituents in the sentence. The system's dictionary gives an indication of the ability of the machine to carry out the necessary operations: full complementation on lexical items is a prerequisite. If the dictionary is very rudimentary (which usually seems to be the case), there is no sound basis for determining the grammatical functions of the words in the sentence.

As things now stand, interactive translation is slower than human translation performed with the aid of a word processor serving as an improved typewriter. And in current interactive systems, human intervention during the translation of a sentence does not remove the need for later human revision of the translated sentence; thus the human element enters the process twice.

- **FAMT** (see section 2.1.3):

FAMT has been shown to be faster than human translation - even taking into account the greater length of time required for revision of the raw output. The following excerpt from the 1980 evaluation of TAUM-AVIATION bears this out (Gervais (1980) pp. 57-58):

- It takes from 2 to 2.5 times as long to revise a machine translation as it takes to revise a human translation.
- Overall, the effort in translator/reviser time is reduced by half in machine translation compared with human translation.

The speed of FAMT is limited mainly by revision time; improvements in parsing methods can be expected to improve the grammaticality of the raw output, with consequent reduction in revision time. Of course, speed is not the only consideration; cost must be taken into account as well. In this respect, FAMT has the advantage of not requiring human assistance, except for revision.

5.3.2 IMPROVABILITY OF THE SYSTEM

In this section we consider the improvability of a system from the linguistic point of view (not of its hardware, printouts, etc.). The user's decision to acquire a system may be influenced by the designer's promise of forthcoming improvements in various aspects of linguistic performance. How can the user make an objective evaluation of the likelihood of these improvements being carried out? In the preceding section we discussed some general limitations on different types of systems; now we consider possible improvements in linguistic capability within those limits.

The user's estimate of improvability will depend on the type of system being evaluated and the kinds of errors that are found in the raw output from the system (i.e., before revision of the translated text). In section 3 we discussed, for each linguistic component, the linguistic phenomena that are particularly troublesome for machine translation, hence likely to produce errors in the raw output. The changes required to eliminate these errors vary from simple dictionary adjustments to major revisions of the parser. **What is needed to gauge the improvability of a system is a classification of errors according to (i) the component in which the error has its source and (ii) the complexity of the linguistic problem that gives rise to the error.**

A classification of errors along these lines differs substantially from the kind which is normally used in evaluating the performance of a system. In the latter case the user is interested in the percentage of errors that seriously affect the understanding of the translated text (both the intelligibility of the translated text and its fidelity to the original) and the burden on the reviser. We may think of this as a **user's classification**: its purpose is to measure the linguistic performance of the system - and it is indispensable for the user. The classification of errors we shall now discuss may be thought of as a **designer's classification**: it pinpoints the source of the error and indicates the effort required to amend the system sò as to prevent future recurrence of the error. The potential user whose acquisition of a system hinges on expectations of improvements in its linguistic performance will also be interested in such a classification. An evaluation of this type requires a deeper understanding of system characteristics (section 2) and linguistic components (section 3), but it may be well worth the effort for the user who plans to make a large investment with a long term commitment to a particular system.

How one should go about grading the complexity of linguistic problems that give rise to various types of errors is not at all obvious. One approach might be to develop a measure of complexity based on theoretical principles within the framework of some model of language. This approach would be in the same spirit as Chomsky's proposal for measuring "degree of grammaticalness" (Chomsky (1965) pp. 148-153). Another approach, outlined below, is more pragmatic: the linguistic problems can be divided into two categories: a) those for which a solution is known and could be implemented in the given type of system, and b) those for which no solution is known that could be implemented in that type of system. They will be referred to as problems of **development** and **research** respectively. Problems of development can be ranked according to estimates of the time required to implement a solution within the system being evaluated.

An error classification of this type was carried out by researchers on Project TAUM at the University of Montreal in 1980 and 1981 for texts in the fields of aviation hydraulics and aviation electronics. The following table summarizes the results obtained in comparing errors made during the translation of texts from these fields[20]. It shows the number of errors per thousand words of text according to the phase in which the error originated and whether the errors are in the development or research category.

PHASE	HYDRAULICS		ELECTRONICS	
	D	R	D	R
ORIGINAL TEXT	0.1	0.0	0.3	0.0
WORD PROCESSING	1.3	0.0	0.2	0.2
PRE-EDITION	4.7	0.1	5.0	0.2
MORPHOLOGICAL ANALYSIS	0.0	0.0	0.0	0.0
ANALYSIS DICTIONARY	20.0	0.1	35.6	0.5
SYNTACTIC ANALYSIS	19.5	16.5	12.6	21.3
TRANSFER DICTIONARY	54.8	24.0	78.0	17.0
STRUCTURAL TRANSFER + SYNTACTIC GENERATION	30.1	13.7	4.3	11.9
MORPHOLOGICAL GENERATION	0.0	0.0	0.0	0.0
POST-EDITION	0.4	0.0	1.7	0.0
TOTAL	130.9	54.4	137.7	51.1

D = development R = research

Table 3

(Figures represent the number of errors per thousand words of text submitted to the given phase.)

Table 3 gives an overall picture of research and development problems within each phase (including, for completeness, errors in the original text). The nature of the errors is specified in an error grid and estimates are given of the time required (in man-months) to correct each type of error in the system.

Further details of the error analysis made during the test of TAUM-AVIATION are included in Lehrberger (1981). In particular, section 3 of that report gives a detailed analysis of the errors in each phase and complete tables are included in the appendix.

The above mentioned analysis of errors was made by the system's designers (the researchers themselves) with the aim not only of measuring the performance of each phase, but also of providing a guide for further development of the system. This was a unique situation; unfortunately, the user who is evaluating commercial systems can not expect to be provided with such analyses. What the user can expect is promises of improvements in the system in the near future. These promises must be viewed with suspicion. The user can form his own idea of the possibility of improvements within a specified time frame if he is aware of the type of system and the complexity of the linguistic phenomena underlying the errors the system makes. Section 3 of the present report provides detailed discussions of these linguistic phenomena.

Improving the linguistic capability of a system entails solving particular linguistic problems. (Genuine improvements may sometimes be confused with successes in translating texts from certain domains; such successes may simply reflect the relative simplicity of highly restricted sublanguages.) The ability to find principled solutions to these problems depends on the system's grammars and dictionaries. Translation errors reveal the extent of grammatical coverage provided by the system; the analysis of errors suggested above, combined with the methods discussed in section 5.2, gives the evaluator access to the system's black box and reveals the grammar inside - not the actual rules (software), but the equivalent grammar in terms of a reference model adopted by the evaluator.

Other aspects of improvability are discussed in **Appendix A**, including the effect of changes in one component on the functioning of other components, the effect of new dictionary entries on the functioning of existing ones, the effect of adding a large number of idioms to the dictionary, and the significance of the error rate in a study of improvability.

5.4 EVALUATION OF USER ENVIRONMENT

After performance and linguistic potential have been determined and the direct costs of a translation chain calculated, the environment of the user-translator must also be evaluated. The costs of this work environment constitute indirect costs for a translation chain. These are either fixed costs (e.g. service contract for hardware and software) or amortizable costs (e.g. building the dictionaries of the system).

In this section, we will deal only with matters that have a direct impact on the everyday work environment of the translator.

5.4.1 MAINTENANCE AND DEVELOPMENT OF THE SYSTEM

Before implementing a translation system, the division of responsibilities between supplier and user must be formally established. Ideally, the user-translator's responsibilities should be concentrated exclusively on the act of translation (for example, human revision of raw translation).

The following are examples of tasks that might be considered in this division of responsibilities:

1° entering texts to be translated:

- initial transcription of texts on computer medium
- conversion of this transcription, if necessary, into a format acceptable to the system
- checking and correcting texts before submission
- development of interface program(s) for texts that are already on a computer medium.

2° maintenance and development of operating software:

- operating system
- telecommunications system
- word-processing system
- optical character reader (if used)
- photocomposition (if used).

3° maintenance and development of application software:

- programming language(s)
- grammars and formalism for dictionaries
- management program(s) for production of translation.

4° maintenance and development of dictionaries:

- development of terminology for texts to be translated
- management program(s) for dictionaries
- program(s) for consulting and checking dictionaries.

5° maintenance of hardware.

6° human revision of translated texts:

- human revision of raw output
- text editing after human revision
- revision and checking final version
- translation quality control
- processing of copy prior to final printing
- printing and publishing final product.

Bearing in mind that the tasks listed above will in some way be divided between supplier and user, the potential purchaser should examine carefully the implications of the following points:

a) personnel training
b) documentation available
c) availability of the required human resources
d) increase in specialized manpower
e) impact of this new product on a non-computerized work environment
f) impact of this new product on an already-computerized work environment.

A description will also be required of the nature, costs and waiting time for after-sales service in the case of tasks that are the supplier's responsibility.

In this section, we will limit our discussion to certain tasks: dictionary building, grammar maintenance and the level of personnel specialization.

5.4.1.1 DICTIONARY BUILDING

In a machine translation system, there are ideally three dictionaries: a source language dictionary, a bilingual source-language / target-language dictionary, and a target language dictionary (see Section 3.1). These three dictionaries may be physically placed in a single data bank (or data file). We would then speak of the dictionary of a system. If there are two or three physically separate data banks, we would speak of the dictionaries of a system. In this section, however, we will use the singular form dictionary as a cover term for the various possibilities for grouping dictionaries.

The SYSTRAN, ALPS, WEIDNER and METEO systems have only one dictionary. We must, however, qualify this statement as regards the METEO and SYSTRAN systems. The dictionary data bank of the METEO system is broken down into three sub-dictionaries: the general dictionary, the dictionary of idioms and the dictionary of place names. The SYSTRAN dictionary is broken down into two sub-dictionaries: the dictionary of single words (stem dictionary) and the dictionary of idioms and expressions (idiom and limited semantic dictionary) (see Van Slype and Pigott, 1979). The TAUM-AVIATION system contains two dictionaries: an analysis dictionary and a transfer dictionary. The analysis dictionary is a dictionary of the source language. The transfer dictionary contains both a bilingual source-language / target-language dictionary and a unilingual target language dictionary (Bourbeau, 1981b). The ARIANE system contains three separate dictionaries (GETA-CHAMPOLLION, 1982).

In a machine translation system, the dictionary is an essential component that is very costly to build compared to the building of a grammar. A potential purchaser should always be very skeptical when a system designer claims that all that is left to do is to build the dictionaries, or that the system will perform even better once the dictionaries are completely finished. It would be more realistic to state that a system moves from the development phase to the operational phase if and only if the dictionaries and grammars are completed.

The complexity of building a system dictionary depends on the nature of the linguistic information recorded in the dictionary. This linguistic information should be encoded using a pre-defined formalism, and each system has its own particular way of coding information. In addition, the intelligence of a system depends on the knowledge it is possible to put in its dictionary (see Section 5.3). Machine translation systems may be differentiated by, among other things, the type of knowledge that can be formalized in the dictionary (see Section 3.1). The more linguistic information there is to be formalized into a dictionary, the more this becomes a job for a specialist (see, for example, Chevalier et al., 1981).

For most current commercial systems the user is responsible for building dictionaries. The designer provides a base dictionary with his system and the user completes this dictionary by adding the entries he chooses depending on the domain being translated. If the user finds himself in this type of situation, he should make sure that he has at his disposal computer tools for the management of a dictionary data bank.

In addition to evaluating the tools provided, the user should receive adequate training and have sufficient documentation to be able to perform this lexicographic work. It is not enough, for example, for the user to know the formalism used to encode linguistic information, he must also have a clear knowledge of the nature, role and function of the grammatical codes to be listed in the dictionary. This means that the system designer must give a detailed explanation of the linguistic model of his system so that the user can easily understand the nature of his work as well as the interrelations between the dictionary and grammars. These should be considered as the minimum conditions to be satisfied before setting users to the task of dictionary building.

5.4.1.2 GRAMMAR MAINTENANCE

Ideally, in a translation system there are three grammars: an analysis grammar of the source language, a transfer grammar for translating the structure of the source language into a target language structure, and a generation (or synthesis) grammar of the target language.

The system designer is normally responsible for the maintenance of his system's grammars. In an operating context the term **maintenance** means technical support for existing rules. In a development context, the term maintenance can also cover the integration of new grammar rules. A clear distinction must therefore be made between an operating version and a version undergoing development. The evaluator should be told clearly whether the potential buyer is looking for a prototype version or an operating version. The evaluator should measure the costs of modifications or improvements to be made to a system on the basis of user requirements. If the installation of a new version of a system is necessary, this should not disturb the production environment of a user already operating a system.

A system designer often proposes to a future purchaser the installation of an entirely new version of the grammars of his system at no extra cost. The reason for this is that it is simpler for a supplier to ensure the maintenance of only one version of his system in all customer installations. This new version thus becomes the "standard version". If a customer asks the system designer to make major changes to the system's grammars on the basis of texts to be translated, this will mean better performance by the system as well as a new version adapted to the requirements of the grammars. This new version gradually becomes a version adapted to the requirements of a given customer. The result is that there is necessarily a widening and occasionally major gap between the standard version and this "custom" version. What happens then? Any number of scenarios are possible, but one thing is clear: the customer will probably have to pay the costs of his custom version.

Before the user assumes responsibility for the maintenance of grammars it is essential that the results of evaluations (cost/benefit, linguistic) and tests be very positive. Accepting such a responsibility means that the buyer is prepared to invest time and money in research and development on the translation system.

5.4.1.3 SPECIALIZATION OF PERSONNEL

A machine translation chain necessitates at the outset the following basic personnel: computer scientist, linguist, translator and terminologist. Each of these persons should have a specialty; for example:

- a computer scientist specializing in natural language processing
- a computer scientist specializing in data bases
- a computer scientist specializing in software engineering
- a computer scientist specializing in telecommunications
- a linguist specializing in computational linguistics
- a linguist specializing in theoretical linguistics
- a linguist specializing in contrastive linguistics
- a translator specializing in the particular domain
- a translator specializing in machine translation
- a translator specializing in lexicography
- a translator specializing in terminology.

Bearing in mind the division of responsibilities between the system designer and the user, the potential purchaser should determine what type of specialists will be needed. If he does not have the required personnel, he will have to make the appropriate investment to train the personnel he has.

For example, we might imagine that the buyer will have to form the following teams:

1° an operating team:
- system operator
- personnel to enter texts for translation
- human revisor(s)
- personnel to process copy
- production management personnel

2° a maintenance team:
- hardware maintenance personnel
- software maintenance personnel
- grammar maintenance personnel
- dictionary maintenance and up-dating personnel

3° a research and development team:
- dictionary development personnel
- grammar development personnel

For each type of task, the number of persons involved, the level of specialization required and the length of training period must be determined.

Given the competitiveness and complexity of this high technology area, a potential purchaser should limit his responsibilities in such a way that his organization provides only the operating team.

5.4.2 "GARBAGE COLLECTOR" FACILITIES

"Garbage collector" facilities, in this context, are strategies that a system designer may develop in order to increase the number of sentences translated. These mechanisms may be considered as a means of forcing the translation of a sentence through even though an error or problem has been detected during processing. How does a system adjust to an unforeseen situation? For some systems the absence of a single word in the dictionary blocks the translation of the whole sentence. In other words, a local error should have a local consequence, while a major error should have a major consequence. In order to have a more error-resistant system (fail-soft system) the system designer must choose strategies that make the system capable of reacting correctly in the most common error situations.

Even though these facilities are part of the inner workings of the system it is nevertheless true that this has direct repercussions on translation quality and consequently on the total work performed by the human revisor. For the translator a good human revision environment makes no sense unless the raw translation is revisable and the percentage of sentences translated is sufficiently high.

The main error situations are the following: a dictionary entry or grammar rule is missing, incomplete or false. There may also be misspellings or syntactic errors in sentences of the source text.

The principal strategies (or mechanisms) may be summarized as follows:

(i) Full sentence analysis but more than one translation produced:

- print all readings of that sentence and let human reviser choose the proper one
- choose one reading automatically and ignore all other possibilities.

(ii) No full sentence analysis:

- relax semantic constraints
- relax syntactic constraints
- produce a partial analysis of the sentence
- make use of interactivity during translation process
- manual pre-editing.

(iii) Neither full nor partial analysis of sentence:

- print input sentence untranslated
- print list of words in sentence with equivalents found in dictionary
- print only the terminological information on technical terms in the sentence.

In an MT system, the error retrieval mechanism(s) might act as a "supervisor" able to observe the breakdown of the sentence analysis process and to take corrective measures. This supervisor should be capable of determining the nature of the problem in order to trigger the appropriate corrective strategy. For example, for an error of type (i), the supervisor would choose to print as the raw translation either all readings (e.g. (26a),

(26b) and (27a), (27b) below), or only one reading (see (26a) and (27b)). If the error is of type (ii), however, the supervisor would then modify certain parameters in order to choose one of the strategies listed in (ii) and re-submit this sentence to the translation system. This operation will not necessarily "avoid" the error and, if all the strategies in (ii) have been attempted without success, the supervisor may then choose one of the strategies in (iii). At the present time the translation systems on the market do not have these error retrieval facilities. Commercial systems do not automatically determine the nature of a failure, except in the trivial case of a word missing from the dictionary.

We will illustrate the application of these strategies in two cases:

(1) multiple outputs for a single input and
(2) incomplete sentence analysis.

COMPLETE SENTENCE ANALYSIS PRODUCING MORE THAN ONE READING

In the March 1979 version of TAUM-AVIATION the parser produced for the sentence in (26) a first reading where we have a combination of noun phrases (26a) and a second reading where we have a combination of clauses (26b). For sentence (27), the system also produced two readings, the first of which is a combination of noun phrases (27a), and the second of which is a combination of clauses (27b). For each of these readings, the translations obtained are shown in (26a), (26b), (27a) and (27b).

(26) **Connect pressure and return lines to pump.**

(a) **Relier la pression et les canalisations de retour à la pompe.**
(b) **Relier la pression et ramener les canalisations à la pompe.**

(27) **Carefully move guide tube to one side and disconnect lines at inlet ports of the two check valves attached to tee fitting at inlet of filter.**

(a) **Déplacer soigneusement le tube de guidage à un côté et aux canalisations de la séparation aux orifices d'entrée des deux clapets anti-retour fixés au raccord en té à l'orifice d'entrée du filtre.**

(b) **Déplacer soigneusement le tube de guidage à un côté et débrancher les canalisations aux orifices d'entrée des deux clapets anti-retour fixés au raccord en T à l'orifice d'entrée du filtre.**

The proper reading of sentence (26) is (26a), while that of (27) is (27b). In an operating context, would it be better to produce a translation for every possible reading and let the human revisor choose the right one, or would it be better to require the system to choose only one reading and thus produce only one translation per sentence? Since the system could only make such a choice on the basis of probabilistic criteria, this means that in some cases it would make the wrong choice. What then would be the best strategy? The best strategy would probably be to offer the two possibilities and let the user choose the one he feels would be the most attractive for his application.

INCOMPLETE SENTENCE ANALYSIS

Any system should at least have mechanisms for processing unknown words (i.e. words not in the dictionary). Some system designers offer the possibility of pre-processing texts in such cases. This consists in running the text through the front end of the system. In the front end the source language dictionary is consulted, resulting in a list of words in the text that cannot be found in the dictionary. The dictionary is then up-dated and the text submitted to the translation chain. It should be borne in mind that this pre-processing mechanism permits the identification only of new written forms, and not of new meanings of a word.

Another strategy consists in submitting the text to be translated directly to the entire translation chain. In such cases the system will make a list of unknown words and the dictionary will be up-dated afterwards. In this strategy, however, the system must also recognize these unknown words by automatically assigning a minimum of linguistic information to them (e.g. lexical category). For example, the morphological component (see Section 3.2) should contain specific rules to account for the linguistic mechanisms involved in the formation of new words. The morphological component can then examine the written form of the word in order to find clues as to its nature and, on the basis of this examination, a series of hypotheses may be submitted to the syntactic analysis component for confirmation.

Sentence analysis may be blocked for reasons other than the presence of unknown words. A parser often blocks because of an incomplete or erroneous semantic description of a lexical item in the dictionary (see Section 3.1.2). In such cases, the supervisor may decide to restart the analysis process while inhibiting the semantic constraints (i.e. "relaxing" semantic constraints). If a complete syntactic analysis is produced this may be used to make the translation.

If this strategy does not produce results the supervisor may decide to relax some syntactic constraints, for example, to accept a certain type of complement not provided for in the dictionary entry for a given verb, or to accept that certain rules of agreement are contravened in order to allow for types of errors that are frequent in the source text, or even to have recourse to a grammar of rare constructions. If one of these strategies produces a complete analysis a translation may be provided on the basis of this analysis.

If there is no way of obtaining a complete analysis of the sentence the supervisor may decide to produce a partial analysis. This is an identification of the immediate constituents (or syntagms) of the sentence. The translation is then based on this partial analysis.

Another strategy would be to have interaction between the machine and the translator during the translation process in order to enable a complete analysis of the sentence to be produced or to choose the translation of a word for which there is more than one equivalent. In this situation the translator replies to questions from the machine. In our view, this type of strategy is not attractive to the translator unless human intervention is solicited only after all the automatic disambiguating powers of a second-generation system have been exhausted, as opposed to those systems which require human intervention as soon as a case of lexical or syntactic ambiguity is detected.

The last strategy that could be used to get around these problems would be to manually pre-edit the text to be translated. This is another form of human assistance in the translation process. In the case of human pre-editing, certain difficulties that the machine would encounter are resolved in advance. This human intervention may be kept to a minimum but it can also quickly become a complex operation.

As an example, manual pre-editing might be limited to disambiguating the period, i.e. the dot marking the end of a sentence as opposed to that forming part of an abbreviation. But it might mean changing the style of the sentence to suit the grammar rules or even inserting symbols in the sentence to mark constituent boundaries. It may even extend to writing the source text using a controlled syntax.

Faced with the range of strategies listed above in (i), (ii) and (iii), the user must determine whether the proposed strategy is adequate and suited to his needs. Whatever the strategy, a system should also be capable of printing messages to advise the human reviser of the strategies chosen by the supervisor.

5.4.3 TEXT EDITOR USED FOR HUMAN REVISION

A word-processing system is steadily becoming an indispensable tool for today's translator. This tool is also a very important element when it forms part of a computer-assisted translation chain. If a translator is required to provide human revision of the raw translation produced by a machine, he should also be provided with a professional word-processing system.

Our objective in this section is certainly not to present a method for evaluating word-processing systems. There are at the present time plenty of reports on this subject in publications dealing specifically with office automation. In the present context it should be sufficient to mention that there are two categories of word-processing systems: "personal" word-processing systems and "professional" word-processing systems (see Marshak 1983). Insofar as machine-aided translation is concerned the translator should have a professional-quality tool for word processing.

Articles appear regularly nowadays in the literature on word processing. Examples that might be consulted are Auerbach (1983), Heintz (1982), Hoffberg (1982), Roman (1983) and Slot (1983), either to obtain a basic list of word-processing software systems, or to have the principal characteristics of these software systems. The subject might also be approached from another point of view by consulting, for example, Jong (1982), Knauss (1983), Marshak (1983), Massaro (1982), Milne (1983), Roberts (1979) or Yencharis (1982).

The conclusion that can be drawn at the present time is that word-processing software for personal microcomputers is a personal tool, while dedicated stand-alone word-processing systems are professional tools (e.g. MICOM, WANG, AES). The user would be at a considerable advantage if the projected word processing system, in addition to being of professional quality, were adapted to human revision operations (e.g. a split screen showing both the source and target texts).

When evaluating machine translation systems the user should thus ensure that the tool provided by the system designer for human revision is a professional tool.

5.4.4 DOCUMENTATION OF THE SYSTEM

Many specialists currently feel that the quality of a computer product may be judged by the quality and professional nature of its documentation. The documentation of a system is a factor that absolutely must not be overlooked.

Documentation may, for example, be used to reinforce staff training, to guide and orient system users, to advise and counsel system maintenance personnel, and to give very detailed information to system development personnel. It should be borne in mind that the term documentation applies here both to computer and linguistic documentation.

Documentation may be classified into four levels of specialization of information:

1° training manual
2° user manual
3° reference manual
4° technical manual.

Bearing in mind the division of responsibilities between system designer and user, the evaluator should determine whether there exists sufficient documentation for each of these levels of specialization. The evaluator might at the same time ascertain whether this documentation is available in the user's mother tongue.

5.5 GLOBAL ASSESSMENT OF SYSTEM'S ACCEPTABILITY TO THE USER

We have examined many details of computerized translation: various types of systems, their theoretical underpinnings, linguistic obstacles to the automation of translation, limitations and improvability of systems, and the practical demands that a system must satisfy to be of use in the real world. We have discussed the details involved in evaluating a system's linguistic performance and its linguistic capability; now we consider, from a global perspective, the evaluation of a system by the user.

The process of choosing (or rejecting) a system may be divided into five phases:

I. Identification of the user's needs

   A. Choice of texts
   B. Identification of type of use
   C. Performance requirements

II. Cost benefit study

III. Linguistic evaluation

   A. Linguistic performance
   B. Linguistic capability

IV. Preliminary use

V. Final judgement

I is the preparatory phase, II and III are the phases of intensive evaluation and IV is the probationary phase. Let us summarize the activities in each phase.

I.A. CHOICE OF TEXTS

The user decides on the domain(s) from which texts are to be taken, since some domains are not suitable for machine translation (for example, where there is a small volume of texts with a potentially very large vocabulary, wide semantic range and complex syntax). The user estimates, for each domain, the volume of texts to be translated per year, the size of vocabulary required, the degree of homography and the syntactic complexity of the texts. He also looks for texts in which normal usage deviates from that of the standard language and notes the kinds of deviation characteristic of various domains.

In effect, the user attempts to identify suitably restricted sublanguages which are prime candidates for machine translation; if the sublanguage grammar is highly deviant, a "tailor made" (corpus based) system may be the only kind that will yield the desired level of automation.

I.B. TYPE OF USE

What constitutes an acceptable translation depends to some extent on how the translated text is to be used. For each domain it is therefore necessary to identify the type of use; this can vary from mere scanning for special information to careful reading for full comprehension, and the intended readers may be specialists who have relatively little trouble understanding the material or non-specialists for whom comprehension may be difficult under the best of circumstances. The user of the translation system must therefore take into account the final user (intended reader) of the translated text before setting up performance requirements for the system.

I.C. PERFORMANCE REQUIREMENTS

The user may decide on a maximum acceptable error rate (or several rates depending on the seriousness of the errors) and a minimum for the percentage of sentences considered grammatically acceptable in the raw output.

The user decides on criteria for quality of the raw output in terms of (i) intelligibility, (ii) fidelity and (iii) style. This is rather complicated since quality is difficult to measure objectively; for a discussion of various methods that have been used, see **Appendix A section A.2.3.3.**

II. COST BENEFIT STUDY

Cost depends on a combination of factors such as initial acquisition of the system, leasing (if not purchased outright), computer processing, maintenance of the system, training personnel to use the system, salaries of personnel required to work with the system (including revisers), dictionary updating, preparation of the source text for submission to the machine and preparation of the translated text for delivery to the final user.

A cost benefit study is not independent of the linguistic evaluation: part of the cost is for revision of the raw output, and the effort that goes into this revision depends on the linguistic performance of the system. Likewise the cost of the human component before revision in an interactive system depends on the system's linguistic performance. As the cost of initial acquisition is amortized, these expenses form a larger percentage of the cost per year. An assessment of long term costs must take into account the improvability of the system, which can only be determined by bringing to light its linguistic capability as well as its linguistic performance (see section 5.3.2).

III. LINGUISTIC EVALUATION

A full in-depth linguistic evaluation is time consuming and expensive. However, with the aid of a specialist in computational linguistics the user may conduct a brief investigation to determine whether a full evaluation of a system is warranted. The user will, presumably, have carried out the studies indicated in phase I, so that he has a clear idea of his needs and constraints. Data for a brief investigation can be obtained in several ways:

- By studying the documentation supplied by the designer.
- By observing the designer's demonstration of the system and raising questions about its characteristics.
- By examining the system's dictionaries (see section 3.1 and section 5.3).
- By working with the system for a short period and submitting test sentences constructed on the basis of information obtained in phase I.

At the end of this investigation the user can decide on the advisability of conducting a full evaluation of the system.

In a full evaluation the user measures all aspects of the system's performance and, in addition, tries to determine the system's potential. In evaluating linguistic performance the user is guided by the requirements specified in the preparatory phase I.C. Of course, it is possible that the results of this evaluation may not be conclusive - especially for the purpose of long term projections. And the designer may promise that significant improvements are on the way. It is in this situation that an evaluation of the system's potential is particularly important. The user can determine for himself the likelihood of necessary improvements being carried out within acceptable time limits. By analyzing the kinds of errors tabulated during the performance evaluation and submitting additional test sentences with particular grammatical constructions, the user can assess the linguistic capability of the system with the aid of an error grid. In this way the user determines the improvability of the system in addition to evaluating its present performance.

IV. PRELIMINARY USE

Before adopting a system for long term use it is advisable to have a trial period, say six months or a year, during which the system is operated on the user's premises under actual working conditions. During this phase the user may

- identify indirect costs not seen in phase II
- observe the effect of longer training in the use of the system by translators and revisers
- make a deeper study of the environmental impact on the work place.

This trial period also allows time for the designer to demonstrate his ability to make improvements in the system resulting in the elimination of errors identified in phase III.

V. FINAL JUDGMENT

The results obtained in phases II and III may now be reviewed in the light of information gathered during the period of preliminary use. The user may also consider the translation system within the global context of the complete computerization of all aspects of production, including:

- printing
    - photocomposition
    - camera-ready copy
- storage of text and reference material
    - manipulation
    - correction
- translation

If the system fits well into the global context, meets the user's needs and constraints, and if the preliminary use confirms a favorable evaluation in phases II and III (or dispels doubts that may have arisen there), then the system is acceptable for acquisition by the given user. It should be stressed that although an evaluation of the kind we have been discussing is based on some very general linguistic principles, its aim is not to establish the universal acceptability of a system, but the acceptability for a user with particular needs and constraints; i.e., the methodology is general, but the results apply to a specific situation.

6. CONCLUSION

What can we conclude about the feasibility of machine translation? Is MT a viable alternative to human translation? Or should we expect the computer's role to be merely that of a translator's assistant, furnishing information on word meanings and usage (a **data bank**) and perhaps analyzing particular linguistic structures (**local analysis**)? Using the computer as a data bank may be a great help to the translator, but that does not constitute **machine translation**; and local analysis is not an effective way to use the computer in the translation process (see **sections 3.3** and **3.4**).

Machine translation suggests that the computer itself performs the translation, which involves at least a syntactic-semantic analysis of the whole sentence in addition to replacing words of the source language with those of the target language. **Machine-aided** translation (or computer-assisted translation), on the other hand, suggests the more modest goal of a translator's helper rather than his/her replacement. These terms were clarified in **section 2.1**, where a more detailed classification was given. In either case the output of the machine or man-machine combination is submitted to a human post-editor - as the translator's output always has been, even before the use of computers in translation.

Returning to the question of the feasibility of MT, we note that the obstacles are primarily linguistic, as detailed in **CHAPTER 3**. Critics of MT often seem to assume that a system should be capable of translating arbitrary texts, which, in our opinion, is too strong a demand. MT has already proven successful with texts from suitably restricted domains where the obstacles create less of a problem. In this respect MT is no different from natural language understanding systems in general (or, for that matter, from space exploration): some successes, many problems, gradual extension to larger, more complex domains.

In any applied science it is normal to find some problems for which no solution is known at the time. Unfortunately, the existence of such problems in MT in the late 1960s led to the abandonment of many projects and curtailment of research, especially in the U.S. More recently, in a number of countries, systems have been developed for limited uses and interest has been revived (e.g., two issues of the journal **Computational Linguistics** were devoted to machine translation in 1985). The question now is not whether MT (or AI, for that matter) is feasible, but in what domains it is most likely to be effective. As new systems are developed the assessment of their ability to cope with specific linguistic phenomena is a useful guide for further research and development. This is an important consideration in the presentation of evaluation methodology in **CHAPTER** 5.

Setting up a global methodology for evaluating all types of computerized translation systems for all users is a task that may not be possible to carry out completely. It requires a blending of linguistics, computer science and human translation while, at the same time, taking into account the wide variety of user's requirements. The present book certainly does not pretend to provide a solution to all of the problems involved. Furthermore, the aim has not been to criticize particular systems or approaches to translation, but to attempt to explain the nature and complexity of the problems of computerized translation by emphasizing the linguistic aspects of this operation.

The reader seeking a universal classification grid or a set of objective questions for evaluating any given system will be disappointed to find no such program offered here. A cookbook approach is too simplistic, given the variety and complexity of MT systems, the grammatical differences between texts from different domains (including texts whose norms deviate from the standard grammar) and the differences in users' requirements (even the minimum acceptable quality of the output depends on the intended use of the translation). We do hope, however, that the reader will now be able to construct for himself the tools he will need to evaluate a particular system for use in a particular situation.

Computer-assisted translation has so far experienced more failures than successes. This is not surprising, since human translation is a highly complex cognitive process. Nevertheless, in the present technological context, computers can certainly provide valuable assistance to the translator. This assistance must, however, be an accurate response to particular needs and constraints. The object of an evaluation is, of course, to determine whether a system permits an adequate response to given needs and constraints. Even though the implementation of the suggested evaluation methodology is a costly operation, it is justified, since the translator must be able to evaluate any proposed high-technology products in order to take a hand in shaping the evolution of his/her working environment.

CONCLUSION

Ideally, an evaluation should also serve to point out a system's specific weaknesses, the areas that need improvement and the limitations of the system. Such an evaluation goes beyond a cost-benefit study and examines the underlying linguistic model. That model may, in some cases, be revealed by studying the errors in the system's output. Such an evaluation can form an integral part of a research and development program.

As for the future of MT, we do not expect any miraculous breakthrough ushering in a new era and displacing human translators en masse. A more likely scenario is the increasing use of computers by human translators who perform the actual translation and, at the same time, an increase in the number of MT systems performing translation in limited domains. As designers incorporate more subtle syntactic-semantic analyses in their systems the quality and reliability of translation performed by the computer can be expected to improve. There will continue to be domains in which the complexity of texts is such that human translation is indispensable; in other domains the human component will consist chiefly of post-editing. The authors are convinced that research on fully automatic systems, with increased emphasis on semantic analysis, will produce the best results for MT in the long run.

NOTES

(1) The passive is identified by some form of BE with the past participle of the verb. These need not be contiguous and BE can be omitted in certain environments such as reduced relative clauses (see sections 3.3.2 and-3.3.3).

(2) In fact, economy in the statement of selectional restrictions between a verb and its arguments in the active and passive was one of the arguments given in support of transformational grammar in the 1950s; see, e.g., Chomsky (1957, pp. 42-43).

(3) In example (19) 'check out' refers to testing for proper operation. The relation also holds for 'check out' when it refers to vacating a hotel room (The clerk checked the guests out. The guests checked out.), but not when it refers to borrowing books from a library, equipment from a storeroom, etc. (He checked out the book (from the library). *The book checked out (from the library).).

(4) The broader the domain to be covered, the greater the risk of this happening. The advantages of restricted domains are discussed in section 2.5.

(5) We have changed the nomenclature slightly here for clarity of presentation. More details can be obtained from the documentation of the TAUM-AVIATION system; (see Bourbeau (1981a, 1981b), Stanton (1981).

(6) This represents the state of the system as documented in Chevalier et al (1978).

(7) See, e.g., King (1980) and King (1982, pp. 139-147).

(8) Although linguists usually assume a semantic level in language and posit a semantic component in their grammars, the role of semantics in machine translation is less clear than that of morphology and syntax. This is an area of active research. At any rate, it is included in (51) as a possible basis for a module.

(9) Sometimes the relations are not predictable and the compound word resembles an idiom (e.g., hook-up, as in 'a national radio hook-up'). In that case the whole word must be listed in the dictionary even though its parts are already there.

(10) For reference to the numerous studies made in the Soviet Union, see W. Moskovich's article "What is a sublanguage? The notion of sublanguage in modern Soviet linguistics" in Kittredge and Lehrberger (1982).

(11) Zellig Harris (1968) has pointed out that the grammar of a sublanguage L' of a language L is not necessarily a subgrammar of the grammar of L ; i.e., the sublanguage grammar may only intersect the grammar of L without being completely contained in it.

(12) This is not the same notion of information content used in communication theory and measured in "bits" (the basic unit, coined from 'bi(nary) (dig)it').

(13) A "literal" translation is given here - the kind usually turned out by machine translation.

(14) The following are simple sentences in English, under the above definition:

The baby is sleeping.
Many statements were false.
Give these horses some water.
A second notice has been sent to each offender.
There are two alternatives.
Can they go?

(15) For example, "a sentence containing only one clause", Quirk & al (1972).

(16) We may take the first argument of an adjective to be the word or phrase that it modifies.

(17) See, e.g., Mendelson (1964, p. 9) for a definition of partial order.

(18) This discussion holds only where the preposition in the complement is 'of'.

(19) In fact, the standard grammar approach does not try to describe the "whole" language, but the standard language (something like Chomsky's ideal speaker in an ideal community). The whole language would include an unknown number of sublanguages plus the standard language; that is not a likely candidate for machine translation.

(20) This is a simplified version of Table A in Annexe B of the report Lehrberger (1981).

APPENDIX A

A SYNTHESIS OF EVALUATIONS OF MACHINE TRANSLATION SYSTEMS

by

John Lehrberger

Montréal
1981

APPENDIX A

TABLE OF CONTENTS

A.1 OBJECTIVE

It may seem surprising that after so many evaluations of machine-aided translation systems[1] over the last few decades, no general methodology has been developed. There is still a strong ad hoc element in setting up an evaluation of a particular system for a particular customer on a particular occasion. In the present paper we examine the diverse factors that have entered into various evaluations of MAT systems in the past.

What is presented here is not an evaluation procedure or a set of procedures, but the elements out of which an evaluation procedure can be constructed once the demands of the potential user of the translation system and the type of system to be evaluated are known.

A.2 BASIC CONSIDERATIONS

Before setting up an evaluation the following points should be taken into consideration:

(i) the needs of the potential user;
(ii) the type of system to be evaluated;
(iii) the elements of the evaluation that need special emphasis, in view of (i) and (ii).

Because of the many different types of translation systems, some of them quite complex, there are a multitude of factors that might be evaluated. Of course, the decision as to which factors are to be given most attention and which, if any, are to be omitted is influenced not only by the user's requirements and the type of system to be evaluated, but by the resources available to the evaluators as well (time, money personnel).

A.2.1 NEEDS OF POTENTIAL USER

The following questions are important to ask when trying to decide whether a translation system meets the needs of a potential user.

---

[1] A machine-aided translation system (MAT) is one in which a computer is used as an aid in the translation process; the role of the computer may range from that of a tool employed by the human translator to a limited extent in what is still basically human translation to that of a fully automatic "translator" producing a finished text requiring only post-editing (such as that accorded to the output of a human translator).

APPENDIX A

- Does the user require high quality text in which style as well as grammatical correctness is an important factor?

- Or does the user simply require fidelity to the original text in terms of information content, with less emphasis on grammaticality and/or style?

- Does the user expect to employ a fair number of translators and revisers to work with the machine, possibly interactively?

- Or does the user expect to perform only a small amount of human post-editing of the raw machine output?

- What range of subject matter must the user translate?

  Texts from a single domain?
  Texts from a number of related domains?
  Texts from a wide range of unrelated domains?

- Will the final users of the finished translations consist of

  . scientists scanning articles for research information?
  . technicians following instructions from a maintenance manual?
  . military personnel reading messages from a command center?
  . people reading job notices in an employment office?
  . etc.

- What is the relative importance of cost and time to the company or government agency making use of the translation system?

  Does the need for a speedy translation outweigh the cost involved?

  Is a large initial investment prohibitive?

  Over what period of time must the initial investment be amortized?

A.2.2 TYPES OF MACHINE-AIDED TRANSLATION SYSTEMS

A.2.2.1 FIRST OR SECOND GENERATION

Translation systems are often classified as first or second generation (and possibly third generation[2]). There is some disagreement about the use of these terms, and the situation is even less clear in the case of so-called third generation systems.

For our purpose we may characterize the translation process in a **first generation system** as "direct" translation. Such a system does little more than plug in a word or expression of the target language for a word or expression of the source language text, with only a limited examination, if any, of the context in which the word or expression occurs in the original text. A string of words in the source language is converted to a string in the target language with minimal or no grammatical analysis.

On the other hand, a **second generation system** analyzes the entire sentence, assigns it a structure, and uses information about the roles of the source language words in this structure to determine their equivalents in the target language and the grammatical roles of these equivalents in the corresponding sentence in the target language.

From a theoretical point of view second generation systems are of greater interest since they convey more information about the sentence being translated. Furthermore, they offer the possibility of an intermediate representation of the sentence and its structure in a **pivot language** - a sort of "deep" structure of the sentence[3]. This pivot language representation can

---

[2] Beyond second generation systems there are experiments with techniques from the field of artificial intelligence. These usually involve a much stronger reliance on semantics, including inferencing both within and beyond the sentence boundary. Looking to the not-so-near future, such systems may provide the best means to obtain fully automatic translation of very complicated texts; but for the moment we will limit our discussion to those systems that seem to offer solutions in the short run.

[3] This is not be confused with Chomskian deep structure. Here we refer to an abstract syntactic-semantic representation of the sentence, containing as much syntactic and semantic information about the sentence as the system's analysis of the source language sentence can provide.

then be used as a basis for generating translations of the original text in a number of different target languages.

Second generation systems may be primarily syntactic, offering no appreciable semantic analysis, or they may incorporate a semantic system to aid in reducing ambiguity and in solving problems of homography. A common method is to introduce semantic features (or markers) which are assigned to a word to indicate the different senses it may have and which help to identify the semantic nature of possible subjects and objects of verbs as well as the kinds of nouns that a given adjective can modify.

A.2.2.2 FULLY AUTOMATIC OR INTERACTIVE

From another point of view, systems may be ranked according to their degree of automaticity. A system may be fully automatic or interactive; if interactive, it may provide basically human translation with some assistance from the machine, or basically machine translation with some assistance from the human translator. This yields the following classification:

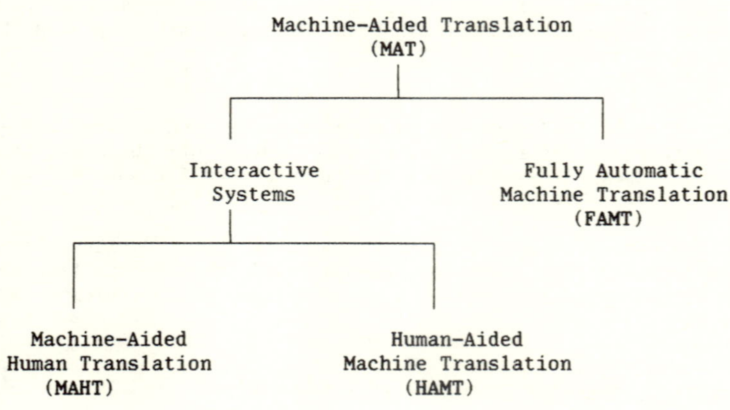

It is not easy to draw the boundary between MAHT and HAMT, but the extremes are clear enough.

At one end of the spectrum, MAHT may simply consist of a word processor with dictionary look-up to furnish the translator with possible target language equivalents for words in the original text. The translator may also have the possibility of updating the dictionary.

In the case of HAMT, the machine performs the translation, but during the translation of a sentence the machine may require information supplied by the human translator. It may, for example, make requests such as the following at certain stages in the translation of a sentence:

- What is the grammatical category (noun, verb, adjective, etc.) of an occurrence of some word in the sentence?

- What is the scope of an occurrence of a coordinate conjunction (e.g., **and**) in the sentence? (I.e., what groups of words are conjoined by the given occurrence of the conjunction?)

- Does an occurrence of a certain preposition in the sentence go with a verb to form a **verb + particle** combination, or does it introduce a prepositional phrase?

There are, of course, many other requests the machine might make; the point is that the human translator supplies some information to the machine after it begins processing the sentence and before it has completed the translation of that sentence.

In the case of FAMT there is no human intervention between the input of the original text and the final raw machine output of the translated text; human revision takes place only after the machine has finished its work.

In a further refinement of FAMT the machine itself decides which of the sentences submitted to it are to be revised, all others being translated and considered suitable as finished text without any human revision (e.g., the METEO system).

A.2.2.3 ANALYSIS, TRANSFER AND GENERATION COMPONENTS

The two broad classifications discussed above (first versus second generation, and FAMT versus interactive systems) are fairly well known in the literature on MAT. Such classifications are of more than academic interest since they give a clue as to the limitations and improvability of a system,- and they may serve as a guideline in setting up an evaluation procedure for a system.

Thus for certain interactive systems, raw machine output may not be a relevant factor in an evaluation. If a system has separate analysis, transfer and generation components, an evaluation of the performance of each component may be crucial in determining the improvability of the system. And if the machine has no semantic component an evaluator may be able to determine that the machine alone will be limited in dealing with complicated texts because of certain problems (e.g., homography, noun-noun compounds, scope of conjunction) which will have to be left to a human reviser.

There are, of course, many particular features of MAT systems that may be of interest to a potential user. For example:

- number and types of dictionaries (building and updating dictionaries for texts in various fields could be very costly);

- kinds of software (it may be easier to incorporate new linguistic rules if the linguists themselves are able to program these rules, and specialized high level languages have been developed for this purpose).

Particular features of MAT systems that enter into an evaluation will be discussed further in A.2.3.

A.2.3 MAJOR FACTORS TO BE EVALUATED

The many different factors that might be evaluated are grouped below under six major headings:

1. COST
2. TIME
3. QUALITY
4. IMPROVABILITY
5. EXTENDABILITY
6. FACILITY

The order of importance of these factors will depend on the needs of the potential user of the translation system and the constraints under which the user operates.

The number and kind of people required to carry out an evaluation will depend on its extent and what factors, if any, are to be omitted. But in the most general case an evaluation may require the services of translators, revisers, linguists, computer scientists, statisticians, and specialists in the field from which the translated texts are taken.

We will now examine the factors 1-6 in detail.

A.2.3.1 COST

- INITIAL ACQUISITION
  - Hardware: Purchase
Installation
  - Software

  Or, if outright ownership is not required:

- LEASING
  - Hardware
  - Software

- COMPUTER PROCESSING
  - Computer cost per word during translation
  - Fixed set-up cost per text submitted
  - Computer cost for making and updating dictionary entries

- MAINTENANCE
  - Hardware
  - Software
  - Documentation updating

- TRAINING
  - Teaching personnel to use the system

- HUMAN COMPONENT OF INTERACTIVE SYSTEM
  - Cost of human translator working with interactive system

- REVISION
  - Human post-editing of raw machine output or of translator-revised output of interactive system

APPENDIX A

. **DICTIONARY WORK**

- Human cost of making and updating dictionary entries
  (a) permanent dictionary
  (b) local dictionary

. **TEXT PREPARATION**

- Putting source text into machine readable form for submission to system.

- Putting translated text (after revision) into final form for delivery to final user.

. **VARIATION OF OPERATING COST WITH TEXT VOLUME**

- Determining the relation between cost of operating the system and number of words of text processed per year.

. **VARIATION OF OPERATING COST WITH DICTIONARY SIZE**

- This does not refer to the cost of making dictionary entries (which has already been mentioned), but to increases in costs due to greater incidence of homography resulting in

  (i) lengthier computer processing,
  (ii) more frequent human interaction, in the case of interactive systems, and
  (iii) increased burden on revisers to correct mistakes involving wrong word choices in translation of homographs.

. **AMORTIZATION**

- When the above costs have been determined, it should be possible to calculate the period of amortization, assuming a certain volume of texts per year.

. **TOTAL ACQUISITION**

- If the aim of an evaluation is to decide whether to take complete control of a system rather than simply pay for its use, then the cost of funding a development team as well as a maintenance team must be taken into consideration. (In some cases it may also be desirable to consider funding research within the framework of the system acquired.)

A.2.3.2 TIME

Cost and time are, of course, interdependent factors. Normally one expects to pay more for more time, although total cost also depends on the ratio of human time to computer time and on how human time is divided between translators and revisers in an interactive system.

It should be noted, however, that there may be some applications where speed of translation is so important that it outweighs considerations of cost and even the quality of translation.

The total time for producing a finished translation, ready for delivery to the final user, can be broken down as follows:

. Time to put texts into machine readable form.

. Processing, or raw output time.

"Raw output" may refer to raw machine output in the case of FAMT systems or to the output of the man-machine combination before post-editing in the case of interactive systems.

. Revision time.

A comparison of the time taken to revise the output of an MAT system and a human translator will be of interest. In the Machine Translation Feasibility Study report to the Secretary of State Department (Gobeil 1981), it is stated (p. 91) that revision of MAT, in the cases studied, generally "took longer than the time required to revise an equal number of words translated by a human translator." An objective method of measuring the difficulty of revising MAT raw output is to compare the time for revising MAT output and that of human translators.

For control, it is desirable to have the same text translated by the MAT system and the human translators.

. Processing time per phase

For information about the internal working of the system it may be useful to know the time spent at various stages in processing a sentence (e.g., analysis, transfer, generation).

A.2.3.3 QUALITY

Judgments of translation quality tend to be subjective and difficult to quantify. Various methods have been used to increase the objectivity of quality assessments and remove variations inherent in subjective evaluations.

The Translation Bureau of the Government of Canada has been using a system for quality control of human translators which is based on the number and seriousness of errors in the translated text, with definite criteria for recording the judgments.

In the 1980 evaluation of TAUM-AVIATION (Gervais 1980) a ranking of the acceptability by potential users was included. Each user established his own ranking criteria.

The evaluation of the 1978 version of SYSTRAN (English to French) for the Commission of European Communities (Van Slype 1979) also included a sampling of users opinions to determine the acceptability of the translation.

Of course, acceptability should be judged relative to the particular situation in which the translated text is to be used: what is considered acceptable quality in one situation may not be so in another.

In order to counteract the effect of extraneous factors on the evaluation of quality, it was suggested in the report of the 1980 evaluation of TAUM-AVIATION that more weight be given to a comparison of the quality of machine translation and human translation than to an absolute measure of quality.

The ALPAC report (Pierce, Carroll, et al, 1966) suggested using at least three or four raters to neutralize the effect of individual variations among raters.

We will now examine three main ingredients of translation quality: fidelity, intelligibility and style.

A. FIDELITY

The fidelity of a translation is the extent to which the translated text contains the same information as the original. The problem for the evaluator is to set up definite criteria for measuring fidelity.

John B. Carroll devised an indirect method[4] for measuring translation fidelity, based on the **informativeness** of the original relative to the translated text: after digesting the meaning of the latter, the rater is then asked to read the original and see how much information it adds to the translated version. If the original is very informative relative to the translated text, the fidelity is low; if the original adds little or no information, the fidelity is high. Carroll used the following 10 point rating scale for informativeness:

9. Extremely informative. Makes "all the difference in the world" in comprehending the meaning intended. (A rating of 9 should always be assigned when the original **completely** changes or reverses the meaning conveyed by the translation.)

8. Very informative. Contributes a great deal to the clarification of the meaning intended. By correcting sentence structure, words, and phrases, it makes a great change in the reader's impression of the meaning intended, although not so much as to change or reverse the meaning completely.

7. (Between 6 and 8.)

6. Clearly informative. Adds considerable information about the sentence structure and individual words, putting the reader "on the right track" as to the meaning intended.

5. (Between 4 and 6.)

4. In contrast to 3, adds a certain amount of information about the sentence structure and syntactical relationships; it may also correct minor misapprehensions about the general meaning of the sentence or the meaning of individual words.

---

[4] See ALPAC report, Appendix 10: **An Experiment in Evaluating the Quality of Translations**, (Pierce, Carroll, et al, 1966).

3. By correcting one or two possibly critical meanings, chiefly on the word level, it gives a slightly different "twist" to the meaning conveyed by the translation. It adds no new information about sentence structure, however.

2. No really new meaning is added by the original, either at the word level or the grammatical level, but the reader is somewhat more confident that he apprehends the meaning intended.

1. Not informative at all; no new meaning is added, nor is the reader's confidence in his understanding increased or enhanced.

0. The original contains, if anything, less information than the translation. The translator has added certain meanings, apparently to make the passage more understandable.

Carroll applied this method to individual sentences; a variant of it has also been applied using textual units. In any case, raters must be given careful instruction and practice in the application of these criteria.

In the evaluation of TAUM-AVIATION (Gervais 1980), fidelity was defined as "the extent to which the information contained in the original text is found without distortion in the translation"; a five point rating scale was used.

B. INTELLIGIBILITY

Fidelity does not guarantee intelligibility, nor does intelligibility guarantee fidelity; these two factors can be evaluated separately.

Error rate may give some clue to the intelligibility of a translation (e.g., the number of corrections made per 100 words of text), but this can be deceptive. Some errors affect fidelity rather than intelligibility, and of those which do affect intelligibility certain types of errors reduce intelligibility much more than others.

A number of evaluations of intelligibility have been made by establishing a scale which raters can use directly to mark the degree of intelligibility; the problem, of course, is to obtain uniform judgments by the raters.

Following this approach, John B. Carroll devised a nine point scale ranging from "Perfectly clear and intelligible" (9) to "Hopelessly unintelligible" (1). In establishing this scale (and also the one for informativeness), before the actual evaluation, Carroll applied a psychometric technique known as "the method of equal appearing intervals" to ensure that points on the scales would be equally spaced in terms of subjectively observed differences. (A detailed description of the points on the intelligibility scale is found in the ALPAC report, p. 69.)

The report of Gervais (1980) defined **intelligibility** as "the degree of clarity and comprehensibility of each sentence". A five point scale was used for rating the intelligibility of the translated text.

A comparison of the time it takes to read a text translated by an MAT system and the reading time for a human translation of the same text may also be used as an indication of the intelligibility of the system-translated text: reading speed should increase along with intelligibility, other things being equal.

The Cloze technique[5], a test of readability based on the gestalt concept and linked with textual cohesiveness, measures the success of a reader in replacing words that have been deleted from a translated text. Subjects are asked to fill in the blanks in the text and then the score is determined by the number of correct responses. A correct response may be taken either as the exact word deleted or as any word that yields a paraphrase of the original text. The words deleted may be chosen from the text on a random basis or every n^{th} word may be deleted (Crook and Bishop deleted every eighth word). Readability of the translated text, as measured by this technique, is assumed to be correlated with intelligibility.

The 1977 RADC[6] final report states: "This factor [readability] was in-

---

5 Devised by W.S. Taylor ("Cloze Procedure: A New Tool for Measuring Readability", The Journalism Quarterly, Fall 1953, pp 415-433) and applied by M.N. Crook and H.P. Bishop ("Evaluation of Machine Translation", Final Report, The Institute for Psychological Research, Tufts University, April 1965).

6 Rome Air Development Center Final Technical Report, January 1977: "The Evaluation and Systems Analysis of the SYSTRAN Machine Translation System" (Battelle Columbus Laboratories).

cluded mainly for a theoretical study of possible effects on interaction among major components selected. One testing technique only has been applied to the component of readability - the Cloze technique. It was to be applied to the testing of readability under the following conditions: regular interval elimination of words from a sample test, and acceptance of paraphrases of the original text."

It can be seen from these different methods of evaluating intelligibility that either the evaluation depends to a large extent on subjective judgments (with certain safeguards to ensure uniformity) or the evaluation depends on the presumed correlation between intelligibility and some more objectively measurable factor.

C. STYLE

The style of a "literary work" (e.g., a novel) depends on the author, but scientific and technical texts, government notices, instruction booklets, etc. usually have a style that depends on the field and on the purpose of the text. For example, in an aviation technical manual those sections describing the theory of operation of the aircraft have a characteristic style and those sections dealing with maintenance and repair of the aircraft have a somewhat different style (purpose = instructions for carrying out certain procedures).

A high quality translation should have a style which is appropriate for the field of the text and the use to which the text will be put.

The style of a text may be rated on some scale, just as in the case of fidelity and intelligibility, although the defining criteria may be somewhat more difficult to specify in such a way that uniform ratings are obtainable over a variety of texts where several raters are involved.

In the evaluation of Gervais (1980) a five-point rating scale was used. The extreme values were established (5 = highest quality; 1 = poorest quality), and the midpoint, 3, was taken as the "passing mark"; 2 and 4 were simply used as intermediate values. A rating of less than 3 meant that the translation was not acceptable. Raters were given practice in using the scale until agreement was obtained on the rating of practice texts.

It may be that there is an essential difference in rating the quality of raw machine output and that of human translators, given the present state of the art in machine translation[7]. A reviser might be inclined to reject out of hand the kind of translations produced by the machine. This can be seen from the comments in the "Summary Report of Revisers' Comments on Machine Produced Translations" (Van Slype, Working Document for the CETIL Meeting (26, 27 March 1979):

> "All the revisers were agreed that their task was at best fruitless and at worst impossible. ... The consensus was that if such work had been presented by a human translator, that person would not have remained long in the employ of the Commission."

Perhaps the conclusion that can be drawn is that revisers need to develop a different tolerance for machine translation, at least for the present, and view the revision of machine output as a somewhat different task. Potential users with cost-effectiveness uppermost in mind will likely expect such tolerance from revisers.

A.2.3.4 IMPROVABILITY

To determine the improvability of a system it is necessary to analyze the performance of its components as well as the overall performance of the system.

- It is easier to make changes in some components of an MAT system than in others. Dictionary updating can usually be done by a translator whereas changes in parsing rules may require a linguist with training in computer programming.

- Changes in one component of a system may affect the functioning of other components. Thus changes in the dictionary may affect certain parsing rules. The effect is not necessarily detrimental: putting more information into dictionary entries might enable the parser to make finer distinctions between syntactic structures or to build semantic-syntactic representations of the sentences in the text that

[7] From an academic point of view it would be interesting to consider the revisable raw machine outputs as dialects (or ideolects) of the target language, each system producing texts having characteristic deviations from standard usage in the fields of the texts.

provide more information for making correct word choices in the target language.

- Within the dictionary component it is necessary to know how the addition of new entries affects the old ones. For example, the statement of predicate-argument relations for existing entries may need revision as a result of new entries. This was the case, e.g., in the feasibility study for extending TAUM-AVIATION to cover the field of electronics (see Lehrberger 1981).

- It is also important to know what problems are "solved" in a system by introducing large numbers of idioms (multi-word expressions) in the dictionary, since this may create some problems while solving others. Often a string of words that forms an idiom in one context is not idiomatic in another context, and false readings may result from entering the expression as an idiom in the dictionary. Thus if **check points** is interpreted as an idiom, **Locate all check points** will be parsed correctly, but **Check points for pitting** will not; it is still necessary to analyze **check points** as a possible verb + noun combination. In short, the introduction of large numbers of multi-word strings as single dictionary entries is not likely to improve performance in the long run unless the system is able to detect "false idioms" in context and re-analyze the sentences containing them.

- The error **rate** (e.g., number of corrections made per 100 words of text) in the raw output of a system offers an objective measurement of improvement resulting from changes in the system (updating the dictionaries, adding rules to the parser, etc.); but the **kinds** of errors remaining will determine how much more improvement is possible. If most of the errors are of types for which solutions are known, and these solutions do not involve changes in the basic design of the system, the prospects for improvement are good. But if the correction of errors depends on basic research in difficult problem areas where no solution is known within the framework of the system being evaluated, the improvability of the system is questionable. A thorough classification of types of errors will help the evaluators decide whether a given system is capable of dealing with texts of a certain degree of complexity and, if so, what amount of effort is likely to be required, in terms of research and/or development, to make the necessary improvements in the system. Clearly, some knowledge of the internal workings of the system and its components is needed to carry out an evaluation of this type.

. LIMITATIONS

Given sufficient knowledge of a system, it may be possible to establish upper limits of improvements in the performance of the system, and to draw up a list of problems that cannot be overcome within the current design. Following are a few examples:

- If a system is designed to translate sentences one at a time, without referring to the content of preceding sentences in the text, then it will not be able to cope with intersentential anaphora. Such problems must then be left to the human translator.

- A system with no semantic capability, or perhaps only semantic markers to help identify complements of verbs and adjectives, is not likely to be able to analyze and correctly interpret noun-noun compounds in technical fields where these abound. For example, in aviation maintenance manuals one finds:

  . fan nozzle discharge static pressure water manometer;
  . No. 2 and 3 nacelle outboard leading edge fillet lower access door blowout door assemblies;
  . pulse analyzer indicator signal conditioning indicator;
  etc.

Such compounding is highly productive in English, so the problem cannot be solved by simply entering all these expressions in the dictionary.

- There is a need to investigate the limit of improvement possible for various MAT systems through dictionary updating. The Rome Air Development Center report (Halliday and Briss 1977) on the evaluation of SYSTRAN concluded (p. 70):

  "Lexical updating produces strong carry-over effects from the test sample to related texts. The rate of improvement appears to be a diminishing one, although the actual rate is not identifiable at present. ... Further research of the same type in one of these technical areas could determine the rate of diminishing return for lexical improvement. The same type of study ... could determine the upper bound of improvement achievable through lexical updating."

Since lexical updating is frequently the main source of improvement, determining this upper bound is crucial in evaluating the improvability of a system.

- Computer limitations are easier to determine than limitations due to linguistic aspects of a system; the relevant factors are storage capacity and memory. As for the number of words of text that can be processed per hour, it should be kept in mind that this depends to a considerable extent on the depth of analysis of the sentence undertaken by the system. A deeper analysis may require more processing time, but it may also yield higher quality translation with less recourse to human assistance.

. RESEARCH AND DEVELOPMENT

Apart from the properties of the system itself, the emphasis on research and development determines the extent to which possible improvements are actually carried out. It will therefore be of interest to note whether the company which owns the system has active programs for extending linguistic analyses and improving the softwares. Flexibility and adaptability of softwares will facilitate utilization of the results of linguistic analyses, and the development and implementation of high level languages will enable linguists to write their own programs.

A.2.3.5 EXTENDABILITY

The application of an MAT system may be extended in several ways:

(A) from a given domain of texts to other related domains;

(B) from a given domain (or set of related domains) to an unrelated domain;

(C) from one language pair to other language pairs.

A. EXTENSION TO RELATED DOMAINS

Extending the text coverage from one domain to a related domain involves expansion of the dictionary to cover technical terms from the new domain and possibly expansion of the grammar if new structures are encountered.

Presumably there will be a "core" vocabulary and grammar common to both domains. It must not be assumed, however, that the lexical entries and grammar rules of a system that deal with this common core before the extension will be unaffected by the extension.

Concerning lexical coverage, "extendability" does not refer merely to the capacity of the dictionary to hold the necessary additional lexical items. As new words are added, some will be homographs of words already present, including words of the core vocabulary. These homographs (words that are spelled the same, but have different meanings) introduce ambiguities that may create serious problems for analysis of the source text and choice of word equivalents in the target language. Extendability depends on the ability of the system to cope with the homography problem.

Even within a single domain homography can be expected to increase as more words are added to the dictionary. If this problem becomes unmanageable as text coverage within a domain increases, extension of that coverage to other domains does not seem feasible.

Grammatical differences between texts may be correlated with differences in **function**. A text whose function is to instruct personnel to carry out maintenance procedures on some equipment will consist mainly of imperative sentences ("Remove cover plate") and conditionals ("If pressure is low, adjust valve"); but a text whose function is to explain the theory of operation of the same equipment will usually consist mainly of declarative sentences, which are apt to be longer and involve fewer deletions of articles (in English). Extending the application of a system to a related domain may not therefore introduce much in the way of new syntactic structures if the texts serve the same function, whereas extending to texts having a different function in the same domain may introduce significant changes in syntax[a].

At any rate, an important factor to investigate in order to evaluate the extendability of a system to new texts is the **completeness** of the system's grammars. True, no computer program is likely to cover all grammatical relations in a natural language, but within certain sublanguages the coverage can be fairly exhaustive. Some knowledge of the properties of specific sublanguages, their lexical and grammatical "overlap", and hierarchical relations

---

[a] Of course, we could say that procedures for maintaining a certain type of equipment and the theory of operation of that equipment are, in fact, different (but related) domains. However, I will continue to use the word "domain" in the sense indicated above, since this corresponds more to the usual practice.

among them is essential for evaluating the extendability of a system to new types of texts.

B. EXTENSION TO UNRELATED DOMAINS

Texts from unrelated domains may differ in vocabulary only, or in both grammar and vocabulary. Generally speaking, however, the problems mentioned in (A) can be expected to become more difficult when extending the application of a system from certain domains to unrelated ones.

Vocabulary differences show up mostly in technical terms characteristic of the subject matter dealt with; there is a "core" vocabulary, including certain prepositions, conjunctions, articles and quantifiers, that is common to most texts. Nevertheless, introduction of many new words outside this core greatly increases the chances for ambiguity resulting from homography. Separate dictionaries for different domains or some form of modularization of the dictionaries is necessary to help eliminate such ambiguities. But this alone by no means guarantees success; it is only the minimum requirement for disambiguating homographs. Ultimately one has to look beyond mere separation of dictionaries to the investigation of semantic relations within, and even between, the sentences of a text. A weak semantic component, or none at all, will hinder the extension of a system to different domains (to say nothing of such problems as noun-noun compounds and scope of conjunction, which also require semantic solutions within a single domain). Lacking an adequate semantic component, a system relies all the more on human translators or revisers to disambiguate words with multiple senses. This must be taken into account when evaluating the extendability to different domains.

It was shown more than a decade ago that subject matter is one determiner of rules of grammar that differ from those of the "standard" language[9]; recent research has added confirmation to this finding[10].

---

9 See, e.g., section 5.9 ("Sublanguage") of Zellig Harris (1968).

10 For example, studies of the grammars of particular sublanguages at New York University (the Linguistic String Project) and at the University of Montreal (Project TAUM).

If a system's grammar is designed to translate specialized texts with highly deviant syntax, that system may not be extendable, without basic changes in design, to other fields. Thus TAUM-METEO could not be extended to cover aircraft maintenance manuals simply by enlarging its dictionary to include terms from the new field; in fact, weather bulletins and aircraft maintenance manuals have radically different grammars.

To evaluate the extendability of a system from texts in one domain to those in an unrelated domain, it is necessary to know (among other things) the grammatical peculiarities of the system. Since there are so many different sublanguages with different grammatical properties, it will be advantageous to be able to describe any of their grammars, as well as the grammar of the system under evaluation, in terms of deviation from or conformity to a grammar of the standard language, expressed in terms of some model of language.

C. EXTENSION TO NEW LANGUAGE PAIRS

Extending a translation system to new language pairs involves writing new grammars, new word replacement rules, etc. - a complex time-consuming enterprise. One way to reduce the amount of work in dealing with many language pairs would be to make use of a universal pivot language into which each source language would be translated and from which each target language would be generated. If there are n source languages, then without a pivot language each target language must be generated directly from n different sources; but with a pivot language, all target languages could be generated directly from one source. This concept of a universal pivot language, perhaps a semantic language of some sort, is a hope for the future; for the present we may content ourselves with a less ambitious scheme which consists of an intermediate representation conforming to certain syntactic constraints, but still containing the words of the source language. The results of the analysis of any source language are put into this general form prior to generation of the target language. In this way, there is at least a general structure which serves as a basis for the generation of all target languages. Such an intermediate representation is compatible with second generation systems (as discussed in section A.2.2.1). For example, TAUM's **normalized structure** is a "pivot language" in this sense; some version of it could, presumably, be used for language pairs other than English-French. Essentially it consists of giving each sentence a representation in terms of its predicate-argument structure, which is a general notion, not dependent on a particular language. In certain respects it resembles the notion of "deep structure" in transformational grammar; in other respects it is quite different.

The presence of some form of pivot language (or intermediate structure) in an automatic translation system should enhance the prospects for extending that system to many language pairs.

A.2.3.6 FACILITY

In this section we consider factors that enter into the actual use of an MAT system by the customer. The following questions are pertinent to an evaluation of "ease of use" of the system.

- Does the system operate in batch or interactive mode?
- Training:
  - How much skill is needed by personnel using the system?
  - What is the length of training required?
  - In what languages is training available?
- Can a monolingual use the system?
  Or does it required a bilingual person?
- Physical strain:
  - Does the type of display used create eye fatigue?
  - Is the printout easy to read?
- Mental strain:
  - Does the quality of the raw machine output disturb or create hostility in the revisers?
  - How well do the revisers adjust to the raw machine output?
- Documentation of the system:
  - What kind of documentation is provided to the user?
  - In what languages is it provided?
- Dictionaries:
  - What dictionaries are provided to the user?
  - Can any user update the dictionaries?
  - Does lexical updating require much special training?

- Interactivity:
  - What is the range of questions the translator can ask the machine?
  - What is the range of questions the machine can ask the translator?
  - Is a KWIC (Key Word In Context) display available to the translator for each word of text?
  - What kinds of temporary files can the translator create (from information stored in the computer as well as information from the text being processed).

- Type of input:
  - Magnetic tape?
  - Diskette?
  - OCR facilities? (Optical Character Reading)
  - Provision for interface with customer's word processing or typesetting system?

- Operating environment:
  - Centralized?
  - Decentralized?

- Does the system keep its own statistics on time spent in each phase?

A.2.4 ADDENDA

- The cost factor is usually of such importance that other factors might easily be overlooked; however, a little reflection reveals their significance in the long run. It is not difficult to imagine situations where speed of translation is of the utmost importance, outweighing even the cost. And whatever the cost estimates may be, the future value of a system depends also on its improvability and extendability.

- Evaluation of components vs evaluation of the whole system. The attitude that the performance of the system as a whole alone determines its value ignores the fact that improvement in the performance of the system and extension to new types of texts are dependent on the limitations inherent in various components, or the complete lack of a particular component (e.g., semantic). The study of linguistic errors sheds light on the adequacy of the various components; this study should be conducted by linguists with a good knowledge of machine translation and a good scheme for classifying errors within the framework of some model of language.

. Self-improvement

A desirable feature in an MAT system is the ability of the machine to examine its own output and take further steps to improve that output without human assistance.

For example, if full analysis of a sentence fails because semantic or grammatical constraints of the system are not satisfied, these constraints may be selectively relaxed until the sentence is successfully parsed[11].

Another example of a system's ability to make self-adjustments involves the listing of translation equivalents for a given word in the source text. If the machine keeps track of the number of times each translation equivalent of a given word is actually chosen to translate that word, then the equivalent with the highest score may be displayed at the top of the list when the given word occurs in the source text next time. In this way, the order in which the choices are displayed comes to reflect their frequency of occurrence in the field of the texts being translated. It is a convenient adjustment to the domain from which the texts are taken[12].

. When comparing the results from two or more MAT systems, using the same texts, care must be taken to ensure that the "arrangements" for the evaluation do not accidentally favor one system over the others.

For example, during the Translation Bureau's evaluation (see Gobeil 1981) of SYSTRAN II, ALPS and WEIDNER, each of the three revisers revised the translations in a different order: (1) SYSTRAN II, WEIDNER, ALPS; (2) WEIDNER, ALPS, SYSTRAN II; (3) ALPS, SYSTRAN II, WEIDNER. As stated in the final report, "This made it possible to counteract the effect of getting accustomed to the text".

---

[11] In the current version of TAUM-AVIATION (1981) selectional restrictions between predicates and their arguments are dropped if full analysis of a sentence is blocked. This has resulted in translations in many cases where no output was obtained before relaxing the restrictions.

[12] This method of adjusting the dictionary to the field of the texts has been used in the Japanese Word Processor (JWP), at Toshiba Corporation, Kawasaki, Japan.

- For control, the same text can be translated by human translators as well as by the MAT system being evaluated. To avoid any interaction, revisers of the two translations should not be the same persons.

It is not inconceivable that revisers, who are former translators, may have some bias against the machine. In discussing revision of machine translations some of the more bizarre errors made by the machine are a natural source of ridicule. Precautions are needed to achieve objectivity. It may be helpful to have the revisers become well acquainted with the machine and spend some time revising its output.

- Before evaluating an interactive system translators must be given sufficient practice so that they can adapt thoroughly to using the machine, hopefully regarding it as an aid rather than a threat.

APPENDIX B

AN EXAMPLE OF A FULLY AUTOMATIC MT CHAIN

Appendix B contains a flowchart of the TAUM-AVIATION system developed at the University of Montreal. High level languages such as Rezo (a version of ATN for parsing), Lextra (for lexical translation) and Q-Systems (for synthesis of the target language) are used to permit linguists and translators to write grammar programs directly in this system. The following legend will help the reader to understand the flowchart.

Underlined	Grammars and dictionaries (data base).
Normal	Processing of data base information before translation process.
Bold Face	Processing executed during the translation process.
CAPITAL	Intermediate data file (Input/Output).
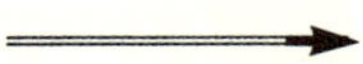	Information flow.
	Sequence of translation phases.
SL	Source Language (English)
TL	Target Language (French)

APPENDIX B

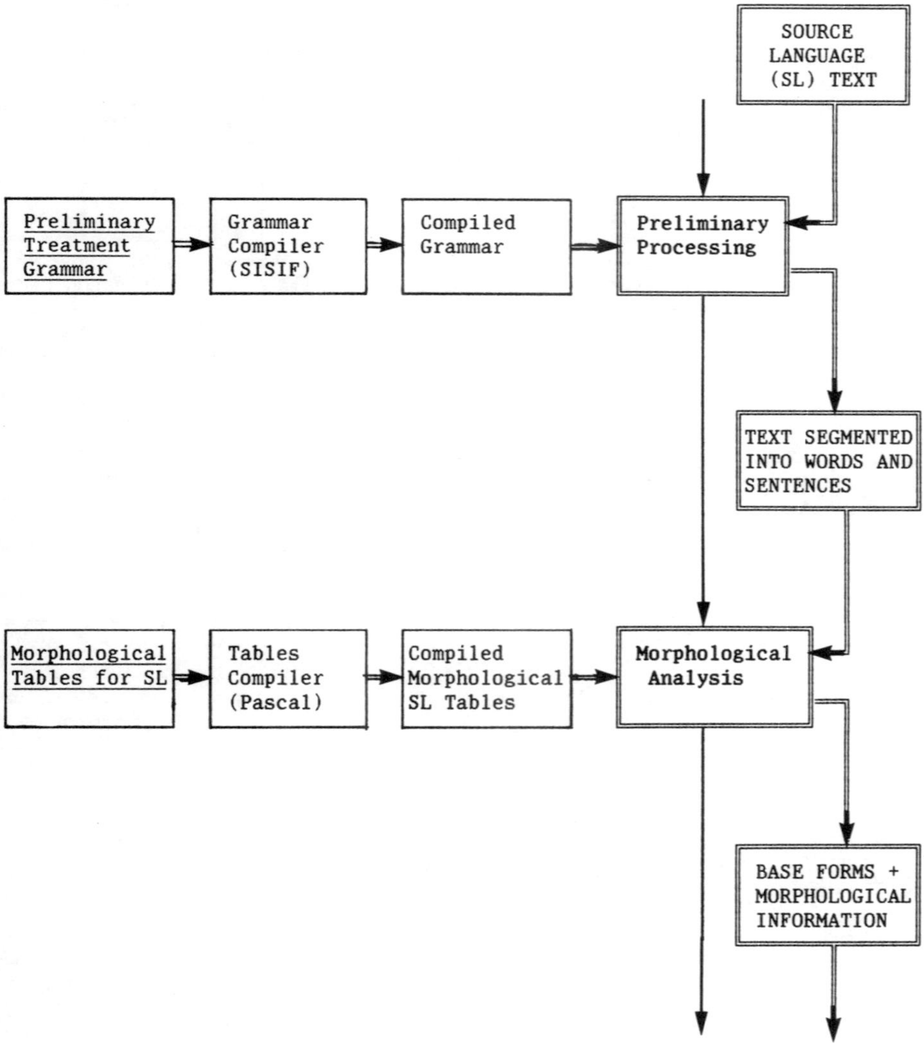
SOURCE LANGUAGE (SL) TEXT
Preliminary Treatment Grammar
Grammar Compiler (SISIF)
Compiled Grammar
Preliminary Processing
TEXT SEGMENTED INTO WORDS AND SENTENCES
Morphological Tables for SL
Tables Compiler (Pascal)
Compiled Morphological SL Tables
Morphological Analysis
BASE FORMS + MORPHOLOGICAL INFORMATION

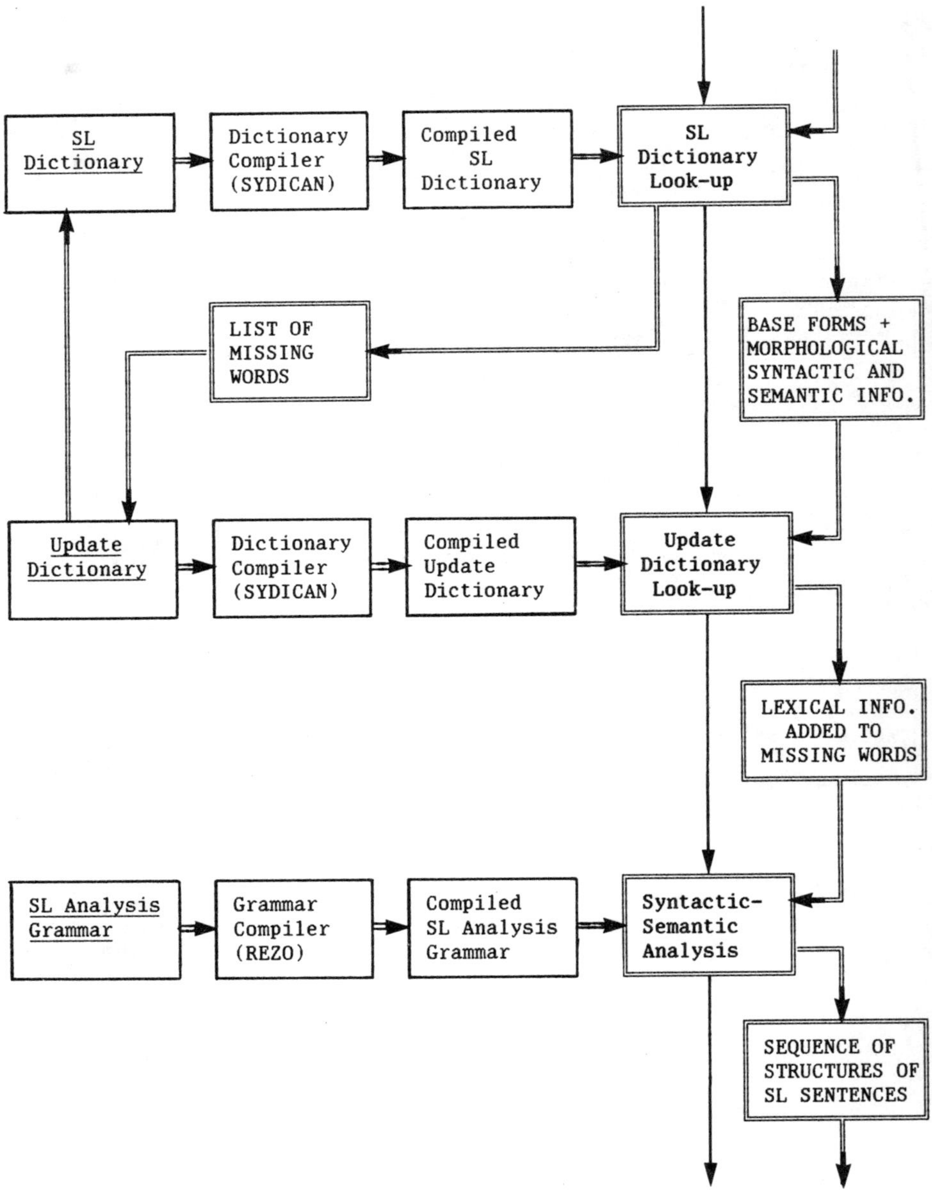
SL Dictionary
Dictionary Compiler (SYDICAN)
Compiled SL Dictionary
SL Dictionary Look-up
LIST OF MISSING WORDS
BASE FORMS + MORPHOLOGICAL SYNTACTIC AND SEMANTIC INFO.
Update Dictionary
Dictionary Compiler (SYDICAN)
Compiled Update Dictionary
Update Dictionary Look-up
LEXICAL INFO. ADDED TO MISSING WORDS
SL Analysis Grammar
Grammar Compiler (REZO)
Compiled SL Analysis Grammar
Syntactic-Semantic Analysis
SEQUENCE OF STRUCTURES OF SL SENTENCES

APPENDIX B

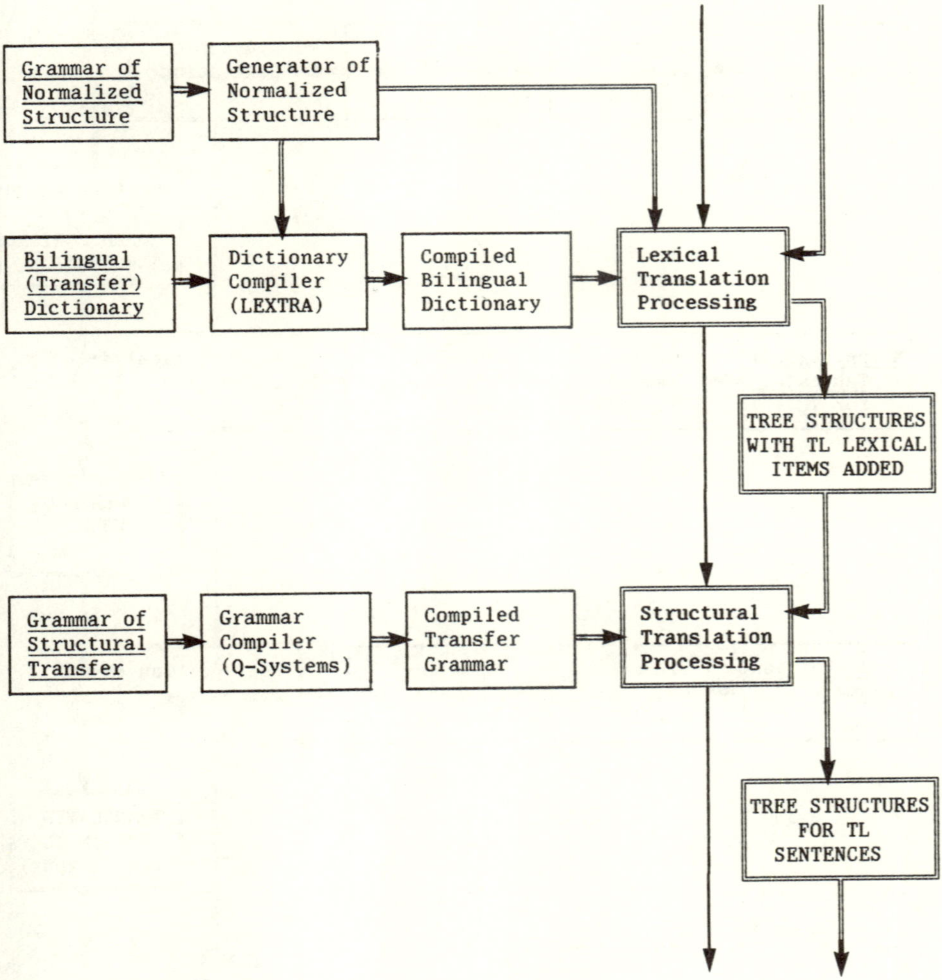

Grammar of Normalized Structure
Generator of Normalized Structure
Bilingual (Transfer) Dictionary
Dictionary Compiler (LEXTRA)
Compiled Bilingual Dictionary
Lexical Translation Processing
TREE STRUCTURES WITH TL LEXICAL ITEMS ADDED
Grammar of Structural Transfer
Grammar Compiler (Q-Systems)
Compiled Transfer Grammar
Structural Translation Processing
TREE STRUCTURES FOR TL SENTENCES

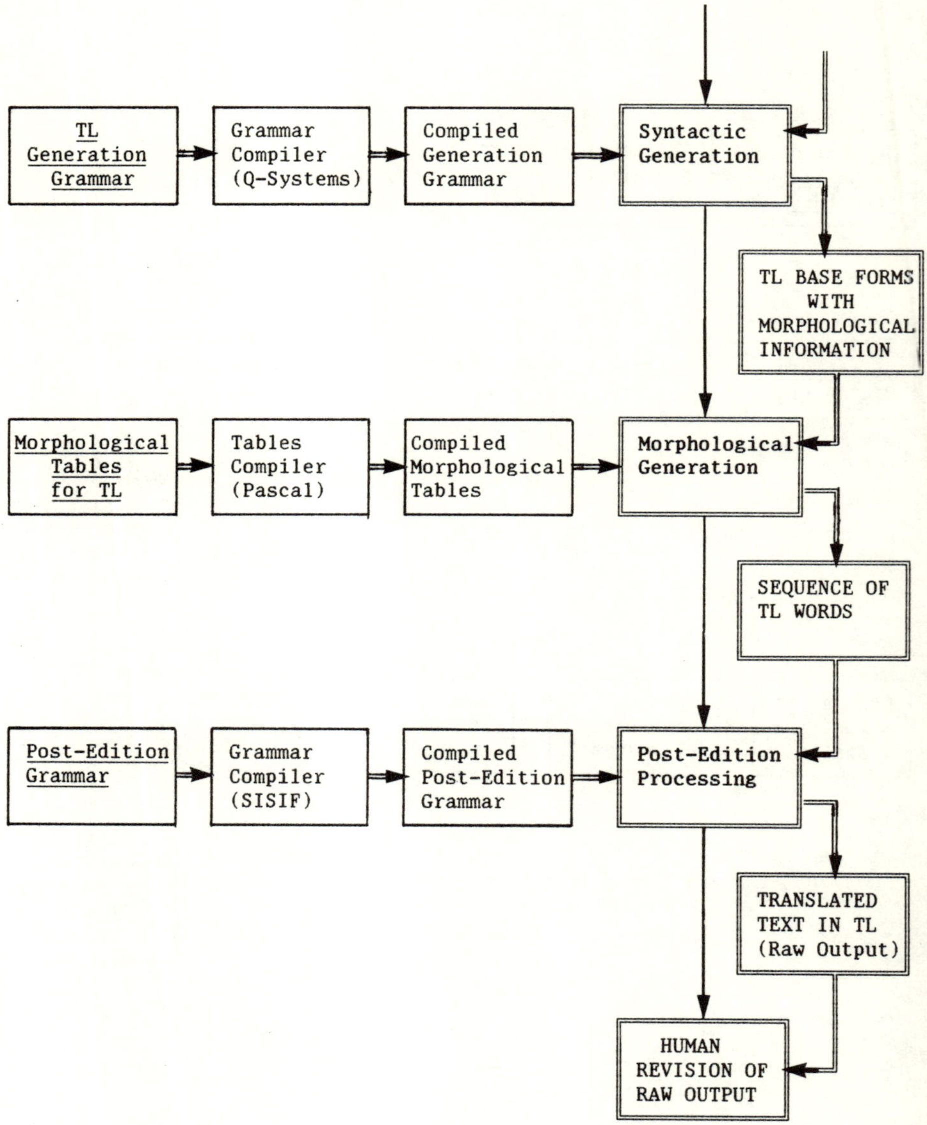
TL Generation Grammar
Grammar Compiler (Q-Systems)
Compiled Generation Grammar
Syntactic Generation
TL BASE FORMS WITH MORPHOLOGICAL INFORMATION
Morphological Tables for TL
Tables Compiler (Pascal)
Compiled Morphological Tables
Morphological Generation
SEQUENCE OF TL WORDS
Post-Edition Grammar
Grammar Compiler (SISIF)
Compiled Post-Edition Grammar
Post-Edition Processing
TRANSLATED TEXT IN TL (Raw Output)
HUMAN REVISION OF RAW OUTPUT

BIBLIOGRAPHY

***[13]

Aronoff Mark, 1976
Word Formation in Generative Grammar
MIT Press, Cambridge, Mass.

Arthern P.J., 1980
Machine translation - a translator's viewpoint
in Lebenden Sprachen 1, 9-14.

Association for Computational Linguistics
Two Special Issues on Machine Translation
in Slocum Jonathan, (Guest Editor)
Computational Linguistics, Volume 11:1, Volume 11:2-3

Auerbach Publishers Inc., 1983
Electronic Office - Management and Technology
Auerbach

Billmeier Reinhard, 1982
Zu den linguistischen Grundlagen von SYSTRAN
(= The Linguistic Principles of SYSTRAN)
in Multilingua 1-2, 83-96.

Bourbeau Laurent, Poulin Guy, 1977 ***
Analyseur morphologique de l'anglais du système TAUM-AVIATION
(= The Morphological Analyzer of English in the TAUM-AVIATION System)
in Project Aviation: Rapport d'étape (Status report) May 1977, Université de Montréal, 327 p., (p. 10-138)

Bourbeau Laurent, (editor) 1981a ***
Linguistic Documentation of the Computerized Translation Chain of the TAUM-AVIATION System.
(= Documentation linguistique de la chaîne de traduction informatisée du système TAUM-AVIATION)
Université de Montréal, mai 1981, (I-VI), 77 p.

---

[13] Any enquiries concerning the documents marked by asterisks should be made in writing to the Technology Directorate, Official Languages and Translation, Department of the Secretary of State, Ottawa, Ontario, Canada, K1A 0M5.

Bourbeau Laurent, (rédacteur) 1981b ***
Documentation linguistique pour la fabrication des dictionnaires du système TAUM-AVIATION
(= Linguistic Documentation for Building the Dictionaries of the TAUM-AVIATION System)
Université de Montréal, (I-IX + Annexe), 1981, 351 p.

Bruderer H.E., 1978
Handbuch der maschinellen und maschinengestützten Sprachübertzung
(= Handbook of Machine Translation and Computer-Assisted Translation)
München/New York

Carbonnel J., Cullingford R.E., Gershman A.V., 1978
Knowledge-Based Machine Translation
Research Report 146, Dept. of Computer Science, Yale University.

Carnap Rudolf, 1956
Meaning and Necessity: A Study in Semantics and Modal Logic
University of Chicago Press, Chicago

Chevalier M., Dansereau J., Poulin G., 1978 ***
TAUM-METEO: description du système
(= TAUM-METEO: a Description of the System)
Université de Montréal, 47 p.

Chevalier M., Isabelle P., Labelle F., Lainé C., 1981
La traductologie appliquée à la traduction automatique
(= Translatology Applied to Machine Translation)
in META 26:1, Montréal, p. 35-47

Chomsky Noam, 1957
Syntactic Structures
Mouton & Co., The Hague, 1957,

Chomsky Noam, 1965
Aspects of the Theory of Syntax
MIT, Cambridge, USA, 1965,

Chomsky Noam, 1967
Remarks on Nominalizations
in Jacobs R., Rosenbaum P.S., 1967
Readings in English Transformational Grammar
Ginn-Blaisdell, Walham, Mass, p. 184-221

Colmerauer Alain, 1971
Les Systèmes-Q ou un formalisme pour analyser et synthétiser des phrases sur ordinateur
(= Q-Systems: a Formalism for parsing and generating sentences with computer) in TAUM-71, Université de Montréal, 239 p., (p. 134-171)

BIBLIOGRAPHY

Crook M.N., Bishop H.P., 1965
Evaluation of Machine Translation
Final Report, Institute for Psychological Research, Tufts University

Donovan Ronald John, 1982
Writing Made Easier with Personal Computers
in Writer's Digest, Sept. 1982, p. 33-42

Esau Helmut, 1973
Nominalization and Complementation in Modern German
in Dik S.C., Kooij J.G., (editors)
North Holland Publishing Company, Amsterdam, 1973, 314 p.

Feigenbaum Edward, McCorduck Pamela, 1983
Land of the rising fifth generation computer
in High Technology, June 1983, p. 65-70

Finin Timothy W., 1980
The Semantic Interpretation of Nominal Compounds
Indiana Linguistic Club, Indiana University, Bloomington, 148 p.

Finin Timothy W., 1986
Constraining the Interpretation of Nominal Compounds in a Limited Context
in Grishman R., Kittredge R. I., (editors) 1986
Analyzing Language in Restricted Domains
Lawrence Erlbaum Associates, Hillsdale, New Jersey

Freigang K.H., Thome G., Wilss W., 1979
Der Stand der Forschung auf dem Gebiet der maschinellen Übersetzung
(= The State of Research in the Field of Automatic Translation)
in Linguistische Arbeiten, Neue Folge, Heft 2, Saarbrücken.

Gérin-Lajoie Robert, 1980
Vérification des manipulations d'arbres en LEXTRA
(= Validation of tree manipulations in LEXTRA)
M.A. Thesis, Computer Science Department, Université de Montréal, 174 p.

Gervais Antoni, 1980 ***
Evaluation of the TAUM-AVIATION Machine Translation Pilot System
Planning, Evaluation and Audit Branch, Translation Bureau,
Secretary of State, Ottawa, 30 juin 1980, 164 p.

GETA - CHAMPOLLION, 1982
Le point sur ARIANE-78 : Début 1982
(= Status Report on ARIANE-78: Beginning of 1982)
Université de Grenoble, CAP SOGETI, France,
April 1982, 62 p. + (Appendices, 79 p.)

GETA - CHAMPOLLION, 1982
Spécifications du système ARIANE-X
(= Technical Specifications of the ARIANE-X System)
Université de Grenoble, CAP SOGETI, France, June 1982, 172 p.

Gobeil Fernand, 1981
Machine Translation Feasibility Study
Planning, Management and Technology Branch, Translation Bureau, Secretary of State, Ottawa, May 1981, 95 p., Appendices A-G

Guilbaud Jean-Philippe, 1980
Analyse morphologique de l'allemand en vue de la traduction par ordinateur de textes techniques spécialisés
(= Morphological Analysis of German for Machine Translation of Specialized Technical Texts), Thesis, Doctorat 3e cycle, Université de la Sorbonne Nouvelle, Paris III, 240 p.

Haller H., 1980
Maschinelle Sprachübersetzung - Hirngespinst oder Hilfe? - SYSTRAN in Europa
(= Machine Translation - a fantasy or an aid? - SYSTRAN in Europe)
in Haller H. (Editor), Maschinelle Sprachverarbeitung Vorträge auf der 10. Jahrestagung der GAL ([West Germany] Society of Applied Linguistics) Mainz, 4-10. Oktober 1979, p. 73-107, Dudweiler.

Halliday T.C., Briss E.A., 1977
The Evaluation and Systems Analysis of the SYSTRAN Machine Translation System
(= Final Technical Report, RADC-TR-76-399)
Griffiss Air Force Base, New York, 70 p.

Harris Brian, 1971
POLYGRAM: Grapho-Morphology Analyzer for English
in TAUM-71, Université de Montréal, 239 p., (p. 46-105)

Harris Zellig, 1968
Mathematical Structures of Language
New York, Wiley, 1968

Hauenschild C., Huckert E., Maier R., 1978
SALAT: Entwurf eines automatischen Übersetzungssystems
(= SALAT: Blueprint for an Automatic Translation System.)
in Sprache und Datenverarbeitung 1, p. 103-114.

BIBLIOGRAPHY

Heintz Carl, 1982
Buyer's Guide to Word Processing Software
in Interface Age, Dec. 1982, p. 40-58

Hoffberg Alan, 1982
A Buyer's Guide to Word Processing Software
in Administrative Management, Sept. 1982, p. 40-58

Hutchins W.J., 1978
Machine Translation and Machine-Aided Translation
in Progress in Documentation, Journal of Documentation, 34:2, p. 119-159

International Resource Development Inc. 1983
PCs versus CWPs (communicating word processors)
in The Clerical Workstation of the Future
Norwalk, 30 High St., Connecticut, USA

Jackendoff R., 1975
Morphological and Semantic Regularities in the Lexicon
in Language 51, p. 639-671

Jong Steven, 1982
Designing a Text Editor? The User Comes First
- A system's power is measured in ease of use
in BYTE Publications Inc., April 1982, p. 284-300

Kay Martin, 1982
The Dictionary of the Future and the Future of the Dictionary
Xerox Palo Alto Research Center, 11 p.

Kempson R.M., 1977
Semantic Theory
London, New York & Melbourne, Cambridge University Press.

King Margaret, 1980
EUROTRA: Technical Specifications
(Preliminary draft, EUROTRA 160/80), Geneva, July 30th, 1980, 82 p.

King Margaret, 1982
EUROTRA: An Attempt to Achieve Multilingual MT
North-Holland, Amsterdam, p. 139-147

Kittredge Richard, Lehrberger John, (Editors), 1982
Sublanguage: Studies of Language in Restricted Semantic Domains
(= Foundation of Communication) Walter de Gruyter, Berlin, New-York, 1982, 240 p.

Kittredge Richard, 1983 ***
Sublanguage - Specific computer aids to translation: A survey of the Most Promising Application Areas.
Planning Management and Technology Branch, Translation Bureau, Secretary of State, Ottawa, March 1983, 95 p.

Knaus Ingrid B., 1983
Setting Up the Office
in The Information Processing Publication, Sept., Vol. 8:9, pp. 10-11

Knuth Donald E., 1978
TEX and Metafont : new directions in typesetting
Digital Press, 1979

Labelle François, 1981 ***
Le modèle linguistique : la structure normalisée et son importance pour le transfert et la génération
(= The Linguistic Model: the Normalized Structure and its Importance for Transfer and Generation)
in Bourbeau L., (editor), 1981b, Université de Montréal, 351 p., (14 p.)

Labelle François, (forthcoming)
Les opérations de traduction dans un système de traduction automatique
(= Translation Operations in a Machine Translation System)

Lawson Veronica, 1982
Methodology Study on the Application of the Systran Computer-Aided Translation System to Texts Translated within the Commission of the European Communities. (= EEC Study Contract TH-47) Final Report, April 1982, London
Volume 1 - A Typology of Texts, 71 p., + Appendices I-III
Volume 2 - A Typology of Machine Translation Errors, 73p.,+ Appendices (p. 74-105) An Ergonomic Analysis, 17 p.

Lawson Veronica, (editor), 1982
Practical Experience of Machine Translation
(= Proceedings of a Conference, London, 5-6 November 1981)
North-Holland Publishing Company, Amsterdam, 199 p.

Lehmann W.P., Bennet W.S., Slocum J., et al., 1981
The METAL System
Final Technical Report RADC-TR-80-374, Rome Air Development Center, Griffiss AFB, New York

Lehrberger John J., 1981a
The Linguistic Model: General Aspects
in Bourbeau L. (editor), 1981a, TAUM, Université de Montréal, 77 p.

Lehrberger John J., (editor), 1981b ***
Etude de faisabilité : possibilités d'extension du système TAUM/AVIATION/HYDRAULIQUE au domaine de l'électronique
(= Feasibility Study: Possibility of Extending the TAUM-AVIATION/HYDRAULIC System to the Domain of Electronics)
TAUM, Université de Montréal, VI + 197 p. + (Annexes 45 p.)

Lehrberger John J., 1982
Automatic Translation and the Concept of Sublanguage
in Kittredge R.I., Lehrberger J.J. (editors)
Sublanguage: Studies of Language in Restricted Semantic Domains
Walter de Gruyter, Berlin-New York

Lehrberger John J., 1986
Sublanguage Analysis
in Grishman R., Kittredge R. I. (editors), 1986
Analyzing Language in Restricted Domains
Lawrence Erlbaum Associates, Hillsdale, New Jersey

Levi J., 1978
The Syntax and Semantics of Complex Nominals
Academic Press, New York

Lieber R., 1980
On the Organization of the Lexicon
PH.D Thesis, MIT, Cambridge, Mass., 212 p.

Loffler-Laurian Anne-Marie, 1983
Pour une typologie des erreurs dans la traduction automatique
(= For a Typology of Errors in Machine Translation)
in Multilingua, Mouton Publishers, Vol. 2:2, p. 65-78

Luckhardt Heinz-Dirk, 1982
SUSY: Capabilities and Range of Application
in Multilingua, Mouton Publishers, Vol. 1:4, p. 213-220

Lyons John, 1977
Semantics
Cambridge University Press, Cambridge, I (pp 1-371), II (pp 371-897)

Lyons John, 1968
Introduction to Theoretical Linguistics
Cambridge University Press, London & New York, 519 P.

Maas H.D., 1980
Zur Entwicklung des Übersetzungssystems SUSY und seiner einzelnen Komponenten (= The Development of the SUSY Translation System and its Individual Components).
in Eggers H. (Editor), Maschinelle Übersetzung, Lexikographie und Analyse Akten des 2. Internationalen Kolloquiums Saarbrücken, November 1979, I. Die Vorträge, Linguistische Arbeiten, Neue Folge, Saarbrücken, Heft 3, (1), p. 7-16.

Marshak Ronni T., 1983
Word Processing Programs for the IBM Personal Computer
in The Seybold Report on Professional Computing, Vol.1:2, March, 32 p.

Massaro Donald J., 1982
Automated Office Hinges on User Acceptance
in Electronic Design, January 1982, p. 180-181

McGraw-Hill
Databook 70 : The EDP buyer's bible
McGraw-Hill Information Systems

Mendelson Elliott, 1964
Introduction to Mathematical Logic
D. Van Nostrand Co., Princeton, N.J.

Milne John, 1983
WP issues in integration
in Office Equipment and Methods, Sept. 1983, p. 35-36

Nagao Makoto, 1982
A Survey of Natural Language Processing and Machine Translation in JAPAN.
in Kitagawa T., (Editor), 1982, Computer Science & Technologies, Japan Annual Reviews in Electronics, Computers & Telecommunications, North-Holland, Amsterdam, 359 p. (p. 64-70)

Pierce John R., Carroll John B., et al, 1966
Language and Machines - Computers in Translation and Linguistics
(= ALPAC Report)
National Academy of Sciences, National Research Council, Washington D.C., 1966, 124 p.

Quézel-Ambrunaz M., 1978
ARIANE : Système interactif pour la traduction automatique multilingue
(= ARIANE: Interactive System for Multilingual Machine Translation)
(GETA), Université de Grenoble, mars 1978

BIBLIOGRAPHY

Quirk R., Greenbaum S., Leech G., Stvartvik J., 1972
A Grammar of Contemporary English
Longman, London, 1120 p.

Ramat Aurel, 1982
Grammaire typographique
(= Typographical Grammar)
Tour de la Bourse, C.P. 408, Montréal, 91 p.

Riesbeck Christopher K., 1975
Conceptual Analysis
in Schank Roger C., (editor), 1975
Conceptual Information Processing, North Holland, (p. 83-156)

Roberts Teresa, 1979
Evaluation of Computer Text Editors
Ph. D. Thesis, Stanford,
Xerox Palo Alto Research Center Report SSL-79-9

Rolling L., 1980
Automatische Übersetzung heute und morgen.
(= Automatic Translation today and tomorrow)
in Umschau 80 (11), p. 333-338

Roman David R., 1983
Word Processing
in Computer Decisions, June 1983, p. 154-182

Sager Noami, 1981
Natural Language Information Processing: A Computer Grammar of English and Its Applications
Addison-Wesley Publishing Company, Reading, Massachusetts, 399 p.

Salkoff Morris, 1979
Analyse syntaxique du Français : Grammaire en chaîne
(= Syntactic Parsing of French: String Grammar)
Amsterdam, John Benjamins B.V., 334 p.

Schank Roger C., 1975
Conceptual Information Processing
Amsterdam, North Holland

Schank Roger C., Abelson Robert P., 1977
Scripts, Plans, Goals and Understanding
Hillsdale, N.J., Erlbaum

Schorr Herbert, 1982
Cost-effectiveness will set the pace of office automation
in Electronic Design, January 1982, p. 172-173

Secretary of State of Canada, 1985 ***
Essai de traduction assistée par ordinateur: Système WEIDNER
Approvisionnements et Services Canada, Projet 5-5462, 59 P.

Selkirk Elisabeth O., 1982
The Syntax of Words
The MIT Press, Cambridge, 136 p.

Slocum Jonathan, 1981
A Practical Comparison of Parsing Strategies for Machine Translation and Other Natural Language Processing Purposes
University Microfilms International, Ann Arbor, Michigan

Slocum Jonathan, 1982
The LRC Machine Translation System: An Application of State-of-the-Art Text and Natural Language Processing Techniques to the Translation of Technical Manuals, Working Paper LRC-82-1,
Linguistic Research Center, Texas University, Austin, 26 p.

Slot Maureen, 1983
Guide to basic word processing
in Software Canada, Sept. 1983, p. 10-11

Smith D.C., Irby C., Kimball R., et alii, 1982
Designing the Star User Interface
in BYTE Publications Inc., April 1982, p. 242-282

Snell Barbara M., (editor), 1979
Translating and the Computer
(= Proceedings of a Seminar, London, 14th November 1978)
North-Holland Publishing Company, Amsterdam, 189 p.

Stanton Jo-Ann, 1981 ***
Description sémantique de la Structure Normalisée du système TAUM-AVIATION
(= Semantic Description of the TAUM-AVIATION System Normalized Structure), TAUM, Université de Montréal, mars 1981, 105 p.

Stewart Gilles, 1975
Le langage de programmation REZO
(= REZO Programming Language)
M.A. Thesis, Computer Science Department, Université de Montréal, 162 p.

TAUM, 1980 ***
TAUM/AVIATION 1980, Université de Montréal, 31 mars 1980, 179 p.

BIBLIOGRAPHY

Taylor W.S., 1953
CLOZE Procedure: A New Tool for Measuring Readability
in The Journalism Quarterly, Fall 1953, (p. 415-433)

Tellier P., Bourbeau L., 1982
Essai opérationnel et évaluation d'un système de traduction automatisé - Rapport final, Translation Bureau, Secretary of State, Ottawa, 250P.

Toma Peter, (1977)
SYSTRAN - Ein maschinelles Übersetzungssystem der 3. Generation
(= SYSTRAN: a third-generation machine-translation system)
in Sprache und Datenverarbeitung 1, p. 38-46.

Van Slype G., 1978
Deuxième évaluation du système de traduction automatique SYSTRAN anglais-français de la Commission des Communautés Européennes.
(= Second Evaluation of the SYSTRAN English-French Machine Translation System of the Commission of the European Communities)
Bureau Marcel Van Dijk, Luxembourg, CCE, DGXIII, November 1978, 179 p.

Van Slype G., 1979a
Évaluation du système de traduction automatique de la Commission des Communautés européennes
(= Evaluation of the Machine Translation System of the Commission of the European Communities)
in 3ième Congrès national français sur l'Informatique et la Documentation, ADBS - ANRT, 1979, p. 66.1-66.5.

Van Slype G., 1979b
SYSTRAN: Evaluation of the 1978 Version of the Systran English-French Automatic System of the Commission of the European Communities
in The Incorporated Linguist 18 (3)

Van Slype G., 1982
Conception d'une méthodologie générale d'évaluation de la traduction automatique
(= Designing a Global Methodology for Evaluating Machine Translation)
in Multilingua, Mouton Publishers, 1-4/1982, p. 221-237.

Van Slype G., Guinet J.F., Seitz F., Benejam E., 1981
Mieux traduire pour mieux communiquer
(= Better Translation for Better Communication)
in Bureau Marcel van Dijk, Prospective study of the translation market prepared for the Commission of the European Communities, Direction générale Marché de l'information et innovation
Bruxelles et Luxembourg, 1981, 174 p.

Van Slype G., Pigott I., 1979
Description du système de traduction automatique SYSTRAN de la Commission des Communautés Européennes
(= Description of the SYSTRAN Machine Translation System of the Commission of the European Communities)
in Documentaliste, Vol. 16/4, p. 150-159

Vauquois Bernard, 1975
La traduction automatique à Grenoble
(= Machine Translation at Grenoble)
Documents de Linguistique Quantitative no 24, Dunod, Paris

Wall Robert, 1972
Introduction to Mathematical Linguistics
Prentice-Hall Inc., Englewood Cliffs, New Jersey, 337 p.

Wilks Yorick, 1973
An Artificial Intelligence Approach to Machine Translation
in Schank Roger C., Colby Keneth M.
Computer Models of Thought and Language
San Francisco, Freeman, p. 114-151

Wilks Yorick, 1975a
An Intelligent Analyzer and Understander of English
in CACM, Vol. 18, p. 264-274

Wilks Yorick, 1975b
Preference Semantics
in Keenan Edward L.
The Formal Semantics of Natural Language
Cambridge University Press, Cambridge, pp. 329-350

Wilss Wolfram, 1982
Methodological Aspects of the Translation Process
in AILA Bulletin, No. 2 (32), p. 1-13

Winograd Terry, 1983
Language as a Cognitive Process - Syntax
Addison-Wesley, Menlo Park, 1983, 640 p.

Yencharis Len, 1982
1982 Technology Forecast : Office Automation
in Electronic Design, January 1982, p. 240-258

Zimmermann H., 1980
Stand und Probleme der maschinellen Übersetzung
(= State-of-the-art and problems of machine translation)
in Lebende Sprachen Vol. 1, pp. 2-5.

In the LINGVISTICAE INVESTIGATIONES SUPPLEMENTA (LIS) series the following volumes have been published and will be published during 1988:

1. FOLEY, James: *Theoretical Morpholoy of the French Verb*. Amsterdam, 1979.
2. SALKOFF, Morris: *Analyse syntaxique du Français-Grammaire en chaîne*. Amsterdam, 1980.
3. PARRET, Herman (dir.): *LE LANGAGE EN CONTEXTE. Etudes Philosophiques et Linguistiques de Pragmatique,* par H. Parret, L. Apostel, P. Gochet, M. van Overbeke, O. Ducrot, L. Tasmowski-de Ryck, N. Dittmar, W. Wildgen. Amsterdam, 1980.
4. LOVE, Nigel H.: *Generative Phonology: A Case Study from French*. Amsterdam, 1981.
5. PAILLET, Jean-Pierre & André DUGAS: *Approaches to Syntax*. (English transl. from the French orig. ed. "Principes d'analyse syntaxique", Québec, 1973). Amsterdam, 1982.
6. LIGHTNER, Ted: *Introduction to English Derivational Morphology*. Amsterdam, 1983.
7. ELIA, Annibale: *Syntaxe du verbe italien*. Amsterdam, 1987. n.y.p.
8. ATTAL, Pierre & Claude MULLER (eds.): *DE LA SYNTAXE A LA PRAGMATIQUE: ACTES DU COLLOQUE DE RENNES*. Amsterdam, 1984.
9. GUILLET, Alain & Nunzio LA FAUCI (eds.): *ACTES DU 1er COLLOQUE EUROPEEN SUR LA GRAMMAIRE ET LE LEXIQUE COMPARES DES LANGUES ROMANES,* 23-26 Septembre 1981. Amsterdam, 1984.
10. ZWANENBURG. W.: *Productivité morphologique et emprunt*. Amsterdam, 1983.
11. LAMIROY, Beatrice: *Les verbes de mouvement en français et en espagnol. Etude comparée de leurs infinitives*.
12. HONG CHAI-SONG: *Syntaxe des verbes de mouvement en coreen contemporain*. Amsterdam, 1985.
13. VERGNAUD, J.-R.: *Dépendance et niveaux de représentation en syntaxe*. Amsterdam, 1985.
14. SUBIRATS-RÜGGEBERG, Carlos: *Sentential Complementation in Spanish*. Amsterdam, 1987.
15. LEHRBERGER, John & Laurent BOURBEAU: *Machine Translation*. Amsterdam, 1988.
16. VERLUYTEN, S. Paul: *La phonologie du schwa français*. Amsterdam, 1988.